Beef, Leather and Grass

Beef, Leather and Grass

by Edmund Randolph

UNIVERSITY OF OKLAHOMA PRESS : NORMAN

By Edmund Randolph

Hell Among the Yearlings (Chicago, 1978)
Beef, Leather and Grass (Norman, 1981)

Library of Congress Cataloging in Publication Data

Randolph, Edmund, 1903–
  Beef, leather, and grass.

  1. Randolph, Edmund, 1903–   2. Antler
Ranch, Mont.   3. Ranch life—Montana.   4. Big-
horn Valley, Mont. and Wyo—Biography.   I. Title.
F739.A57R367   978.6'38   80–18818

Contents

Illustrations

Preface

THIS IS A BOOK ABOUT the modern West (1940s–1950s) with particular reference to large-scale cattle ranching in southeast Montana on the Crow Indian Reservation, where Edmund Randolph
spent twelve years as a partner in the Antler Ranch on the Little
Big Horn River near Wyola. Before that, he had been in partnership with another important ranching enterprise some fifty miles
due east in the Tongue River valley, during the 1920s and 1930s.
In all, he has had more than fifty years of close connections with
southeast Montana and the adjoining Sheridan, Wyoming, area
to the south and has been a Montana landowner since 1925, when
he filed on public domain under the Homestead Act. Probably
he is the only born Manhattan Islander who holds a U.S. patent
(not a deed) to part of the Louisiana Purchase. He now lives in
Denver, but still holds his property near Birney, Montana.

The Antler Ranch lay within the borders of the 3,800,000-acre
Crow Indian Reservation, of which the Antler range comprised
some 385,000 acres of practically self-renewing leases (whites
not being allowed to buy much Indian land, and the Crows being
prone to favor an incumbent lessee at renewal time). The Antler
deeded land, centered mostly around the ranch headquarters,
comprised about 50,000 acres, with the Little Big Horn River
running through it. The ranch passed out of the original family
hands in the 1960s.

The general area of the author's interests, therefore, was
bounded roughly from west to east by the Big Horn River and

the Tongue, with the Little Big Horn and the Rosebud rivers in between, all flowing northeastward as tributaries of the Yellowstone River. From a north-south standpoint, the boundaries might be considered as the latitudes of Billings, Montana, and Sheridan, Wyoming.

This area has long been historically important, from the days of the early fur trappers, the Lewis and Clark Expedition and the Indian wars, the Custer Massacre and the general lore of the Sioux, Cheyenne and Crow tribes. It is the land of Sitting Bull, Crazy Horse and Buffalo Bill Cody. It was also the mecca of the great cattle barons who trailed their vast herds from Texas to greener and better-watered grazing lands in the north. Cattle ranching is still a very prominent industry here, though today it must share honors with sheep raising and sugar beets and other agricultural pursuits.

Now the energy era has come along and with it the great boom in coal, from which it is hoped to squeeze electricity without the smoke of present methods. There are practically unlimited deposits of lignite coal, unsurpassed in low-sulfur content, and it has been said that two-thirds of the nation's energy requirements eventually will originate here.

Thus, this land has again become an important battlefield, with industrialists pitted against conservationists, and the Indians returning to their old domains, digging up old treaties and claiming water rights, fortified by money and ready to go to court.

In this still sparsely settled area, the Antler Ranch was one of the most important institutions, one of the greatest beef producers in the United States and one of the most fearlessly innovative enterprises anywhere in the West.

Yet very little has been written of this area and its people in comparatively modern times, and nothing by any other author who has spent years of individual contact with the land and its inhabitants, or personally engaged in their endeavors, successes and sorrows.

Beef, Leather and Grass deals with this situation in a unique manner, not as a fictional account of a ranch, a would-be "Western" or an autobiography, but from personal observation. It is a bit of biographical history, a first-person, factual description of places, people, customs and a form of American life that had its being in pioneer days and is now almost gone. It seeks to show today's youngsters what that part of America was like before the highly vaunted hand of "progress" interfered. The book shows up the Wild West Syndrome for the fake that it is and replaces the image with bare facts, some pleasant, others not so pleasant, but all true experiences.

Only the names have been changed, and for obvious reasons: out of respect for the dead or the privacy of the living. The characters themselves have not been changed. They are recorded exactly as seen through the eyes of the author. Actual conversations, of course, cannot be verbatim, but are reconstructed according to the situations as closely as memory will allow and within the reasonable limits of creative license.

In the words of the author:

"There's nothing particularly new in the idea of young easterners coming west and entering the livestock business. From the 1870s on, there were a number of instances where noted people followed this pattern: British and Scottish noblemen, sons of prominent eastern seaboard families, such as Theodore Roosevelt, Chicago and midwestern millionaires, not to mention small fry like myself. The story of 'Go West, young man,' reaches far back and too often had a rough landing. However, in my particular case, I was lucky enough to adapt a slightly different approach, which had a happier outcome.

"I had no great fortune behind me; no organization, stockholders, board of directors or advisors. I had just $10,000, (mostly borrowed) in each of my modest ventures, on Tongue River and on the Little Big Horn. The difference was that I never went into competition with the native cattlemen. I always went into partnership.

"Our ventures met with good times and bad, but on the whole, they were decidedly profitable. There were also fringe benefits in terms of better health, interesting travel in the United States, Mexico and Europe, dealings with unusual characters and a sense of contributing to the war effort in the production of beef, which carried a high priority.

"In general, *Beef, Leather and Grass* seeks to record what history probably won't: a vignette of American times and customs that may soon be forgotten, but shouldn't."

Beef, Leather and Grass

1

Getting Back to the Rangeland

MY SOPHOMORE TERM of activity on the cattle ranges of southeastern Montana began in April, 1940. Nearly twenty years before, I had passed through my freshman stage along the Tongue River, which rises in the Sheridan, Wyoming, area and flows northeast into the Yellowstone at Miles City, Montana, a distance of some 130 miles. Headquarters had been about fifty miles along this route in the vicinity of Birney, Montana, which was and still is just a post office area, not a town, most easily described as where Hanging Woman Creek joins the Tongue.

Now, in 1940, my old livestock partners having a fully stocked range, I was on my way north of Sheridan, again looking for grass, but this time along the banks of the Little Big Horn. My good friend Albert Harris of the long-established Tongue River cattlemen's clique was taking me to meet an old cowpuncher friend of his youth, one Matt Sheardon of the Antler Ranch, who was now a big operator on the Crow Indian Reservation and had "a world of grass."

Albert Harris had been my first benefactor on Tongue River. He was a short, heavyset man whose correspondingly short steps, tempered with the remnants of youthful military training in a Virginia military academy, blended into a peculiar, determined gait, while his smile preceded him like the ray of a searchlight, ever brighter with the glow of kindliness as he drew nearer. His approach reminded one of the pistons of a steam locomotive with their short but determined and powerful strokes, such as those hauling the Burlington freight train puffing along on our left. It was struggling upgrade toward Parkman, the straining of the three huge compound engines belching thin smoke and live steam high into the air, with all that old fascination of the steam age.

The main problem in starting any range operation is grass: who has it, and how do you get it? If you don't own it yourself in fairly large acreage — a cow and calf require 36 acres to survive properly —you lease it, or you contract with some grass-rich ranch to run your cattle for you. This is a particularly good way to start off a small operation of fewer than five hundred head, such as I had in mind. That is, it's good if you can find the right man with the right amount of grass, who is also willing to sign the right contract.

Albert Harris, looking out from under the broad, brown brim of his faded beaver Stetson, that seemed as if it could have been with him for most of his fifty-five years, exuded confidence that he had the right man in his sights, Matt Sheardon. His large, soft eyes took in the makeup of the freight as we passed it — flatcars of lumber, gondolas of coal, loads of farm machinery. Then there was a string of slat-sided cattle cars. He started counting them under his breath, concluding, "Twenty-six carloads," after a terrifying mile or so of serpentine driving, sometimes perilously close to the ditch, as he was a notoriously lackadaisical driver even when not counting anything. "Mexican cattle . . . low-grade *corrientes* . . . and I'll bet they're going just where we're going . . . the Antler."

It was a reassuring omen that Matt Sheardon did, indeed, have "worlds of grass," as several sources of information had indicated to me. But Matt himself had been a bit vague on the point in the one very short letter he had written in answer to several of mine from New York. Albert was a good correspondent, but Matt did not have Albert's education, and his disdain for the pen was widely known. He had answered my query as to how many head of cattle he could run for me in what seemed the most remarkable and unbusinesslike way. His exact answer had been, "Any number." There was something intriguing about the idea that the biggest operator on the Crow Reservation could be so casual and inexact about a proposed business deal. After another letter on the point had brought no response at all, it had seemed best to meet him through Albert and to get the information from him face to face, which was the purpose of our trip.

"If Matt has the crack outfit on the Reservation, why is he shipping in low-grade cattle from Mexico?"

Albert grinned. "Of course, that doesn't mean I agree with him. Nobody down Tongue River does. As you know, we're all straight cow-and-calf outfits. We stick by our native Herefords, and we know that every time a cow has a calf she pays for herself. Matt was brought up that way, too, but he's an experimenter. Now he says that was okay when we were kids on the open range, with practically free grass because the public domain wasn't fenced off and labor was cheap. But not anymore."

"How's his theory been working out lately?"

"Well, he's just about the biggest beef producer in this state and only a few years ago he was flat broke. I guess we have to admit that he's ahead of us right now. Maybe there *is* more profit in doing it his way, buying steer calves down in that drought country along the border. Then, of course, he has a corner on this cheap Indian grass at fifteen cents an acre to run them on and more water than we've got."

"Why does he go so far to buy his calves?"

"Because it's a drought country, especially for the last few years. Cattle so poor they're about to keel over, especially the calves. Their mothers don't have enough milk for them. By the time they're weaned, some of them don't weigh 250 pounds. No point in anybody down there buying them. They couldn't graze them, and the rivers are damn near dry. So Matt buys them . . . by weight, of course, and cheap . . . and ships them up here where he's got all this grass and water. Believe me, it's a buyer's market down there along the Río Grande."

Albert kept watching the freight in his rearview mirror with a peculiar interest that seemed to suggest memories of the big beef shipments his own ranch used to send over these same rails before the "hard winter" of 1919, when they were rated as a million-dollar outfit—in gold dollars. That was the year that broke their fortunes; but now their range was stocked to full capacity again, and the cowman's creed of never giving up seemed justified once more. Then, "You know what?" he suddenly announced, "We'd better be getting across that track at Wyola before that shipment gets there. If those cattle are for the Antler, we'll be caught on the wrong side of the track while they're being unloaded." He then shot forward and drove at a frightening clip, figuring out loud, "Twenty-six carloads . . . that'd be twelve to fourteen hundred head. They load about fifty to fifty-five head per car. Must be for Matt."

It was uncanny how much these western stockmen seemed to know about each other's business. They weren't like other types of businessmen, learning from the Wall Street Journal; they had more of a genuine and deeply rooted interest in each other's welfare, carried along by some kind of invisible grapevine system. It was like the custom of branding each other's slick calves before some rustler got them, in the old open range days.

We got over the grade crossing at Wyola in plenty of time and started up the ten-mile dirt stretch to Matt's headquarters. "Matt's got so damn much range, you never can tell where he's going to unload . . . maybe Benteen or Spear Siding. From here on, Matt either owns or controls most of the land on both sides of the Little Big Horn."

"How does he work that?"

"Nobody knows, exactly. He's just got a way with the Indians. These Crows seem to love him. He's on the gray list."

"What's that?"

"A kind of ranking system. Sort of like the difference between common stock and preferred. Preferred makes you more gilt-edged. That's the gray list."

"You think that accounts for the hold Matt has on all this Crow land?"

"Some of it, at least. Anyway, they sell or lease him almost everything he wants, and he buys up every dead-Indian allotment that comes on the market."

"How many acres does he own, anyway?"

"It's not so much what he owns as the range he controls. Why own anything if you can lease and control it for less than what your tax bill would be? He has strategic patches tied up that control water and, indirectly, other leases that give him lots of range. Actually, he only owns the Antler headquarters and a few small ranches north of here. Perhaps fifty thousand acres in all, but his leases run up into the hundreds of thousands."

Obviously, then, Albert had been faithful to our long-standing friendship and had almost certainly solved my grass problem. His complete dependability broke upon me as cheerfully as the sudden, shrill little bursts of melody from the meadowlarks that

Boss and bear

darted, dipped and hovered around us or sang from the fence posts.

No special evidence indicated that we had arrived at the Antler —no sign, gate or mailbox with a brand on it. Albert simply announced, "Well, here we are," and turned abruptly onto a narrow, rutted road. A few yards ahead on our right was a small man apparently locked in combat with a large brown bear. Man and beast staggered about, the bear's paws on the man's shoulders, the man's hat on the ground, a small, gray felt hat that looked particularly unranchlike. Then we could see that the bear was licking the man's face.

"That's Matt now," said Albert. "Looks like he's got a pet bear. He's a great animal lover." We pulled up to watch until Matt saw us, pushed the bear off and came over to the car. Albert made a hurried, casual introduction.

Matt also seemed to take it as casually as if he had expected us, giving the impression that somehow, through the brotherhood blanketing all livestock men, the three of us were as one. This despite the fact that he hadn't seen Albert in many years and had never seen me at all. "I've been expecting Ned to show up one of these days," he said warmly. "W've been having some correspondence."

The correspondence had been exceedingly brief and left hanging more or less in midair, and he now referred to it with a sort of half-apologetic look, more like that of a repentant schoolboy who had skimped on his lessons than a man in his sixties, but pure goodwill glowed in his eyes. They were of a remarkably twinkling gray, set rather far back, so that the lids made little overhanging folds slanting down toward the outer corners and giving the whole eye a triangular effect.

"Sorry I didn't get around to answering that last letter of yours," he apologized, "but we've been pretty busy shipping in calves all month and lambing. We've got some sheep around here too."

Later, "some sheep" turned out to be about sixty thousand head, a mildly startling revelation in view of the time-honored and much touted enmity and even "wars" between sheep- and cattlemen. But Matt, ever experimenting, had found out that the two operations could be handled on the same ranch by separating them with a mountain range. He was, in fact, operating twenty-six sheep wagons, each with its band and herder.

The bear was sprawled out happily in the background near a sort of den that had been dug out for him. He had a collar, made from an old harness strap, and a light, very long, chain ending with a metal peg lying on the ground.

"How do you like my new pet?" Matt asked. "Porky loves people. Happy as a clam out here, greeting everybody that comes in and out of the ranch. Scares the daylights out of newcomers sometimes." He tapped the peg into the ground lightly with a stone, explaining, "He sure hates to be tied up fast. He knows he can pull this anytime, but he's trained not to. That's what keeps him so good-natured. Once in a while he pulls loose and breaks into the commissary, though, and raises hell. It sure bugs the cook when he bats those five-gallon cans of honey around. He knows what's in them . . . damndest thing." He had taken time out from business to stroll down and play with his bear. No wonder so many of my letters had gone unanswered. "Come on up to the house and we'll have a drink." He picked up his by then battered little gray hat, clapped it jauntily on his head and got into the car.

The ranch headquarters loomed up as a small emerald patch in a vast sea of sage green set against a background of misty and still snow-trimmed mountains. To the east lay a vista of irrigated fields and small ranches stretching across the flat lands of the Reservation, through which the Little Big Horn River wound its way toward the waters of the Big Horn, which then flowed in a generally northeastern direction to the Yellowstone. From a high hill near Matt's house there was a wonderful view of the head-quarters. Standing on the top, one could see the bright green lawn dotted with small white buildings, the log corrals, bunk-house and cattle pens, the mess house, office, commissary and huge machine shop, with its first-aid facilities for fixing anything on the ranch from shoeing a horse to retreading a Caterpillar tractor.

Higher up, on a flat across the shallow river valley, one could see the skeleton of a large hangar forming against the skyline. Matt, who, like Albert, deplored the passing of traditional ranch-ing methods, was, nevertheless, aware that the light private plane was rapidly becoming a ranch tool. Not that it could ever replace the mounted cowpuncher in handling cattle, but because, quite to the contrary, it could help both man and horse in their work. Many a highly paid man-hour and many a pound of horseflesh were wasted in riding useless miles over the vast range for cattle that simply were not there, as a sky puncher could have warned.

From this lofty hilltop perch one could see almost the whole physical layout of the ranch headquarters and could feel even more. As the eye roved its full radius of some thirty miles, scooping in what one knew to be only a small part of Matt's domain, so taken for granted that there was no definitely marked boundary, just a gradual fading of one type of land into another—lawn to irrigated alfalfa fields to sage-covered range to distant timbered mountains—one could feel the subtle changes of history that had occurred in only four or five generations since Lewis and Clark explored this area for Thomas Jefferson. And one could wonder where these changes might eventually lead.

Close at hand was the lush lawn, with a yardman walking briskly behind a softly put-putting mower, the very symbol of modern suburban, as were the three small, white clapboard homes of various family members, Matt's own home being set off by a magnificent, ten-foot-high white lilac hedge.

This hard-core suburban nucleus was bounded by a less suburban, unpaved dirt drive, with branches leading off toward the mess house and corral areas, where there was diminishing lawn. The green finally ran out beyond the mess house around the cook's and the accountant's quarters.

The next general boundary was the narrow river, gurgling away softly through groves of cottonwood and box elder, occasionally venturing out into the prairie to flash through the sagebrush on its way to the scene of General Custer's fate, actually not very far off.

Beyond the river the landscape was pretty much as God had made it, and when one's eye reached up into the mountains, he saw exactly what Lewis and Clark had seen. Moreover, he breathed the same clean, crisp air from which the pioneers had drawn much of their strength, with its life-giving tingle as distinct from civilized air as is a deep breath drawn in mid-ocean. Above and around all there was an incredible, restful, yet somehow vital stillness, punctuated by the meadowlarks.

Matt directed Albert to his little white house nestling between the lilacs. From the kitchen refrigerator he fished out a black-labeled bottle of Scotch, then took three small highball glasses from the cupboard, poured generous drinks into them, and nodded toward the sink. "If you want any water with it, it's right over there." He put an ice tray on the drainboard.

The living room was spare, with a mail-order-catalog look — overstuffed sofa and matching chairs unnecessarily big and out of proportion to the room, their dreary, mud-colored plush upholstery making them look even bigger. There were nondescript tables of no particular design laden with livestock periodicals and gaudy trivia. The entire decor was an honest admission that sophisticated taste had just not come to the Little Big Horn. The very honesty of it, the lack of excuses, pretense or embarrassment of these simple ranch people, was itself impressive. They were unashamedly what they were, ranch people, and they were good at it. Ignorance was bliss, quite harmless, and could even have a certain challenging fascination.

The cheerful notes of a rope-operated dinner bell rang out boldly. "There goes the first bell," Matt announced. "Fifteen

minutes if you want to wash up," as he poured a light splash of
Scotch into each of our glasses. Then he led the way out the back
door, along the irrigation ditch, across a little gully on a narrow
wooden footbridge, past his mother-in-law's neat, clapboard house,
and so to the mess house, which looked like a small country school,
with its bell pole and a porch cluttered up with muddy overshoes
of both the boot and clodhopper types. A cowpuncher was ringing
the second bell as we arrived.

Inside was a bare board table some twenty-five feet long with
wooden benches on either side. A few motley chairs were scattered about, occupied by very earthy-looking men, who glanced
up shyly from their tattered magazines and smiled. Others were
rather more dapper-looking fellows in high-heeled boots and with
a general appearance just ragged enough to be believable as
authentic cowpunchers, who projected a distinctly more carefree
aura. Matt mentioned the names of a few close by. Others smiled
or waved from a distance, but there were no formal introductions
or explanations. Instead, there was a sort of psychic feeling that
it didn't matter much who one was, because all present must in
some way be friends of the outfit, or they wouldn't be there, and
that the main thing was to get along with the eating.

This idea was carried out with no delay. No particular seats
were assigned, but the irrigators and other earthy types tended
to gravitate toward one end of the table, where they ate silently
though mightily, passing a large platter of beef and dishes of
vegetables up and down the line, keeping the coffeepot moving
briskly, and occasionally calling for more.

The women of the kitchen, who kept things going, were a
mixture of family, in-laws and hired help, who would chat briefly,
or introduce themselves while flitting by with extra mounds of
food or refills of the two coffeepots. They brought other huge
loads of provender for our end of the table, with Matt at the head,
Albert and me on either side of him.

In between the earthy end and the managerial end were the
cowpunchers, two office workers, the stoic Japanese yardman,
two who seemed somehow connected with the Antler sheep operation, a Burlington freight official, a local bank manager and the
Crow Indian agent.

Albert was right at home talking old times with Matt, and the
others were politely careful to include me in their conversation,

which showed a kindly interest in my plans to rejoin the ranching industry, especially with Matt, whom they held in a sort of brotherly awe.

Then, as suddenly as the meal had begun, it was over—at least, for the lower echelon. The earthy ones took their last hurried gulps of coffee, swung their legs back again over the bench, trudged out to the porch and their overshoes, and were whisked away in pickups or trucks, for all Antler hands commuted to meals at headquarters unless they were out on the range at the roundup wagon or at a sheep camp.

The office people went back to their books and voluminous files of Indian leases, the Japanese to his mowing, the irrigators to their meadows, headgates and laterals. All seemed eager to get back to what they had just rushed away from. Matt lingered on a while, then suggested that we go over to his private office.

The space partitioned off from the back of the commissary seemed a very modest allotment to serve as Matt's private office. There was barely enough room for the three of us. At one end of this compartment was a plain, old worn flat-top desk, littered with copies of the *Montana Stockman.* Also on it were helter-skelter little piles of loose papers, some weighted down with boxes of ammunition, and a disorderly pile of unopened mail. Behind the desk in the end wall of the building was a window. At the other end of the office some slickers hung on a nail. Several rifles were stacked in one corner, and a saddle lay on the floor.

"I don't know how in the hell that saddle got there," Matt said apologetically. "Someone just left it here months ago." He squeezed around between the wall and his desk and sat in his swivel chair, pawing through the papers. "Don't know what I did with that last letter of yours . . . funny, I saw it here just yesterday. Was going to answer it today."

"Never mind. It was about grass: whether you could run a few steers for me, and what sort of deal . . ."

"Oh, here it is." He picked out the familiar-looking envelope, with its seal as intact as it had been when dropped into a New York mailbox some three weeks before. "Damned if you didn't beat it out here," he added, smiling and slitting it open, although the New York and Wyola postmarks might have contested this theory.

Even the round, steel-rimmed spectacles he picked off his desk and clapped on his nose—severe though they were—did not suggest the executive type of American businessman. Yet, here was the boss of a small empire, a considerable fortune in livestock and a range into one mere pasture of which Manhattan Island would fit quite loosely. It was like an optical illusion. He didn't even have a secretary.

His perusal of my letter was swift but thorough. "Yes," he said, "I remember our other letters," and then apologized, "Sorry I couldn't get around to answering this one sooner, but we've been pretty busy receiving cattle from Mexico, and I've needed the accountant, who does the typing, up at Benteen, when we weigh them off the cars. I only write about three letters a year. I'm not very good at it."

This suggested that he had put me in a distinctly preferred class among his correspondents, to have received even one letter, and made me feel much better; or, at least, not slighted. He put my letter on a pile under a box of .30-30's, as if to signify that one more matter had been attended to, and continued, "As far as grass is concerned, we don't have any problem. All during the recent hard times—those droughts and plagues of crickets and grasshoppers—I've kept up my leases here on the Reservation, even though I couldn't use them all. So I've kept my priority with the Crow tribal council. Nobody can outbid me except an Indian. I have the right to meet all other bids. The Crows took some range back for themselves, but not much. They're not good livestock operators on this scale. No organization. They'd rather take my money and let us do the work. Matter of fact, I've just renewed all these leases."

He pointed to a huge government plat of the Reservation, which covered most of one wall of the room, and which Albert was already studying. It showed vast areas from the Montana-Wyoming line north almost to Billings, divided into "Units" of various sizes and shapes and subdivided into strips of township lines, range lines and squares for the "Sections," or square miles. Great stretches of land were marked with the Antler brand, a sort of shallow "U" with hooks at either end.

"About how many head does this all work out to?"

"Well, Ned, you know, it takes thirty acres or more to support a cow and a calf in this country. There's about four hundred thousand acres in those leases, so we could run ten thousand cows and

calves, what with the sheep. But since we've shifted over to a
straight steer operation, the grass would support a lot more, maybe
double with lots of rain. The way things stand now, we can easily
take on another five thousand head. How many would you want
to deliver?"

"Only about four or five hundred to begin with."

It sounded like very small potatoes, but Matt politely ignored
this and asked, "Have you bought them yet?"

"No, but I have a broker working on it. I wanted to make sure
of the grass first."

"You can count on us. That's one commodity we don't figure on
running out of right away. And these are six-year leases. When
would you be ready to deliver?"

"I've been letting that hang fire for a while to check on the
market. They tell me eight to nine cents a pound for steer calves
weighing four to five hundred, and seven to eight cents for yearlings around seven hundred. It sounds high."

"It *is* high. But then, you're talking about these native cattle.
They're heavy and high per pound, so they have a big price tag.
That's my point here at the Antler, and I stay away from them. I
buy down along the Mexican border, where they're light and
cheap by the pound, because nobody wants them. There's no grass
after all that drought, so they have a small price tag."

"Then why doesn't everybody else do the same thing?"

"Because of the low quality. People up north here are scared
of it. Most of them have the old dream of topping the beef market
with a uniform herd—all solid colors and straight backs. A rubber-
stamp herd. And I'll admit it, it does make some difference. But
not much profit. It's mostly psychological. Oh, I know that people
around here make fun of my Mexican billies when they only see
them being shipped in: slab-sided and all shapes, sizes and colors.
But nobody makes fun of my balance sheet when they're shipped
out, with their weights tripled on this cheap grass I've got tied up
on six-year leases. Grass has gone sky high everywhere. You know
yourself how hard it is to get."

There was a stack of correspondence in my files to prove that.

"You know," he rambled on, "it's nice to build up a fancy reputation for winning blue ribbons and prize money at the Denver
Stock Show. But those ribbons and checks and all those fancy
pictures in the newspapers don't support an outfit. It's putting

cheap weight on an animal that makes your money. And there's only one way to get cheap weight: cheap grass and lots of it. That's what I go for here. Not the idea that every time a cow has a calf she pays for herself."

At this, Albert quit his perusal of the plat, turned toward us and grinned. "I guess we've both learned that the hard way, haven't we? We've both gone broke on cows and calves. Remember the Hard Winter? Remember pouring hay and oil cake into cows all winter, and then having them die in the spring, with their calves still inside them?"

So Albert, backbone of the old Tongue River cow-and-calf outfits, was beginning to contradict himself and to see some flicker of truth in Matt's wild, new challenge to tradition. It was encouraging, just sitting there and hearing one old-timer convincing another, while both were giving me a free lesson in the economics of animal husbandry, which could not possibly have been gleaned from any university at any price. It was too good an opportunity to be marred. And so, as Albert turned back to the map and pulled out his sack of Bull Durham, Matt went on uninterrupted.

"As a matter of fact, getting a calf—that is, future beef and profit—by old mother nature's process can be the most expensive way to do it, because you're supporting three animals to get one chance at that profit: the cow, the bull, and the calf. You wait nine months for the cow to produce the calf. Then you wait another six months for the calf to be weaned and old enough to be put out on the range, where it can even begin gaining the weight that makes your money. Meantime, your capital's tied up for fifteen months, earning interest for your bankers at these high rates, maybe even 7 percent. All that and the labor. Of course, there's more labor on a cow outfit than on a straight steer deal. All that goes into the price per pound of the weaned calf you put out on the range, before he even starts working for you.

"That may have been all right in the old, open range days, but it just doesn't always work out today. Now, you've got to cut corners, double up, and hustle. You can't always wait for mother nature, and she won't hurry up. Why, for what it costs to put a home-raised steer on the range around here—maybe twenty cents a pound—I can have three Mexican billies eating their heads off and gaining weight just as fast. After double-wintering they might even gain more. And if I lose one, I'm only losing the five

or six cents a pount I've got invested in him and the grass he's
eaten at fifteen cents an acre. That's the basis we operate on here,
and if you'd like to come in with us, any way at all, we can draw
up a contract. What did you have in mind?"

"Something, perhaps, like what Albert and I operated on fifteen
years ago. I thought we might all discuss it."

Albert pulled the only other chair across the room to the desk
and sat down. "It was a standard form of deal we used on Tongue
River in the old days," he explained, "but for cows and calves at
that time, naturally. Our company was still broke from the Hard
Winter, like everybody else. The banks had us all sewed up. Some
of the other outfits went over to dudes, but we didn't. Well, Ned
here came to us out of the East as a weekend guest. He'd run into
an old acquaintance at Eaton's Ranch, a wild young fellow from
New York, who'd had some sort of run-in with his family, and
was working at our ranch. Ned liked the country and wanted to
stay on. He hadn't been too strong but felt better and wanted to
get into something. We couldn't hire him because we didn't have
any spare cash, but we did have a small herd built up again by
that time, and he had some money coming to him that he wanted
to invest. So we got together on a deal, and I drew up this contract."

To my surprise, Albert reached into his jacket and produced a
copy of the old document, wherein I had put up ten thousand
dollars, and his ranching partners had put up a thousand acres
of range for the purchase of three or four hundred additional cows
and calves to be run under a fifty-fifty partnership brand, V Bar C.
It had worked well enough for its day and age, what with all their
other range.

Matt glanced over the contract and handed it back, smiling.
"Fine for your situation in those days. But things are different
today, and the situation now is steers, not cows and calves. We
have a form of contract that we use with several partners on deals
like this." He turned to me and added, "I think you'll find it tailored to order. If not, we can make it fit. Who are your lawyers?"

"The Marshall firm in Sheridan."

"Good. I'll have my lawyers in Billings send you a copy, and you
can have Barry look it over."

He gazed at the old Seth Thomas on the wall ticking away the
half-seconds with its little, twitching pendulum. "We've got a

shipment of twenty-six cars unloading at Benteen today, and I ought to be up there now to receive them. Sorry if I have to run along. Come back any time." Then he led the way to his little house in the lilacs by the ditch, where we got into our separate cars and drove along together. At the highway by the Wyola station he pulled over to wave us good-bye. We turned south for Tongue River, and Matt turned north toward his beloved Mexican billies.

2

Tongue River Panorama

AMONG THE CATTLE-RANCHING PEOPLE of the Montana-Wyoming area, rivers and their tributary creeks (usually, *cricks*) were the main points of reference and probably always will be to some extent. At least, they will be until a great many more cities spring up as better reference points in these two huge states totaling more than a million square miles, with a population of less than a quarter million souls as of 1970. That makes a distribution of about one person to every four square miles, or 2,560 acres, even after the recent, nationwide population explosion.

Therefore, people tend to group themselves and each other according to creeks and rivers. The most western of this particular area system would be the Big Horn River and Little Big Horn River people. They tend to be the larger operators of the encroaching machine age and the less closely knit socially: reservation people who, besides working with livestock, also lean toward great agricultural operations, especially in sugar beets and wheat. They are paved-road people, whose beat is the U.S. 87 highway mostly between Billings and Sheridan, where no one would ever consider stopping to offer help to a stalled car.

To the east of them would be the Rosebud River people. They are mostly of cheerful, hardy, old-time cattle families. They have beautiful green valleys with a few millionaires nestled among them and a creek appropriately named Cache Creek nearby. They have more timber and shale roads. They almost always stop to help each other or—until the 1960s, anyway—just to talk and be pleasant.

18

Then come the Tongue River people. They have both shale and gumbo roads and can almost always be spotted in town by their muddy cars. They are most likely to stop and help each other or even strangers on the lonely stretches and high divides between the Rosebud and Miles City. They are friendly and warm to an unusual degree for this day and age, and they never lock their doors.

Next come the Otter Creek people with mostly gumbo roads, who are always rescuing each other. They are separated from Tongue River by the high land of the Custer National Forest, dominated by its widely known butte, Poker Jim, which accommodates a key Forest Service lookout station fire tower. They don't visit back and forth very much with the Tongue River people. No hard feelings. It just isn't the custom.

A tributary tribe of the Tongue River people includes the Hanging Woman Creek dwellers. They count as original, basic Tongue River, with its pioneer aura and hospitality, not only among their own families but to later settlers and temporary visitors as well.

All these people are resourceful and fiercely independent, above the bourgeois concept of social distinction by automotive scale. They don't even wash the mud off their cars very often. They are people whose money, or lack of it, doesn't show and isn't important as in a sort of silent, unplanned aristocratic pattern.

Still farther east are the Pumpkin Creek and Powder River people, who stretch out into the unknown hinterland beyond the limits of our present consideration.

As related to the few population centers that do exist in our area, the people around Billings are the most urban and industrial. They have passenger trains, a multiflight airport, a petroleum industry, a ballet school and interior decorators; and they lean toward city clothes. They are flatland, Yellowstone people.

Miles City people are the only other urban Yellowstoners. Theirs is the little-sister city to Billings. They are more the old-west type, pioneer cattle-ranching families, less industrially minded. They have the same railroad tracks and passenger service, but big-time flight schedules are a passover situation.

For a period well up into the 1950s, Miles City also had a remarkable district on an island in the river on the edge of town. There a few neat, white houses with cheerful window boxes of geraniums, nestled around a simple restaurant known for the most delicious and reasonably priced Sunday steak dinners on the Yellowstone, char broiled by a Chinese cook.

But only on Sundays could the city notables bring their wives and families for a simple treat in this idyllic nook. That was the one day when the girls caught up on sleep and tended their window boxes instead of the welfare of humanity through easing the tension of mankind's most fundamental requirements.

"The Island" was a model of law and order, a haven of peaceful, hygenic relaxation, and often a very practical information center for ranchers. The popular cattle brands, as well as liquor brands, were all represented. Crime, violence and narcotics were unknown. The whole atmosphere of the place was a relic of that old-fashioned American common sense and tolerance now so rapidly being crushed under the cruel, misguided heel of so-called progress.

Sheridan has always been an attractive western magnet for easterners. With modest population and blissfully free from highly mechanical or technical industry, it is still relatively unspoiled even though dangerously close to the new, horror-sized super-highway, with ghastly coal-mining operations pushing paved roads from its northern doorstep through once quiet cattle country for thirty miles down the Tongue River valley to the northeast. Nevertheless, it retains a nice east-west flavor balance with an economic base of cattle ranches and people ranches that operate at the foot of the Big Horns and south to include its satellite area of Big Horn, Wyoming. There the eastern flavor of registered show cattle, blooded horses, polo and family silver is slightly more noticeable as it blends charmingly into the best that the old west had to offer, flavored with some inherited money and affectionately called the Mink and Manure concept.

Sheridan proper is referred to as "downtown Sheridan." No one has ever heard of "uptown Sheridan." The only place it could possibly be is the airport, which is officially designated the Municipal Airport, although there is no other or any very likely place to put one. A northbound and a southbound plane stop by daily, and there is a brisk business in private and charter planes.

The Burlington Railroad abandoned service long ago but kindly left a huge compound double expansion steam locomotive on its now defunct passenger station lawn as a fond memorial to the decades throughout which it sent its Numbers 42 and 44 passenger trains proudly puffing east every day, while its Nos. 41 and 43 puffed west.

At sixty miles Sheridan is the nearest town for the Tongue River people, who have their immediate nerve center and post office, Birney, at the junction of Hanging Woman Creek and the river, complete with grade school, church, two general stores and a few small homes. All rolling hills and red shale buttes, the area consists of sage- and timber-covered cattle country, mostly owned and controlled by a few large, old-time livestock outfits, of which Albert's was one of the original, founded by his father, a veteran of the Civil and Spanish-American wars.

In the early 1920s my father's estate sold our house, and I had a living problem, which Albert and his family solved in more ways than one by their hospitality. Among them was Albert's guidance in enabling me to file a claim on 653 acres of public domain adjacent to his ranch, with an attractive building site overlooking his own house. He even gave me an abandoned cabin up in the hills to move onto the site. It had no roof or floor, but its logs were sound, well fitted, and would enclose an area twelve by twenty feet—plenty large enough to start a home—and there was certainly room for expansion, considerably more than the area of the Principality of Monaco.

After a somewhat unglued childhood and adolescence, spreading over nine homes—town and country, leased and owned—with education stabs at seven schools and two years of college, I felt that I still hadn't learned anything, had no meaningful home base, and was probably difficult. A short note to Princeton authorities had conveyed my farewell, which undoubtedly delighted them.

At that point, the log quadrangle, carpeted in sage and roofed by sky, clouds and stars, seemed a gift from the gods and suggested the old lyrics, "Oh, give me a home where the buffalo roam . . . ."

That winter an odd, semirecluse type of bachelor in his fifties, who had a cabin across the river, and whom I hired for the moving and reconstruction, contracted a couple of Cheyennes with a team to skid the logs down on the snow. Next spring, with lumber and supplies shipped out from Sheridan, we finished the transformation, having first (as old Fred insisted) built an outhouse. Then we built a one-car shed and a coal shed. Our color scheme was green for window trim and shed walls, red for shed and outhouse roofs, with a native red shale roof on the cabin.

By summer I had the place furnished with a cot, a coal stove,

a table, three bare hardwood chairs, two galvanized water buckets, a dipper, a wash basin, some coat hooks screwed into the logs,
and two oil lamps. Then I moved my meager possessions up from
the ranch house and had a home of sorts, except for meals, which
I took at the ranch.

That fall I made my first wildly extravagant purchase: four
hundred dollars for a foot-pumped, pneumatic upright player
piano. This called for a housewarming. With moonshine liquor
easily available for a short horseback ride up nearby Harris Creek,
music right at hand, and food brought up from Albert's house, the
rest was easy. Albert and his family came, with two houseguests,
their bunkhouse crew of three—including my charming but badly
behaved friend Tom Sithers—and old Fred.

Wonderous melodies, ranging from Beethoven's "Moonlight
Sonata" to the "Twelfth Street Rag" and "Flaming Mamie, the
Sure-fire Vamp" floated out over the cool, still night air, down
the hill and across the alfalfa meadows, until Tom got boisterous.
Denied access to the jug (which had been carefully hidden outside by then) he produced a pint bottle from his hip pocket and
challenged me to keep him from drinking his own liquor.

I told him that he could go outside with his pint but could not
drink it in my cabin. Whereupon he raised it to his lips, and I
grabbed it. In the ensuring tussle he managed to throw the pint
into the stove, which had a bed of live coals in it. The high-proof
rotgut exploded, blowing open the firebox door, which was ajar,
and belching coals out onto the floor, with a shower of sparks
blasted up the stovepipe high into the air outside. A neighbor,
who had driven by just then, later reported it as an odd sight,
assuring him that the cabin was at last in full operation. On this
note the housewarming broke up.

The following year I enlarged the compound by tacking on
another cabin seventeen by twenty-four feet. Fred had advised
me that it would be an excellent investment, which he could
arrange at a good price through friends. This time it was a brand-
new building, deserted in the process of construction, just long
enough ago so that the logs were well seasoned. He had disappeared on horseback for two days, returning to announce that
he had bought the logs for fifty cents apiece, with the ridge log
thrown in free because it had a slight bow in it. "But we can lay
it with the bow up, and it'll be that much stronger," he had

chuckled. This made my investment come to nineteen dollars for the basic materials and a few trimmings needed to round out a very adequate living space for one man.

The new purchase was about four miles away, up Dead Man Creek. Again Fred contracted for the moving and then applied his own considerable skills as architect and builder. A husky Norwegian stonemason and his helper came from Sheridan and boarded down at Albert's ranch, where we all ate.

Fred commuted to work back and forth across the river on his fat, dark brown gelding, Fashion, with his enormous (and also gelded) striped yellow cat, Sport, riding on the swell of his saddle, clutching the horn. Every morning they could be seen easing through the hay meadows at a slow walk, such as would not be uncomfortable for Sport, and which might also give him a chance to spring at grouse, as Fred had taught him.

The stonemason and his helper spent the first three days blasting sandstone out of the neighboring hills and hauling it in on a stoneboat with a team kindly loaned us by Albert, while Fred and I, with the help of an occasional Cheyenne or two from the nearby Reservation, manned picks and shovels. We dug a twelve- by five-foot excavation eight feet deep at one end of our planned floor space for a future vault and laid pipe in a trench five feet deep, running into the area from a likely direction, for a future water supply from a source as yet undetermined. Then we dug a generously proportioned three-foot-deep pit for the foundation of a fireplace. Fireplaces were the stonemason's famous speciality.

Up went the logs. Down went blocks of white sandstone carefully fitted to form the vault with its reinforced concrete floor, a ceiling supported by steel I-beams with concrete poured between them and, eventually, a specially built, heavy steel trapdoor. As the logs went up, so did the fireplace and chimney. We laid sleepers and flooring. Then with saddle horses, throw ropes and skids, we hoisted the roof logs.

We placed the long side of the new room up against one end of the old cabin, with the log work carefully dovetailed together. Thus, after roofing, chinking and otherwise finishing the new part, we had only to saw a large opening in the old part and put in a pair of double doors. The old homestead cabin then became a mere future kitchen. So we moved the player piano and the bed out of it.

Interior of Edmund Randolph's cabin, looking from kitchen (original homestead cabin) into living room

Old Fred, thumbs hooked into the outrageous bib overalls which he insisted on wearing despite all western sartorial tradition, and rocking back and forth on the heels of his scuffed, early twentieth-century mail-order-catalog high shoes, surveyed his handiwork and concluded, "Hell, Ned, we've got to jerk that heating stove out of there and the roof jack, so we can put in a brick chimney for the cookstove."

No one had mentioned a cookstove, but it now seemed certain that there was one in my future. Fred didn't wait for me to ask about it.

"If we're going to live here, we've got to have a cookstove." He made it sound like a simple, commonsense, everyday remark and went on to embellish. "You see, it'll take a six-inch stovepipe, so we'll need a fireproof brick flue. That's why I ordered more of that Denver firebrick than we needed to line the fireplace."

There had, indeed, been a great surplus of yellow fireproof brick lying around unexplained.

He produced a cheap, crumpled notebook and began a long process of thumbing through it. "There's some other things we'll need, too, some day when we get to town. I've sort of been jotting them down."

Indeed he had. It was a dizzying list that he read off, complete to the most remarkable extent in every field: furniture, bed linen, rugs, tableware and other necessities, large and small, from the cookstove itself (our greatest expense, $161) to kitchen matches with which to light it, and extra mantles for the Coleman lamp.

Fred had always used the inclusive pronoun as a cozy way of suggesting that I was not left out of his building plans. But now the "we" began to have a special meaning. Was he gradually getting Sport accustomed to a new home, into which he himself would also move?

Hating trips to town, he had made sure of including all needs in his list, so as to avoid a possible second trip. We even delayed for two or three days to try to think of more things. When we finally did go in the old touring car, it was a thorough buying spree lasting two days, with nothing omitted. We brought back as many of the small items as would fit into the car, including great quantities of canned goods, and had the rest freighted out.

Now that we had an extra folding spring bed, it was natural for Fred to suggest that he should hang around awhile to straighten things out, as this would cut down his commuting time and enable him to get more work done. Also, he had noticed some mouse signs already. "When colder weather comes, field mice always try to get indoors. And fussing around with mousetraps don't pay. All that cheese just attracts more. For every mouse you catch, two more come along and finish up the bait. You can prove that because the first mouse gets killed before he has a chance to eat anything, and there's never any bait left after you catch one."

"Really? I never noticed."

"Well, son, you just look next time. That's why I didn't want you to buy all them mousetraps the hardware feller sold you. I don't care what people say to sell mousetraps; there's nothing like having a good cat around. When you do, mice just naturally seem to know it and stay away." He looked at old Sport lovingly. "He'll keep mice out of your oatbin better than a hundred traps."

"Oats?" I had only two saddle horses, and Albert very kindly let them run with the ranch cavvy. I had never owned an oat. "What oats?"

But Fred had turned away and was heading for a little sage-brush flat nearby in his slow, rolling gait, his shoulders working like the walking beam of an old side-wheel steamer. As he passed by where his saddle lay on the ground, he stooped over and un-limbered a nondescript-looking canvas container, which swung heavily at his side as he progressed to where Fashion was staked out. He buckled the nose bag over the old brown gelding's head and lumbered back toward his work, while Fashion munched contentedly.

We built the brick flue and set up the coal range, which had a hot-water jacket designed to heat the usual tall, round hot-water tank that once stood near every kitchen range. But we had no water system to supply it so Fred took the large oak barrel we had bought, together with some plumbing fittings he had ordered for it, and ingeniously produced a crude but well-functioning system by which we could eventually dip bubbling hot water from the barrel, thanks again to Albert for letting us use his well.

Fred beamed at the first bubbling barrelful with the joy of accomplishment. "That sure beats heating it up in a kettle, don't it?" Then he made a neat wooden cover for the barrel.

Sport, with feline curiosity, had been watching the process intently. When the cover was in place, he jumped up on it to investigate and purred approval. From then on it was his favorite perch, where he lay curled up most of the time blissfully ignorant of the existence of mice or our need for hot water.

"Some day, when you get your own water supply, this'll be the most comfortable little cabin on Tongue River," Fred forecast, glancing around at his brainchild approvingly. "Not so little either. Lots of families live in less space than you've got just for your-self here. Why, hell, boy, it's plenty big enough for two."

"Who knows, Fred? I might get married some day."

He shook his head disapprovingly. "For God's sake, don't do that. This place is no good for a woman. Women wouldn't appre-ciate it. They've got to have a lot of fancy stuff like an indoor toilet and a vacuum cleaner and a washing machine with an engine to it like that goddam thing down there on the back porch. Every washday, when they crank it up, I can hear it across the river at my place. Sounds like somebody riding a motorcycle around. And all that smoke and stink. No, this is no place for women. Ideal for bachelor quarters though."

He seemed to speak the truth. An unattached man was likely to become a roamer, with no appreciation of established life values, wasting his energies and his family's money on luxuries that soon wear thin; perhaps even becoming a sort of remittance man like Tom Sithers. A bachelor needed some place he could call his own, no matter how simple. Even Fred had his hundred-and-sixty-acre homestead. He always claimed that he would never sell it, even though it might be worth a lot some day if the predicted railroad ever went through. "There's just something about these old hills that I couldn't do without," was the way he had put it.

Visions of the possibilities of my own water system kept appearing. Without it life would have to continue on a camping basis: carrying four buckets a day up the hill; throwing dishwater out on the sagebrush; depending on the neighbors or the river for baths, or waiting for the next trip to town where, if one did not stay overnight a bath could be had anyway, for seventy-five cents complete with soap and towel, in the rear of the O.K. Barber Shop. That was one jump better than living on a roundup wagon, but not a bright lifetime prospect if it could be avoided.

Albert assured me that it could. He had a fine, deep soft-water well of inexhaustible supply, pumped by a gasoline engine. Tired of struggling along on his former small attic tank system (and there being then no rural electrification), he had started excavating for a large reservoir on the hill and had bought a lot of pipe. Then the Hard Winter and financial woes had dashed his plans. The excavation was well started, and the hill was now part of my land. If I wanted to finish the job, he would donate the pipe, a team of horses and slip for the digging, and some help from his own men, plus the water and pumping machinery. This would provide an ample supply and also fire protection for both our homes.

Spurred by Albert's generosity, I lay to the task with a will, hired an ever-changing labor force of some dozen Cheyennes, another team and slip, and recalled the stonemason. Fred became a sort of self-elected straw boss, overseeing the Indians as they dug the large hole on the hilltop, finally digging themselves out of sight at about the six-foot level, when only the flying earth from their shovels could be seen by the watchful foreman.

If it did not fly fast enough, he would make a trip up the hill to see if they were loafing down in the hole. Tiring of the climb, he took to shouting at them through a small megaphone he had made out of an old Victor phonograph horn sawed short. One day, exasperated, he sent a .30-30 bullet whistling harmlessly high, but none the less audibly, over their heads. The salute was acknowledged by lively spurts of earth flying out of the hole for a record spell.

More sandstone was blasted, hauled by our teams on the stoneboat, laid and lined with a smooth inner surface, which was then coated with water glass to insure against leakage. The result was a circular tank ten feet deep and twelve feet across, into which the supply and drainback pipe from Albert's pump house entered far below frost line. We had a special rain-catching cover made for it in town.

Fred, now hydraulic engineer on the project, had insisted that the ranch supply-and-demand line be set not less than two feet above the bottom. This, he pointed out, would guarantee us a reserve of some two thousand gallons should the ranch go dry from faucets carelessly left open, accidental leakages, or from pump failure. "It's a cinch they'll get the pump fixed before we ever run out of water," he predicted reassuringly. The situation never arose, but Fred was a careful planner.

Naturally, this sudden and tremendous push for "our own" (as he called it) water supply projected his thoughts into the future. How were we going to handle it when we got it? There would have to be a kitchen sink and, of course, a bathtub. That, he had noticed, was one of the things I valued most. "You can't figure on going through life without a bathtub," he pronounced, although he himself had foregone the luxury at least since he had arrived on Tongue River just after the turn of the century, during which time the river in summer and a washtub on his cabin floor by the stove in winter had seen him through in fine health.

Moving the outhouse indoors, so to speak, was at this time only a dim possibility in the distant future. But even so, the whole mysterious structure of the plumber's world—with its drains, sewer pipes, cesspools and vents—which caused one to hurry past plumbing shop window displays in town, rose up as a specter to haunt my dreams. Would my gorgeous new ten-thousand-gallon reservoir turn out to be just a Pandora's box? There were times when the barbershop bath seemed so sensible.

On thing was certain. No matter what happened, I would need Fred's expertise, and he knew I knew it. He had been casually moving more and more of his personal belongings across the river.

"Where in hell are we going to put the bathtub, when you haven't even got a bathroom?" he asked one morning, while I was still waking up.

It was indeed a reasonable question, and he went on to answer it himself before I had a chance.

"I've been figgerin' . . . we've got two natural corners on the outside now, since we tacked this new room on . . . inside corners, I mean. That means we've got one end and one side of another room already built and two choices where to put it. We don't want to spoil our view, so I'd say to put the bathroom facing the road, wouldn't you?"

"Yes." It was the only possible answer, and it made me feel that I was partially committed to this new "figgerin'" already.

"That's why I put the waterline in at an angle under here. It comes up right where we want it. There's plenty of room for a water heater in the corner by the stove. We hook right into the water jacket, bore through the logs, and you've got hot water for your bath."

I could almost feel myself soaking in the tub.

"That'd do away with the barrel. It'd be tough on old Sport. But then, I could fix up another place for him. He settles down easy most anywhere. And it'd give us room for a kitchen sink."

He got out of bed, a huge, gray bulk of long-handled union suit underwear in the pinkish dawn, shook the ashes down with the grate crank, put some wood in the firebox, and opened the drafts.

"Poor old Sport." He stroked his pet, curled up on the warm barrel cover. "You won't be having that nice warm bed much longer." Then he got dressed and started mixing his flapjack batter.

Fred had been a roundup cook in his day. He was full of range stories and the ubiquitous good humor of the roundup wagon. But in later years, forced to lead a more sedentary life as a builder specializing in log work, a house painter and a jack-of-all-trades, he had been somewhat soured by the changing times. Some said that he had been disappointed in love and had become a hermit, living all by himself across the river. But he did have a few old-time cronies who commuted around among themselves on horseback and came to visit him.

Perhaps he was genuinely lonely and was seeking a source of companionship for his later years, offering his humble skills in return, seeing that I needed but lacked them. Actually, at that time I could not even make a flapjack, and I was duly impressed by the discovery that he baked delicious bread. He was also one of the few surviving old-timers who could whip up a sort of legendary roundup wagon stew, traditionally known as "sonofabitch," without hyphens. It had no other name and no recorded recipe.

We discussed further building prospects at breakfast. Of course, it would be a shame to forego a bathroom two sides of which were already in existence. Fred knew where he could get some more good, solid, straight, well-seasoned logs for the same price, logs that could be cut and fitted to order free. We would need only seven or eight for the long side — what with a down-sloping roof — cut twenty feet, with two small window cutouts, also free, and they could be hauled by wagon on short notice for $3.00. The end wall needed only a few short logs, which could be easily bargained for. Fred was thus emerging in the guise of a log broker.

It all added up to the prospect that he would be needed around the property — at my instigation, of course — for a considerable period, especially since he was by that time beginning to talk about adding a porch on the opposite side of the kitchen to utilize *that* corner in the interests of architectural equilibrium or to "sort of balance things up," as he put it.

More lumber and supplies were hauled from town. More Indians dug more trench for waste lines and also a cesspool. Some Cheyennes had now pitched tents nearby for semipermanent residence. Fifteen hundred feet of hand-dug trench five feet deep and wide enough for a man to work in, pipe laying and filling in, excavating, rock hauling and handling had been a labor bonanza for them, and other pickings were good. The ranch had killed an old sick cow and let them have the carcass. Before it was cold, they had opened

Randolph cabin in 1960, and as it is today

it up gleefully and rolled out the large, purple paunch, a great delicacy with them.

The new bathroom was a decided improvement, and the gleaming, full-size white enamel tub, mounted on its high ball-and-claw cast-iron feet, a real vision of luxury. Fred got into it as soon as it was unloaded off the truck to try it out for size. That was the only time I ever knew of his being in it, as he abhorred the thought of the mechanical chores required to pump water up from the ranch and used as little as possible. So he always stuck to his old bathing technique of the washtub on the kitchen floor.

The space was way out of proportion for a bathroom, being twenty feet long and only four feet wide, but Fred allocated it masterfully into areas for the tub, a storage closet, an icebox — Albert had a fine icehouse — and (in the dim future) a toilet.

"That still leaves quite a lot of extra space down at the far end," I suggested.

"We'll put the oatbin down there . . . you know, for the horses."

The horses, plural. . . ? This reminded me that, besides Fashion, he had other horses, which he raised for sale on his own homestead across the river.

"You might want to keep your own horses around here instead of letting them run with the ranch cavvy. It'd be much handier if we want to go someplace in a hurry. Then we won't have to depend on the wrangler running them in."

It was a farfetched theory that we would ever have to go anywhere on horseback in such a desperate hurry that I could not make arrangements with the wrangler in time. He wrangled early every morning and brought the cavvy in right past my door around six o'clock.

So I told Fred, "I think they're better off with the cavvy."

"If we keep them around here," he insisted, "we could feed them oats in the winter . . . right out of the oatbin through this window onto a feeding table without ever going outside ourselves. It'll sure be handy."

"Let's hold off on the feeding table for a while and get on with building the porch. If you want to keep some oats here for Fashion, fine. But I don't want a lot of horses messing around right outside my bathroom window."

He turned away silently to his other chores with a sort of hurt expression, and I had the feeling that this matter would require further settling.

3

Shopping for Steers Nets a Stallion

ON MY RETURN from the Antler trip with Albert Harris, I found a letter from Skel Baxton, a local cattle broker with whom I had been corresponding and who had lined up several bunches of steer calves "worth the money." He wanted to know if I would look him up in town. A few days later there was a letter from Matt's lawyers in Billings, enclosing the draft of a suggested contract with the Antler Ranch.

Fred seemed consumed by curiosity as I looked over the contract. "That about your new business?" he asked bluntly. "Bought any cattle yet?"

"Not yet. But it looks as if there are some steers around the country worth the money, according to Skel Baxton here."

"Hell, these cattle brokers all tell you that. Anything's worth the money to them as long as you buy it and pay their commissions. They're a slippery lot. Watch out. . . . And say, isn't that feller more of a horse trader, anyway?"

"His letter says that he's a general livestock operator."

"Them goddam fancy handles they hang on their names nowadays," he sneered. "He's a common old cow buyer. That's what he is. And probably a renegade like most of them. If it was me, I'd watch out just the same, or you could take an awful beating. These cattle are sky high, and the market's going plumb wild. I hear they're asking ten cents for steer calves at Miles City."

"Eight to nine's the information I got back east."

"That's where they were three weeks ago. Who're you going

33

to run them with, if you do get them? Albert said he thought you could make a deal with Matt."

"It's all right in here, if I want to take it. Have a look."

He waved the contract away. "I don't savvy that law jabber. All I know is you've got to have lots of hay and double-winter them calves. And you don't want to get mixed up in a deal with somebody else's brand. Have you got a brand to put on them?"

"Albert said I could have our old V Bar C brand."

"You'd better make damn sure there isn't anything still in it."

"How could there be? He says they shipped the last of the V Bar C's eight years ago."

"They'll have to prove that up in Helena before the brand office'll make the transfer to you personally. It'll take a lot of time. You'll never get your brand registered in time to put it on any critters you're going to buy right away."

He had always been a sort of devil's advocate on any kind of cattle deal, looking for the worst even fifteen years before, when I first went in with Albert. Now he was frowning and slowly shaking his head as he rolled a Bull Durham, spilling the tobacco over his marsupial belly. "You know, I don't like this whole damn steer business that's going on up on the Crow: shipping all them southern cattle up here to this northern climate. It's too risky and too hurry-up. I kind of wish you was going back into cows and calves. It may take longer to make money, but then, every time a cow has a calf she pays for herself."

"I understand that there were a hell of a lot of them around here back in 1919 that didn't."

"Yes, that was a fright, all right. A dry summer and not enough hay put up to start with. Then the Hard Winter that started in October, with all the hay gone by February, and a crust on the snow that would hold a man on horseback and no grass under it anyway and no way to haul oil cake out from town until it was too late. Cattle busting through the fences and coming in around the house, looking in the windows at you, bawling for food, and freezing to death standing up. I seen it with my own eyes. So pitiful it'd make you feel sick . . . but that was an exception."

"How about the blizzard of 1887 that put all those big cow outfits down in Wyoming out of business, and Teddy Roosevelt, too, right over the hill here, in Medora?"

"Well, there's some exceptions like that. But in the long run, as any old-timer'll tell you, every time a cow has a calf she pays for herself."

"Maybe for old-timers they did, in the old-timers' days of the open range that they talk about, with practically everything free. But old-timers are getting pretty well thinned out, and so's the open range. In fact, I've never seen it, and even you haven't seen much of it. The big grass deals are all gone."

"They've still got a lot of it up there on the Crow. Of course, mostly, it's cut up into little pastures of ten or fifteen thousand acres, but that don't hurt any. It just means the boys on the round-up wagon get more sleep. They don't have to ride night guard so much."

"Anyway, I'd like to get the V Bar C back again just for old-times' sake. Albert said he'd give it to me for a Christmas present."

"Which Christmas? He means to, all right, but you know how forgetful he is. Then again, they might want to keep that brand themselves, for old-times' sake. It's one of the oldest in this country. Used to be on a string of cattle over here on Otter Creek, that belonged to the foreman of that English earl. They bought out the cattle and the brand, too, like they did with the Rocker A. If I was you, I'd go up to Helena and register my own brand and not buy any cattle till I had it ready to slap on them."

The contract from the Billings lawyers was clear, concisely written in well-known cattleman's language, with a minimum of legal terminology, and seemed eminently fair. I would agree to notify the Antler Ranch of a delivery date for so many head, free and clear; the ranch would agree to receive them, brand them with my own brand, run them for a period to be mutually agreed upon, finally market them and assume responsibility under a 2 percent loss clause on the tally. That is, they would agree to account for ninety-eight percent of the animals (allowing for winter kill, predatory animal loss, or other unavoidable losses). For the range fees and all handling charges I was to pay at the rate of fifty cents per head per month. Incidentally, this grass, under their Crow Reservation leases at that time, figured out to only about fifteen cents an acre for what must be very close to the finest cattle range in the United States. If extra hay had to be fed in winter (such as, perhaps, for a hospital bunch or in case of extremely severe weather) it would be provided at cost.

Antler Ranch irrigated lands produced an annual hay crop of

six thousand tons. Actually, however, not much hay was needed, thanks to a series of nearly open winters.

Those were, roughly, the terms suggested for running my cattle, for which operation Matt was to be responsible, and concerning which, therefore, he was to be the final authority in case of any dispute. There never was a dispute.

On the financial side, returns from sales were to be handled in what also appeared to be a square-shooting arrangement. All sales checks would, naturally, be made out to me as owner of the brand. Running expenses (range fees, hay, labor, and so on) would then be deducted. After that, I would be entitled to a guaranteed 5 percent return on my investment in the cattle. Then Matt would be entitled to the same return on any money of his own which he had invested. The remainder would be net profit, which we would divide equally.

The Marshall law firm in Sheridan passed on this contract, with a few minor changes acceptable to both sides, and from then on, I was in business with Matt. The first hurdle—grass—was overcome. The next challenge was to find cattle "worth the money." I called Skel's headquarters, but he was off on a buying trip. Whoever answered the phone said that he would be calling in from Miles City next day and would probably be coming up Tongue River soon on his way back to Sheridan. So I left the message that I would be ready to join him if he wanted to stop by for me.

I knew Skel only casually, and he had never been to my place before, so he drove down to the ranch house first, then turned and came back up the hill, raucously tooting his horn, which disturbed Fred from his perusal of the *Pathfinder,* his Bible among periodicals, over the top of which he looked disapprovingly as Skel got out of his car.

Skel was never one to stand on ceremony, and when he burst into the kitchen it was as if a spring storm had blown the door off its hinges, filling the place with tingling air and promises of sunshine to come. His sharp blue eyes glinted appraisingly about the cabin; his booming voice had a mischievous tone as he flitted about comically in his high-heeled boots, like an overgrown Peter Pan. His somewhat stocky build showed the beginnings of the standard middle-aged cattleman's starch-and-fried-food paunch just showing over the silver belt buckle, which was modeled after a longhorn steer's head with tiny, chip ruby eyes. "Just been looking for you down at the main house. Didn't know you were staying with Fred up here."

"I'm not staying with Fred. Fred's staying with me."

Fred obviously didn't like this sally, as, concerning it, he later said, "The sonofabitch knew all the time you weren't living at the ranch house. He just went down there looking for information about you." But at the moment he contented himself with giving Skel a cool reception, merely grunting at him over the top of his *Pathfinder.*

I packed a bag hastily and threw it into Skel's car. Fred came out on the porch to see us off and mumbled a warning to me under his breath. "Don't tip your hand. And if you buy any stock, make sure they weigh out right."

Skel, although he had been in the car and apparently out of earshot, later seemed to have sensed Fred's words. He turned up his collar and laughed gaily as we drove away. "Thought I felt a cold draught back there. Bet I know what he's been telling you: 'Keep away from steer deals; every time a cow has a calf she pays for herself.'"

"Yes, Fred's a real cow-and-calf man, all right."

"These old-timers are all the same. They'd rather sit down in the sagebrush with an armful of cows and starve to death waiting for the old days to come back, than ride over the hill to look at a new idea that might pay the taxes. You know, cows and calves don't grow a damn bit faster now than they did in 1890, but taxes have speeded up a lot. So once in a while, you've just got to jump out and buy some of these calves ready-made, so long as you've got the range to turn them into beefsteaks real fast."

"I figure that I've got plenty of range lined up."

Skel smiled knowingly but asked no questions, so I took it for granted that he probably knew all about the matter. Skel just looked straight ahead and sped on down the river road, presently adding confidently, "I tell you, partner, we're going to see some calves that're really worth the money."

"Where are we heading?"

"Oh, just down the road. Sheridan first. We'll stop in at the auction sale there and get a few prices. Then south."

We didn't stay long at the auction. After witnessing a few high-priced transactions and meeting several grinning, gold-toothed individuals with big smiles but no reasonable prices, Skel nodded

38

toward the door. He clucked and shook his head as we climbed back into the car, mumbling disconsolately, "They're higher than a cat's back!" I had a vague feeling that this was a softening-up process to prepare me for relatively higher prices all along the line, which might or might not be justified. But Skel's merry voice soon brushed these thoughts aside. "Let's slip on down the road. We can do better than this. I've got an option on a nice little bunch of mixed steers and heifers near Gillette."

The prelude to inspection of these cattle included several long-distance telephone calls, to facilitate which we patronized one of the more elite drinking and gambling establishments. There, Skel called the operator repeatedly, pumped the receiver hook, changed his hat positions, registered the whole gamut of facial expressions, lighted or crunched out cigarettes and, occasionally, worked the booth door back and forth for ventilation. I sat for awhile idly at the bar. The patrons all seemed to be full of quips about changes in their bodily appearance as they wormed their way into middle age. A hat would be lifted here to display a bald spot, or a stomach punched there, with the remark, "Looks like you sure wintered good!"

Skel, his telephoning finished, bounded out of the booth, and soon we were heading southward through Wyoming. But the little herd near Gillette didn't look like much, and after supper in town we continued on over the great, starlit plains rolling endlessly before our headlights. Suddenly Skel pulled up to a dilapidated little hotel. "It ain't much to look at," he apologized, "but the beds are good."

Later, upstairs, one of the beds collapsed in the joints as he sat on it. He put the joint together again and tested it gingerly, explaining, "You see, it ain't used to so much action. This is the one they save for undertakers' conventions to lay out the corpse on."

We crawled between cold, gray patched sheets and settled down to a sleep undisturbed by any sound coming in the open window. There was only the strong, dry, sparkling air sweeping in from the plains and smelling of sage.

By the first faint streaks of dawn, Skel lit the lamp, which gasped for oil and threw wan rays on us as we dressed and splashed in the wash basin, Skel apologizing for the accommodations. "Can't expect much in this kind of a place, where there's so little going on the hoot owls have to make love to the prairie chickens, just for a change."

Cheyenne . . . Denver. It was the same. We dropped in at stockmen's bars and wandered through hotel lobbies looking for likely
brokers. Skel haunted the telephone booths and finally suggested,
"I've located a good buy down near Pueblo. We ought to make it
there by suppertime. Friend of mine has the stock on a little
ranch just this side of town."

Toward sundown we reached Pete Drake's ranch, a few hundred acres of irrigated farmland which was once range not so very
long ago, but was now cluttered with fences, chopped up into
small pastures, sprinkled with modern, "store-bought" houses and
served by city electricity. What had once been a ranch was now no
more than a farm on the outskirts of a small city. There, where
men once rode horses, now they rode tractors. The conquest of
the plow-jockey was complete and to it he had raised, as everywhere throughout the land, his standard victory monument, the
silo.

Some of Pete Drake's paddocks held a few head of Hereford
steers—heavy, tame and expensive-looking—browsing about on
luscious green grass. But most of the paddocks held blooded
horses, with a Denver Stock Show look about them. Strangely
enough, Skel passed up the cattle with only a casual glance in
their direction but stopped in front of the horses and eyed them
searchingly. "Trotters," he mumbled absentmindedly and drove
on, looking inquisitively all around. "Doesn't seem to be anybody
around. Let's go look in the barn."

"Nobody around here either," I said, as we entered the caver-
nous building.

"Quite a spread, eh?" Skel kept looking about, and his eye fell
on the ladder to the hayloft. "I wonder how much hay he's got up
there? Come on, let's go see." And he led the way up the ladder.

The huge loft was about half full. The end doors were open to
the setting sun, and a cool, dry evening breeze blew in, mingling
with the sweet scent of hay. Skel went to the opening and looked
down into the barnyard below, steadying himself on the hay hoist
tackle. Then he jiggled the tackle, rolling it back and forth on its
overhead track, like a child playing with a new toy. "The last time
I was here," he mused, "a bunch of us had one hell of a fight in
this barn over a band of ewes that Pete and some of his friends
tried to sell us."

"What was wrong?"

"Oh, they just wasn't up to contract, and the sellers didn't want

to return our deposit. So we took it out of their hides. Locked ourselves in here with them, broke all the light bulbs and fought
them on and off all night in the dark. We'd fight a little while, then
sleep a little while. Then get up and fight some more. They got
to jabbin' around at us in the dark with pitchforks, so along about
dawn, we caught one of them and busted his pitchfork over his
head and strung him up by the heels from this hoist." He rolled
it back and forth affectionately. "Then we eased him out to the
end of the track and let him dangle over the barnyard awhile, so's
he could have a good bird's-eye view of the ewes and see how many
old gummers they had tried to run in on us, that we wouldn't
accept. When we finally hauled him back in again, he was the
scaredest sheep salesman you ever saw, and I'll bet he ain't
touched a pitchfork since." He paused a moment for me to absorb
the lesson of how well he defended his customers taking delivery
of livestock from Pete Drake, then added hastily, "Come on, let's
get out of here," and led the way down the ladder. We got back
in his car and he started off in a direction away from the ranch
house.

"Where to now? I thought we just had time to make supper."

"Well, I'll tell you, Ned. This old bastard's got another little
pasture a couple of miles down the road here, that he thinks I
don't know about. Might be something interesting down there."
When we reached the pasture, he took a pair of binoculars from
the glove compartment and stared through them.

"What are you looking at?"

"Want to see a pretty golden palomino stud?" He handed over
the glasses. "Way back up at the far end against the fence."

I focused on the stud, admiring the flax mane and tail waving
gently in the breeze, a setting sun bringing out the burnished
gold in his sleek coat.

"Ain't he pretty?" Skel asked impatiently. "He's won prizes
all over the country. Got a pedigree as long as a railroad track.
That's *Looey's Door.*"

"Louise *what?* Who'd ever call a stud *Louise?*"

"Not *Louise* . . . *Looey. Looey's Door.* I know it's kind of silly,
naming a horse after a door, but it's one of them fancy French
names that don't mean what it sounds like."

I took a long look at *Louis d'Or* but couldn't see what he had
to do with our cattle-buying junket.

"*Looey* should have been up at my ranch long ago," Skel pouted as he turned the car around and fell into a silent streak, heading back toward Pete Drake's house.

Pete got there at the same time, driving up in a trotting gig behind a fine chestnut gelding. He was a smallish fellow with a dark complexion, grayish hair and beard stubble, probably, I thought, in his sixties. He sat bolt upright in correct driving posture, but was too hard-bitten–looking to make a good picture for the sports sheet. "Been expecting you all afternoon, and when you didn't show up, I put off supper and took this horse for a workout," he announced, flashing a gold-toothed, hard-bitten smile. Then he took us into his little house, furnished in bad bachelor's taste, and the housekeeper put on a passable supper. During supper I became disillusioned about the possibility of making a cattle deal with Pete.

By next morning it was certain that there would be no deal, and the talk turned to horses, Skel asking innocently, "Say, Pete, what did you ever do with that pretty palomino stud, *Looey?*"

"Oh, I've been breeding him."

"I thought I was going to get to use him as part of our last deal? I've still got quite a few good mares up in Montana that I think would appreciate *Looey.*"

"Bring 'em down any time. There'll be no stud fee. You can use him awhile for nothing."

"It's quite a haul, though. I thought the deal was that you were going to drop *Looey* off at my ranch when you brought him down from Canada."

Pete was silent a moment and then explained, "I was, but it got too close to winter. And anyway, I couldn't locate you at the time. He'll be going back up that way after awhile, I guess. One of those Montana copper kings around Butte made me a pretty attractive offer for him, and *Looey* can stop off at your ranch on the way. In fact, I'm flying up to Butte this morning to talk it over. Be gone about a week."

We drove off right after breakfast and as soon as the car door was shut, Skel asked anxiously, "You're a witness to what he said about *Looey,* aren't you? He said I could use him for a while, remember?"

"That's what I thought he said. Why?"

"Well, the sonofabitch said that once before, and I never got to use him. And it was through me that he got *Looey:* part of a horse deal I put him on to up in Canada. He made lots of money out of that deal, but now he's doing me a favor to let me ship my mares all the way down here to *Looey,* or else wait for him to ship *Looey* up there. Why, if he sells *Looey* to that copper king, he'll be so anxious to get him delivered and paid for that he won't let him stop off at my ranch any more than he did the other time."

Skel kept on mumbling about *Looey* and the Canadian deal until we were well on our way north again. Then he suddenly turned in at a gasoline station and began telephoning madly while the car was being filled up. He came out of the telephone booth wreathed in smiles, and I felt sure that, this time, he had really located some cattle to buy. But we reversed course and headed south again. "We're going back to get *Looey,*"he explained simply.

"How about the cattle? Aren't we going to buy any?"

"Sure. They're as good as bought right now. We've got an option on that bunch at Gillette, and about 30 percent cheaper now. I just been talking to the boys up there. Been getting information on that herd all along the line, and I know we won't find any better buys down here unless we go plumb to the Mexican border. Then I called Pete Drake's ranch."

"What did Pete have to say?"

"He'd just left for Butte, but I spoke to his man and told him Pete said we could use *Looey* for my mares, so we were coming to get him."

"I thought Pete said you could use *Looey* when he was on the way up north."

"Well, he's on his way right now," Skel laughed. "And *this* time there won't be any slipup like before, when old Pete just couldn't wait to get him down here and collect all them fancy stud fees. We'll just take *Looey* right along with us and save Pete that much freight. We ought to charge him for it."

As we headed north again, towing *Louis d'Or* in a rented open horse trailer, I mentally reviewed the circumstances of our loading the valuable stud without any papers. "You know, Skel, I thought Pete's man looked kind of surprised when we came back for *Looey.* I understood him to say that they were expecting some mares for *Looey* in a few days."

"Must be a mistake somewhere," Skel smiled. "But he'll have plenty of good Montana mares soon. We might even breed him to a few of these farmers' work mares on the way up, and pick up a little extra cash toward our hauling costs. . . . Why hell, partner, we could visit all over the country free, if we wanted to, and just let *Looey* pay our bills for us as we go along. We're hauling a gold mine."

"Suppose some mares come in to Pete's ranch before you can get *Looey* back there?"

"Well, in that case, I'd give a whole lot to see old Pete's face when he gets back from Butte and finds the corrals full of fancy mares from his swell customers, and *Looey* off on a trip to Montana. . . . By the way, he'll need goggles and a blanket in this open trailer. We'll stop in Denver and get him outfitted."

I could see that Skel was enjoying his revenge to the full and began to wonder what the real object of our trip was: this revenge or buying cattle. But when we pulled up to the pens at Gillette again, there were the cattle, all right. The sellers and their agents were also waiting, lined up on the corral gate like a bunch of expectant cormorants, their high heels hooked over the rails for balance. As we drove up, I could feel that Skel held the center of the stage with his two exhibits: a high-priced stud and an investor from New York.

"What you got there, a stud?" said the nearest cormorant, getting down from his perch and standing on the mudguard of the trailer to peer into it.

"Sure. Twenty thousand dollars' worth," Skel tossed off lightly.

The cormorant went around to the other side of the trailer, climbed up on that mudguard, and looked over again. "Sure a dandy, ain't he? Where'd you git him?"

"Just shipped out from the east."

"Got a brand on him?"

"Hell, no. These eastern horses don't have brands."

A second cormorant eased up casually. "Eastern horse, eh? I don't savvy how they keep track of them eastern horses without brands. Looks to me like something worth twenty thousand dollars would be worth keepin' track of."

"Why, that ain't much money back east, where my partner here comes from. His old man was one of them long-whiskered financiers with pearl button shoes that hunts bulls and bears up and down Wall Street with solid gold buckshot." He slapped the cormorant in the belly playfully.

It seemed best to overlook this imaginative and highly inac-
curate metaphor and let Skel set the scene his own way and do the
trading. After all, the trading was what he was being paid a dollar
per head commission for. Besides, after standing so long in the
trailer, *Louis d'Or* might appreciate being turned out to roll around
and limber up a little. So I unloaded him and was about to strip
off the heavy traveling blanket we had bought for him on the
way through Denver.

"Better leave that blanket on," Skel called out. "He might have
a little touch of shipping fever." There was to be no chance of
the cormorants' seeing *Looey's* brand. As he watched the handsome palomino water and caper about the sagebrush flat on the
end of a long lead, he seemed more interested in the horse than
in the cattle negotiations. Then suddenly, he signaled to load
Looey back into the trailer, and we drove off with only the briefest
of farewells to the cormorants.

"Well, did we get the steers?"

"No. But we will, or we'll get something. I made them an offer.
They're going to see their bankers and telephone us in Sheridan
. . . whether they can accept it or not. They'll accept it, all right."

"What kind of offer?"

"Well, they won't come down under forty-five dollars per head
on their yearling steers. That's too risky a price, so I told them to
skip it, as you were buying a big interest in some of Sheardon's
Mexican steers at way less than that."

I marveled at how Skel had gotten this idea and decided that it
must have been through the cattlemen's grapevine. After a short
silence, he asked, "That's right, ain't it?"

"Not exactly, just now. But Sheardon's expecting another big
shipment of Mexican billies this week. He told me I could brand
any number I wanted at delivered cost. And I know that won't be
forty-five dollars."

"I told them that we'd take six hundred and fifty of the heifers
at thirty-five dollars a head, if they can gather that many and they
weigh out right, laid down on the Reservation."

"*Heifers?* . . . Six hundred and fifty? Who said anything about
heifers, or buying six hundred and fifty head of anything?"

Skel smiled confidently. "It's this way. These boys have some
heifers up their sleeve, and there were a few in that back corral,
as you probably saw. The heifers are a better buy than the steers

now, and they'll bring within a penny or two of the same price on the beef market. They're a better grade. Then, if this market breaks, you've got a chance to protect your investment. You can always breed them. Some are bred already, a few showing calf if I know anything about it, but most are still open heifers. If you should happen to get caught in the market, you can always breed them, and their calves will help to pull you out of the hole. In other words, you can go two ways with them . . . see?"

"But six hundred and fifty! That's nearly twenty-three thousand dollars plus freight. I don't want to spend that much right now. You let them get the idea that I'm some sort of millionaire, with all that talk about *Looey* and Wall Street."

"That's the best thing for them to think. These guys never try to skin a millionaire too bad the first time. They want him to come back. It's more profitable in the end. And as for the heifers, I'm taking half of them myself. If you don't want the rest, I'll take them all. I've got a little banker up the road there, who'll finance me."

We stopped in at a little bank to see the little banker, himself an old cattleman. He was wandering around his establishment behind a low railing, with a sheaf of papers in his hand. Skel gracefully vaulted the railing, lifted the little banker up by the armpits, carried him into his private office and sat him down gently for a quiet, heart-to-heart talk. When he emerged, the little banker had agreed to finance him for whatever heifers I would not take. I decided to take half if the cormorants accepted our bid, so Skel was to take the other half.

Soon we were back in Sheridan with the cormorants on the wire, and the deal was finally made. I telephoned Matt Sheardon about delivering the cattle. Then Skel said casually, "You know, I hate to see you unload those cattle on the Reservation."

"Why?"

"Because I could make you a lot more money out of them, and a lot faster, up the line a bit, where I'm going with mine."

"Aren't you unloading at Sheridan and running them on your own outfit?"

"No, I'm taking mine on up the line to Lewistown, Montana. Got a much better deal for them up there. Why not let yours ride along too? We can turn our money over in about ninety days. You'll never do that on the Reservation."

"But I've just made my arrangements to deliver to Matt Sheardon."

"You can postpone it, can't you? He'll wait ninety days. Then you can deliver twice as many, because you'll have twice the money to buy more with. Matt don't care. He won't miss the deal. It don't mean that . . ." he snapped his fingers . . . "to him. In fact, he's doing you a favor even to bother with it."

The problem loomed more clearly. Was it worthwhile risking the loss of a safe deal with Matt in order to take on a blind deal with Skel in the hope of becoming a ninety-day wonder?

Matt knew that I had spent months in locating range. In fact, I had written forty-one letters on the subject, probably more than he had ever written in his life. What would he think if now, for no obvious reason, I called the whole deal off?

Here was my chance to match Skel Baxton's theories against Matt Sheardon's. I need only split my cattle between the Antler and Lewistown.

Skel was having fun when I dropped in at his ranch a week later to ask about delivery of the heifers. "Wait till you see my pet coyote that I found orphaned in the hills. I'm educating him. . . . Here, Jackie!" He clapped his hands, and a coyote pup appeared out of the sagebrush a hundred yards away. Skel fed him some meat and shooed him off. "Now, go hide again!" The pup ran off. "Ain't he a smart little devil, though? I've put in a lot of time training him."

"What for? What are you going to do with him?"

"Oh, knock him on the head when he starts chasing chickens, I guess."

It all seemed so futile. "How's *Looey?*"

"Say . . . he's really working over my mares. Going to have the prettiest bunch of foals you ever saw next year."

"What news about the heifers?"

"Oh, yes. I tried to get in touch with you about that. Well, the boys down there plan to load them out this week, and they want to get straight on the billing. Why don't you let yours go right along up to Lewistown with mine? I talked to the railroad, and they'll give us a better run nonstop, and we'll save all around. Then, I've got this guy, Paul Langer, up there to receive them. Plenty of cheap range and buyers all lined up. I tell you, we can double the money in ninety days."

"I'll try to split my end of it, Skel, but I'll have to talk it over with Matt first. After all, I've got a contract with him, and I've made one change already, from steers to heifers. Although that might make a difference to him, he was pretty decent in not mentioning it. Now, if I'm going to change numbers, too, I'll have to ask him first. As you say, he's doing me a favor to begin with, and if I cut the numbers down very much, the deal might be too small for him."

"The phone's right in my den." He waved toward the house. "Help yourself. I'm going over there to check on Jackie. He's beginning to sniff around the henhouse."

This allowed for a quick but more careful assessment of my proposed commitments. The whole deal was beginning to take on a slightly more speculative aspect than I had first planned.

When I had telephoned from Sheridan, I undoubtedly loaded onto Matt some small differences in his figures, as the end product value would be changed and also, possibly, the methods of handling range matters. He had shown an honest interest in my welfare by immediately asking about my brand. Of course, the V Bar C had not yet been transferred to my name, so now I was in a brand dilemma. But from this he quickly released me. "It's too late now. We can't wait. But don't worry. The Recorder of Marks and Brands in Helena is an old friend of mine. I'll fly up there tomorrow and get him to fix up a brand for you out of whatever's open and bring the papers back with me. And, by the way, that big shipment of Mexican billies have just come in . . . at the lowest price ever . . . and if you'd like to get in on some of them, too, we'll brand as many as you want with your new brand. I'll have our blacksmith make up your branding irons."

On this second phone call, everything was again fine with Matt. The decision was that I'd deliver two hundred heifers to him instead of three hundred and twenty-five but would hold off, for the present, on any Mexican steers.

"I'll throw in with you for a hundred and twenty-five heifers on the Lewistown deal," I told Skel when he came into the house.

Skel had a peculiar psychological habit of playing "deadpan." His face could suddenly become as immobile, noncommittal and uncomprehending as some frame from an old Laurel and Hardy comedy film stuck on the screen by a jammed projector. Possibly, it was one of his poker-playing assets, but occasionally, he used it in other situations, both joking and serious. Now, he turned it on full force.

I took it for disappointment, but after a chilling instant, he broke into a sunny smile. "And they'll make you twice the profit you'll get out of the other two hundred."

He had arranged for earnest money to hold the six hundred and fifty heifers, so now I gave him a check for the balance on my end of the deal and another for his own personal commission. He looked at the commission check wistfully and offered it back. "You're just a little bit doubtful about this Lewistown deal, aren't you? . . . Well, I don't want your money till you're satisfied with the cattle and make a profit on them. That'll be time enough to pay me." When I wouldn't take the check back, he added, "Anyway, I won't deposit it till you're well out of those heifers, and you can stop payment any time. Come on, now, let's have a little scamper-juice, for luck." Then he busied himself hunting around for a bottle of bourbon. "My wife hides all the whiskey around here from the hired man, and when she's gone, I have hell getting a drink myself."

Judging by the air of disarray about the house, I had suspected that he was "batching" and asked, "Is she in town?"

"Damned if I know. She's been lathered up about a lot of things lately. The fire's been out a long time, anyway. Then old Pete Drake phoned the other day. That put a burr under her tail, and she took off. Probably gone back to her folks in California, hopping mad. Never left a note or anything. . . . Well, anyway, here's the Old Sunnybrook."

"How's Pete? . . . Missing his stud?"

"Say . . . talk about people getting hopping mad . . . he's really jumping up and down in his harness about *Looey*. We sure put over a good one on him that time."

I didn't care for the "we" approach, having by then reflected on the full implications of the *Looey* episode, and I suddenly felt something akin to a twinge of sympathy for Mrs. Baxton who, evidently, was also disenchanted with the idea of being connected with this quite illegal operation. For, in plain language, it meant the serious offense of moving a valuable, branded animal across not one, but two state lines without brand inspection, any papers, or even the owner's consent. No wonder "we" didn't take the blanket off *Looey*, because he might have had "a little touch of shipping fever." Also, perhaps, because where cattle are corralled for sale or shipping, there's likely to be a brand inspector hanging around.

Skel, however, went on blithely, "Serves that sonofabitch right for trying to pull a deal like that on me. Then, to top it off, telling me there wouldn't be any stud fee for my mares . . . like he was doing me some sort of favor."

"When's he going to get *Looey* back?"

"Whenever *Looey* gets all my mares bred. Then, I'll just send him a postcard and tell him to come get his stud whenever he wants to, and there won't be any pasture bill."

He pulled the cork from the Sunnybrook and poured a couple of drinks. "Well, here's to old Pete!"

4

Nine Thousand Wild Horses
and the Silent Domain

THE ANTLER ARRANGED to receive and look after my two hundred heifers, so Skel and I took off for Lewistown to receive the other four hundred and fifty and turn them over to Paul Langer. Skel had the time schedule from the railroad, showing approximately when the freight train would be due and the numbers of our ten cars of cattle.

I had learned from Matt Sheardon that my new brand was recorded as "Reverse RN." The R is reversed, and its upright coincides with first upright of the N, making the letters connected to form a neat, compact stamp iron. It was the nearest approach to my own initials that could be worked out, and an altogether appropriate brand (even better than the V Bar C, requiring two irons). It is a left rib brand for cattle and is also registered for horses on the left shoulder. Later I got the V Bar C also (registered for cattle only), and both these brands are still valid in my name until the re-recording date in 1981.

We spent the night in Billings, planning an early start the next morning to be sure of reaching Lewistown ahead of the train.

During supper I sketched my new brand on the back of an envelope for Skel. "What do you think of it?"

"Not bad," he pronounced, giving it a quick scrutiny. "What does it stand for, Royal Navy or Registered Nurse?"

Obviously, he was still not brand conscious. "When are we going to put it on my heifers?" I pursued.

He studied the question a moment and then said noncommit-

Randolph's personal brands: *left,* V Bar C; *right,* Reverse RN

tally, "We'll talk that over with Paul Langer in Lewistown tomorrow. I don't know just how he's set up for branding. You see, he's
just got a small, family outfit, no real cowpokes. I'm a fair roper,
but you might have to wrastle. Then, of course, we'd have to make
some irons, or at least one. You should have gotten a couple of your
new irons to take along if you wanted to brand."

"I never thought of it. They could have dropped the irons off
at the Wyola Garage for us to pick up. Do you have your irons
with you?"

"No. But then, I don't figure on branding my stock."

"No? . . . Why?"

"Because it don't seem worthwhile for such a short time when
we've already got a bill of sale for the brand that's on them now.
Why, we'll be rid of these cattle in sixty to ninety days. So I figured
we might as well save the expense and that much shrink on top of
the shipping shrink they've already had to take. And so soon after
shipping too. Then, they'll take more shrink being moved from the

railroad to Paul's range. All that extra, unnecessary handling and branding's just going to knock the pennies off them, and I don't see where it would pay when they're going to be in good hands on a nice outfit. Of course, you can brand yours if you want to."

This sounded logical enough, but I still liked the idea of having my own brand on an investment in faraway places with strange people, no matter how nice they might be, since the law stated that checks for proceeds of sales have to be drawn to the order of the brand owner.

Skel changed the subject amiably and in a tone mildly suggesting the possibility of some further windfall that had just entered his head. "Of course, you know," he said with a wink, "now that I come to think of it, some of these heifers might just happen to get bred by accident. Lots of the fences in that big, lonesome country up there don't get much upkeep, and there's a lot of weak spots, especially around Paul's range. In springtime, like now, some of the neighbors' fine, big bulls can't resist trying out them weak spots, when they're full of that green grass and get to feeling kind of lonesome. Sometimes, a bull just naturally figures, well, 'first come, first served,' and he ain't educated up to reading brands. He don't even notice whether the heifer's brand's the same as his own, or not. So you see how it is that you might have some unexpected calves to put that fancy new brand on along about next February."

"That's a hell of a time to have calves born in this country. Let's not count on it. Anyway, I'd rather make my money on purpose, not by accident."

Next morning, speeding through the unbelievably empty country which then was—and to a great extent, still is—that vast area encompassed generally by the Missouri and Musselshell rivers and their tributaries in central Montana, we picked up a long plume of smoke and followed it until we overtook the double-header freight laboring toward Lewistown, the two huge compound engines roaring a varied pattern of chugging, as their pistons got in step and then out of step with each other.

Skel ran ahead of the freight, stopped the car and got out his binoculars. He glanced intermittently through the binoculars and at a slip of paper with our car numbers on it, as the freight dragged slowly by. "Sure, there go our cattle, all right . . . them ten cars next to the front engine, just where I ordered them to be. . . . You know, livestock's got a right to ride next to the engine, don't you?"

I didn't, but nodded anyway, while he went on to explain that it was the safest place, especially on a long train . . . the least jerking from taking up slack in the couplings, both slowing down and starting up.

We reached the Lewistown freight yards well ahead of time and confirmed with the yardmaster which track our train would be coming in on. It was an outside track, separated by a dilapidated slab fence from a trucking alley, along which we were walking when the train pulled in. It was a relatively short train and had dropped the pusher engine at the top of the Snowy Mountains divide. As the last of our ten cattle cars went by, something caught Skel's attention. He ducked through a shaky section of the railroad fence and, as the caboose went by, shouted through his cupped hands, "Hey, brakeman, fix that stockcar door! It's busting open!"

The brakeman yanked a cord, and the train, which had just about lost headway anyhow, shuddered to a stop. Cattle surged up against the broken door, which had run off its lower track and was flapping outward from the upper one. Thirty or forty of our heifers were thus admitted to the great outdoors. In no time at all they were loose on the town, running up the alley along the railroad tracks and deploying into side streets.

Skel spied some stockyard hand's pony hitched to a post. Without saying a word, he untied the reins, swung into the saddle and booted the pony into a dead run to get around ahead of the heifers and hold them up. Railroad yardmen, a few willing bystanders and I gradually bunched the little herd and moved them gently into some receiving pens.

Paul Langer, who had been hanging around the yards, waiting for the freight to come in, showed up. He was a long, loose-jointed, grimy-looking stockman in faded blue jeans, runover boots and a raggedy slouch hat. A big grin bisected very plain and somewhat knotty features as he exchanged a few perfunctory remarks with me about a nice rain they'd had and how good his range looked. Then he went into a huddle with Skel, obviously about the cattle and, I hoped, about branding my end of them, but nothing special seemed to come of this.

When our stock was finally bedded down for a rest, with plenty of hay and water, Skel motioned me to follow him out to where we had left the car parked. "No use hanging around here," he said. "We won't move them for a couple of days. Let's get going."

We had a quick bite of lunch and got back into the car, which Skel soon throttled up to a brisk pace. It didn't take long to get out of Lewistown, and soon we were bowling along a deserted highway, flanked on either side by the flattest and most uninteresting country I had ever seen: just a sea of sagebrush. "Where are we headed for now?"

"We're going to spend the night with some friends of mine that have a ranch up the road a ways. They want to see me about some business, and they haven't got a phone. So we'll just kind of drop in. They're working a big herd of cattle, so it might be interesting."

"And after that? . . . I suppose Paul Langer will be branding?"

"You don't have to worry about them heifers, Ned. I tell you they're in good hands and also in pretty good shape. I damn near winded that little fat stockyard pony trying to head them off, even after forty-eight hours on the rails. They're light, but they're tough. So we don't have to rush back there. In the meantime . . . well . . . how'd you like to drive on up to Saskatchewan? We could be there in another day or so."

"What for?"

"Horses. I've got the best deal you ever saw waiting for me up there at a little ranch just across the border. You know, we've got to find another deal to double the profits we're going to make from these heifers. I was going to cut old Pete Drake in on this, even after that dirty trick he pulled on me about *Looey*. But after the way he talked to us when we were down there, and the prices he put on his cattle, I decided to get me a new business partner. Now, I know a big horse outfit up north, here, that's got nine thousand head we can buy for next to nothing."

"But I don't want nine thousand horses."

"You wouldn't have to take them all, just a few thousand. Say, two or three. I'd take the rest."

"I couldn't even use two thousand horses, or even two horses. I've got a couple of good, gentle saddle horses of my own at home, and Matt tells me the Antler cavvy has plenty of horses I can ride. Most of these half-broken broncs they try to sell you in this country, or Saskatchewan, I suppose, would just buck me off."

He put on the mock-serious, frozen face and stared straight ahead. "Oh, we'll fix that!"

"How?"

A puzzling silence reigned, as if he were in deep thought, until he decided to relax into his humorous mood. "You know, there's just a hell of a lot of these wild horses that gets over the bucking habit . . . once you pop them into a can."

The idea of horsemeat had always curdled my stomach, but I knew that European armies relished it. Obviously, the rounding up of wild horses for canneries, which was big business during World War I, had started up again in World War II.

"No, Skel. No horses for me. I want to stick to the beef business."

"You want to make money, don't you? And now that you're a livestock man, I don't see what difference it makes what kind of meat you trade in. Look at your partner, Sheardon. One of the biggest cattlemen in the country, but I notice that he runs sheep on the side."

"Yes, but sheep aren't like horses. You don't ride them."

"You don't ride these horses either. They're wild as caribou, and they don't belong to anybody, no more than game does. Never had a brand on 'em. It's a last chance. The only big herds left are up in Canada, this here country's getting so damn crowded."

"Let's get the profit out of these heifers first, before we decide how to invest it."

"Oh, I was just thinking ahead a little bit, like you've got to if you're going to make a fast deal once in a while. Why, we can double our money on these heifers in six or eight weeks and then triple the profits on just this one horse deal. Well, anyway, we don't have to decide right now. Here we are, at the ranch," and he drew up abruptly at a wire gate.

"What ranch?" I asked, getting out to open the gate, which was not marked in any way. There seemed to be no way of identifying any kind of ranch from the rest of that sprawling, empty country we'd been driving through for hours. Except for range and sky and the three-wire fence, there was nothing in sight anywhere.

"This is old Bill Delane's outfit, where we spend the night. Silent Bill, they call him. You mustn't be surprised if he don't talk much to you. That's his way, and he's just naturally extra shy with strangers. He don't mean nothing by it, like a lot of these old-timers. And he's got lots of good cattle around here."

We bumped along over Silent Bill's range for another half hour without seeing any cattle at all. Then a newborn calf wobbled to its feet and staggered away from our approaching car. Skel stopped to look it over, remarking, "His mother's hidden him while she's gone off to water."

"She must have gone a long way. We haven't seen any water yet."

"She's got to be around here somehwere . . . oh yes, over there," and, pointing to a speck on the horizon, he took his binoculars from the glove compartment. "Yes, that's her, all right. She keeps looking back to where she cached the calf. Can't see her brand, but she must be one of Bill's." He switched off the engine and got out of the car to steady his elbows on it and have a better look.

I got out, too, glad to stretch my legs and peer around through the glasses, searching for more cattle. But aside from the cow, the calf, the range and the sky, there was absolutely nothing to see. It was just Silent Bill's domain. No wonder he had grown to be like it.

"Where does he hide his cattle?" I asked. "We haven't seen anything yet, except that one cow and calf."

"He's got about two thousand head of mixed stuff in this pasture, but there's quite a scatter on it. This time of day, you'll find them mostly along the creek bottoms. I'd like to spot some. I'd like to make a deal for his yearlings." Apparently Skel was already figuring out how to double or triple the profits from his forthcoming wild-horse deal.

The ranch house, when we finally reached it, was something of a shock. Originally a log cabin, it had been tacked onto in all directions haphazardly without rhyme or reason or any matching materials or much benefit of carpentry inside, where there were practically no partitions. From without, the eye was assailed by a hodgepodge of roofs: slabs and batten strips, corrugated iron, tar paper and, on the old part, sod with sprouts of vegetation. A double-barreled outhouse with turkeys roosting on its peak was silhouetted grimly against the distant sky.

Inside, the general floor plan was that of a stable: a large central tramping area with stalls leading off from it. Down the center of the tramping area was a long, wooden table with benches at either side, while other parts of the area were discreetly screened off by canvas tarpaulins strung on wires. Off one end was the kitchen, which seemed full of people going in and out with scuttles of coal, armfuls of wood and buckets of water. At the other end was Silent Bill's office: a small room, mostly filled by a large rolltop desk strewn with disorderly papers and surrounded by tall stacks of old magazines, reaching from the floor to well up over the desktop level. At the desk, with his back to the door, sat a spare, white-haired figure immersed in his reading, silent as a tomb.

"That's Bill, if you want to meet him," Skel said. "But it don't matter much. He won't say anything." So we skipped the introduction.

There were many other people in the ranch house, most of whom nodded to us or said a friendly word, but not much more than necessary. It seemed that Silent Bill had cast a spell over all of them. Women struggled in the kitchen, with children underfoot. Oldsters sat about, quietly knitting or whittling. Cowpunchers came in from the corrals, throwing their chaps and spurs down on the porch and lunging through the kitchen door with easy grace, to gather in knots, squatting on their heels along the wall, and talking shop. Skel moved from group to group among them. "They're working a big herd," he explained to me later. "That's why there's such a hell of a mob around here. Lots of reps from other outfits."

About fifteen minutes before suppertime, the cook gave several lusty yanks on the bell rope, and a series of peals floated out over Silent Bill's domain to summon stragglers from the range, unlikely as it seemed that there might still be any, in view of our large complement.

"There goes the first alarm," Skel announced, contemplating the mounds of steaming meat being placed at each end of the long table, ready to be passed around.

Incredibly enough, a few more riders wedged their way in through the kitchen before the cook reached for her bell rope again. Skel, eyeing her, poked me and whispered, "Here goes the gun! . . . Take the nearest seat you can get." I did, and he got the one next to me. There was a mild commotion as the other boys swarmed around the ends of the table, swung their legs over the benches and eased down into working positions. One end of the table, toward the kitchen, was left empty to facilitate replacements of the rapidly diminishing food.

At the other end, near the boss's office, Silent Bill remained standing. He was uncommonly tall and lean, with a sort of dewlap of loose skin hanging down under his chin, which was covered with a thin, white stubble of beard. The dewlap waggled slightly as he looked up one side of the table and down the other, his dark, deep-set eyes like small, polished chestnuts, but completely inexpressive, bathing us as a group in a gaze of Arctic frigidity. Some of the men waved a knife or fork at him, nodded, or said a pleasant word if they were near enough, while most paid no attention. A few winked at each other. But Bill did not wave or nod or acknowledge the existence of any of us. He simply gazed at us silently, his mop of white, tousled hair and cold, flashing dark eyes surmouting, in weird contrast, the quiet, somberly·dressed frame that towered above the tabletop, in shirt-sleeves with arm bands. A heavy gold watch chain was anchored by a cross bar to a buttonhole in his open vest, which looked as if it had been hand-tailored by whoever made the roundup tent, out of surplus overcoat material.

Paralleling the tabletop, and a good foot above it, was his waistline, set off by an old, scratched-up money belt of cowhide, folded over at the bottom, saddle-stitched at the top and of a general silver dollar width. Its well-worn, somewhat clumsy buckle arrangement was designed so that the tongue strap, before passing into the buckle itself, first sealed off the hollow belt's end, so as to prevent the accidental escape of coins in unforeseen circumstances. Relieving the horizontal motif were the black and gray gamblers' stripes of his generously cut trousers, which by then needed a little slack taken up.

When Bill had finished his survey of us, he hauled forth his railroad conductor's type watch, pushed on its crown to snap open the lid, and studied its face gloomily. As he snapped the lid shut, he hung his head and mumbled something in a low, rasping voice, his lips moving almost imperceptibly. The effect, as he sat down, was almost as if our doom had been sealed, and we had only a short time in which to prepare for our demise.

During the entire meal he uttered not a single word of conversation, although on a few occasions he did supplement the pointing of his bony finger with more low, rasping sounds suggesting various foods he wanted, and after which, on at least two occasions, he gurgled a death-rattle version of "Thank-ee."

The meal was noisy enough without Bill, but somehow its din couldn't quite drown out an occasional thought of our host, and most of the men glanced up at him once in a while. Every time I did so, he seemed to skewer me with a drilling stare. As the meal progressed, I felt smaller and smaller, more and more guilty of I knew not what, until finally, wrenching my eyes away, I caught an amused look from Skel, who whispered hoarsely, "He's getting your number, boy!"

Just before the meal was over, Bill, who ate sparingly, arose, gave us all a final, accusing glance and retired again to his dusty office, with his back to the door. I later followed him there to thank him for his hospitality. The boys presently told me that his reaction to this amenity was unusually warm, for he had actually turned his swivel chair a quarter way around, looked up at me and nodded before returning to his perusal of the *Montana Stockman*. But not a muscle of his face had moved.

Skel later assured me that there was no cause for hurt feelings, since Bill had not spoken to anyone in forty years, when, after a brawling, gun-toting youth, he had been converted to law and order by a passing woman evangelist and later became a U.S. marshal. "The shock just knocked him plumb speechless, except for once, just before World War I, when he had all his teeth pulled and took time out to cuss the dentist. . . . Well, I've got a little business to attend to. Have to make some phone calls."

Handily enough, there was a telephone twenty-four miles down the road, and for this objective he departed with two cowpuncher friends, suggesting to me as he left, "They'll be turning in pretty soon, before I can get back. But you and I'll bunk in together over there." He pointed to a large, iron double bed in an ell of the house and rushed out. The ell was spacious. It contained, besides the double bed, several cots and a few bedrolls, amid a litter of chaps, spurs, ropes and hackamores.

The main body of cowpunchers trudged off to the bunkhouse, only extras, the kitchen crew and a few guests being left to share the stable-like arrangements of the ranch house. But we were still a goodly company and taxed its facilities to the utmost. Silent Bill had magnanimously offered his own room (one of a few with doors) to the cook's relatives, who had some small children with them. He himself put out his Coleman lamp in the office soon after supper and, without saying a word to anyone, strode over to our ell, pulled off his boots, stripped down to his union suit and dug himself into one of the cots.

The cook was next. She had also turned over her room (another one with a door) as part of the nursery arrangements. She was a large woman and fearsome to behold in her corsets, as she prepared for the night only partly shielded by the tarpaulin of her alcove. A few men came into our ell, and one modestly pulled the tarpaulin along its wire, mercifully shutting off my view of the cook as she was struggling with the last of her laces.

The lamps were blown out, but there remained a faint afterglow of sunset, in which I followed the general pattern of casual disrobing, lulled by the sounds of this communal retirement: the creaking of bedsprings, the thud of boots dropped on the floor, the unbuckling of bedrolls, all against a sonic background of cattle bawling in the distance. There was one cot still unoccupied near old Bill's, but soon a woman, armed with a large bedpot, slithered deftly out of a substantial, horse-blankety wrapper and got into it, at the same time shoving the bedpot underneath, rather noisily. She was one of Silent Bill's granddaughters, who had been toiling in the kitchen and later in the nursery department. Before long she was joined by two children. One wanted to use the pot and was immediately accommodated, together with appropriate whispered instructions. The other was accommodated several hours later.

At the time of that second accommodation, in that deepest darkness before dawn, there were great whisperings and mumblings in several other voices. Somebody else wanted to borrow the pot. "Bring it back here," the somebody was instructed, as his shuffling, stumbling footsteps faded away. This took some time. The borrower must have gone outside, I thought, hearing the screen door of the kitchen bang softly. After a while it banged once more. Now he's back, I concluded, as the same footsteps grew louder again. Then there were mumblings, including a man's voice, demanding his turn. Evidently it was being passed around. I wondered whether, by some miracle, I might at last have heard the phenomenon of old Bill's voice and made a mental note to check up with the cowboys in our ell.

At the first faint streak of dawn, I was awakened again, as Skel flounced into the bed, his telephone calls having led him into a party. From then on it was solid sleep until half past four, when the cook got up and started shaking down the stove grates. The rest of us lolled in bed until five. But on the whole I was almost as tired as when I had gone to bed.

A hearty breakfast soon cured that, however, and by seven o'clock Skel and I were headed back toward Lewistown to make our arrangements with Paul Langer for the heifers, in my part of which I had decided to skip branding and rely on my bill of sale. We fell to talking about Delane and our uniquely one-sided leave-taking from him, during which he, of course, had said absolutely nothing. "It seems hardly worthwhile to thank a man like that," I suggested.

"He's sure no chatterbox, is he? About the only man in the world who said his last words forty years before he died: that's the reputation he'll have some day."

"What do you suppose his last words were?"

"According to the talk around here, that was back about 1905, when he shot a man in a saloon. Well, they asked him what he did it for, and old Bill just said, 'He had it a-coming,' which was true enough, all right. But nobody ever heard him say anything after that."

Having checked up with cowpunchers, I could now state authoritatively, "Skel, you'd better get up to date on that. As of early this morning, Silent Bill's last words were, 'Please pass the pot.'"

5

Sheardon's Domain
and Fred Lauby's Wisdom

WITH A FINAL PLUG for the nine thousand wild horses, Skel dropped me off at Wyola, where I picked up my car and headed for the Antler.

"Well, how are things up in Lewistown?" Matt asked, when I found him out in the corrals with his men, branding.

"A little confused."

He smiled, knocked down a bar of the squeeze gate with a side-swipe of the iron, to expose the proper spot for the brand, and applied the iron with professional calm. "Turn her loose!" he called to the cowpuncher on the Johnson bar, who eased it up, releasing the pressure of the squeeze gate, while another boy unlatched the headgate and allowed one of my heifers to scamper away, with a neat Reverse RN on her left side. "Did you get this brand on those heifers up there?" he asked me.

"No, I didn't think it was necessary for such a short time. Skel figures on turning them over for a pretty neat profit in a few weeks."

"Well, we never go broke taking profits, do we?"

The remark was not too encouraging, but I let it go at that and said confidently, "Of course, I have my bill of sale for the brand that's on them now."

"A bill of sale's all right . . . so long as it's in apple-pie order." He looked pensively at the branding iron in his hand and con-cluded, "But there's nothing like one of these things." Then he put it back in the fire and picked out another, while the next heifer struggled into the branding chute.

"What do you think of them?" I asked, nodding toward the cattle.

"They're all right . . . but they're light. Very light," he answered, thoughtfully eyeing the little herd in the corral. "They must have taken a hell of a shrink on the railroad. Just now, you've got quite a little invested in them by the pound. Looks like over thirteen cents. But they'll gain back that weight pretty fast, once we get them out on the range. Eventually, they'll come through just fine. You'll see."

Obviously, he was encouraging me as much as he honestly could, but I remembered something he had said on the telephone about having only seven cents a pound invested in some of his Mexican billies, and I had a sneaking suspicion that two mistakes were apparent in this venture right from the start. First, as Benjamin Franklin's childhood anecdote went, I had "paid too much for my whistle." And, second . . . well, there were the branding irons—those symbolic proofs of ownership—glowing in the fire.

When we finished up, he took me on a short tour of the headquarters. From an area that was just sagebrush forty years before, he had set up, almost single-handed, a complete system for what was generally considered the largest beef-producing ranch in the northwest. There were none of the pretensions to the life of ease sometimes evident in older ranches to the south, or on plantations where lush climate, cheap labor and generations of experience brought such about naturally over the years. There was no *mañana* idea; no guitar-and-siesta effect; no hint of polo playing or winters spent in Paris; none of those Argentine or Mexican traditions of Eaton and Oxford for sons of the rich ranch owners. Most men of Matt's generation never got beyond grammar school, for the good reason that, in their day, there were no other schools. Matt never left a roundup wagon until he was twenty-six years old.

Everybody worked at something for the good of the outfit, as and when needed, which was almost continually. Whether or not a salary was involved or an interest in the cattle made no difference in the person's status. A partner in the business or a member of the family or Matt himself would as willingly shoe a horse or brand or drive a truck to town as would the ranch blacksmith, a cowboy or someone hired for a fairly specific purpose. It was just a question of what had to be done at the moment, and whether anybody was around who could do it.

In a yard behind the blacksmith shop, the mess wagon was

being groomed to go out on the range. In his glowing forge the blacksmith heated new iron tires to be shrunk on its wheels, which were pulled while the axles were being greased and new brake shoes affixed. Several cowboys were busy checking harness and shoeing dozens of horses, while the cook hovered about, exercising his traditional authority over this vehicle. Later, on the range, he would call for the wheels to be pulled and the axles greased every fifty miles (or whatever he thought might be fifty miles).

The bed wagon was undergoing similar treatment, and so was the roundup tent, temporarily pitched near the two wagons and being inspected for faults or needed stitching. The wagons and their paraphernalia were to be loaded on large trucks and hauled about forty miles out on the range, where the first camp was to be set up, while horse wranglers would be driving the cavvy by a shorter route. From there on, the wagons would follow the herd under their own horsepower.

"I suppose you'll be coming out on the roundup with us this year?" Matt asked.

"Yes, I'd like to, if I wouldn't be in the way too much. Haven't been with a roundup outfit for fourteen years, though, since I left Tongue River. I might be kind of rusty, and I can't rope worth a damn."

"That don't matter. I think you'll get along with our outfit. Jerry Flynn's a fine wagon boss . . . best in the country. Strict as hell, but even-tempered. He may be a little hard to get to know, but that's only because he's shy and doesn't usually talk much at first. But you'll get to like him. How're you fixed for horses?"

"I could bring over a few."

"Never mind." He waved the suggestion aside. "We've got plenty, and lots you'll be able to ride, even if you do feel a little rusty. I'll have the boys cut out a string of gentle ones you won't have to worry about."

"When are you starting?"

"Any day now. We've got most of the new cattle branded. There's one small shipment due in tomorrow. They won't take long to brand and rest up."

He took me into his immaculate little house for a drink with his family before supper and showed me my quarters for the night, a tiny, glistening upstairs room with such an enormous double bed that there was barely room enough to walk around it and a ceiling light fitted with a one-hundred-and-fifty-watt bulb bathing it in an almost painful glare.

It had been decided that I should return to Birney and reappear in a few days, with my roundup bed and tack, to join the wagon.

Back at the cabin I found old Fred still brooding over the turn of events. He wasn't satisfied with life at all, or, at least, with mine. I'd been doing too many things without consulting him. He was worried because election year was always a bad year to go into the cattle business, and what made it worse was my association with "that renegade," Skel Baxton. The whole cattle picture just wasn't right for him. He had it straight from some Cheyenne that a series of hard winters was due. And how did I know how much hay the Sheardon ranch *really* put up, or how much might be mortgaged or sold? Just seeing it in the stacks wasn't enough. The whole outlook, as he analyzed it, was just too shaky. So there was no use in my getting all set for an indefinite stay in the cabin and making a lot of fancy changes, like bringing the outhouse indoors, just because we had a little water to work it with . . . damn little. It was best to wait and see how things turned out first. There was always plenty of time to make changes.

In other words, it didn't suit him to do any of the cleaning I had suggested or pump water up from the ranch house, even though Albert had installed new pumping equipment down there. Fred would rather scatter his dishpans and cooking utensils around under the eaves to catch what rain he could. That made it *his* water, and there was never enough of it to "waste" any by mopping.

Fred was enjoying a siesta after having made a gain of eight or nine gallons in a cloudburst that was almost over before he could swing into full action. The window shades were pulled down all around, and in the half-light I could see the curve of his stomach rise and fall gently as he talked. "You know, some of my ancestors was Spanish away back, and damned if I don't think this siesta idea is pretty good. They got it all figured out long ago that a man needs a break in the middle of the day. He can work much harder that way. It comes from living in that hot climate, where you can't get nothing done real good around noontime."

"What do you find to do around noon in wintertime, when I'm back east?"

"Oh, well . . . of course, I feed the horses their oats then, so I
don't have too much time, what with getting my snow water in
and watching for the mail stage, always expecting a letter from
you . . . and all. But sometimes I take a little rest like this just to
keep in practice for the summer. You know, it ain't good to change
your habits too much. That's what the doctors say. I seen it in the
Pathfinder. And *you* better be catching a little extra rest too if
you're going out on the range with that Antler wagon. You'll need
all you can get now, 'cause you're not going to get much up on that
goddam wagon, I can tell you that, boy."

"I never rode with any wagon to get rest. I want to see how this
outfit works, and what happens to my heifers, and I don't know
any other way to do it, Fred. It's not a question of rest."

"You've never been on any other wagon except these Tongue
River outfits years ago, just after the hard times, when they all
took on a few dudes to help out with their cattle losses. Now,
mind you, I ain't got nothing against dudes. God knows, it was
that eastern money that kept a lot of these cattle outfits from
going bust after the Hard Winter, and dudes is nice to get along
with. They're sure comical. But what I mean is, they got to be
pampered. I understand that some of them gal dudes wanted to
lie in bed till five o'clock in the morning. The hands couldn't go
into their tepees to drag them out, and it was hell. They'd just
have to knock the tepees down and make a joke of it, or they
wouldn't get any cattle rounded up all morning. Now, that's just
child's play compared to the outfit Sheardon runs. They ride three
circles a day instead of two. Why, he's got so much range up there,
some of his own cowpunchers don't know where it all is. I know
all about it. I got it firsthand from Jigger McCabe. Antler hands
get more pay than any other outfits to take the strain. And half
their horses ain't fit to ride outside of a rodeo. You just wait and
see. Take my advice and get a little extra rest now."

Jigger McCabe was that rare type of ex-cowpuncher who had
saved his money and now, at approximately Fred's age, had a
little stake invested in cattle. Jigger did what he wanted, which
was usually very close to nothing, except for snooping. Self-elected
roving reporter of the range, he rode the grubline everywhere and
was always welcomed as good company. His short, rotund, chin-
whiskered and somewhat raggedy figure pitched slightly forward
in the saddle, could be encountered almost anywhere, slowly
jogging along on his sorrel mare.

Lately, Jigger had taken to frequenting the Crow Reservation. Some hinted that he was in the employ of the government, watching out for overgrazing, checking on brand inspectors and smelling around for rustlers, but he would never admit to being any kind of range detective, though he clearly enjoyed being suspected. A confirmed bachelor, he lived up a side creek tributary of the Rosebud which, in its day, had sheltered several shady characters. After the *Pathfinder,* Jigger was Fred's most respected source of information.

"How in hell am I going to watch my investment if I don't go out with the wagon? Through a telescope? Or, should I depend on Jigger McCabe?"

"You don't have to worry about your investment with Matt, son. That's one man you *don't* have to watch. He'll look after your heifers, all right. And if any of them should happen to get bred, you can bet he'll brand the calves for you. Personally, if it was me, I'd breed them all and go into cows and calves. Why do you want to sell them for beef so soon, just for a quick profit? You ought to get at least one calf out of them, because every time a cow has a calf . . ."

"I know, I know, Fred. But that's just it, she *doesn't* pay for herself nowadays. You've got to help that cow out. The best she can do is drop one calf a year, and you've got to find another now and then if you're going to make any kind of profit worth all the risks. At least, that's what Matt says, and he ought to know, if anybody does."

"Yes, he knows, all right. But he's been wrong before, and he'll be wrong again some day. You just want to watch out, that's all. Matt's got so many interests that he can go broke on one, and the others can pull him out. Besides the cattle, he's got those sheep. I don't know how many thousand, but Jigger claims he's running twenty-five or thirty sheep wagons . . . just as a sideline, mind you, and raising sugar beets, hay and flax . . . that's the latest . . . and he owns that little bank, too, and God knows what else. Jigger tells me he's even got an interest in the Crow buffalo herd . . . donated thousands of acres of range to them that he wasn't using for cattle, when the Yellowstone Park herd outgrew their grass. But you've only got those cattle. You got to watch out, and fooling around with a straight steer outfit is risky business."

"But I've got heifers."

"You may have heifers now, but you'll wind up with steers

sooner or later. That's what you came out here for, isn't it? The only reason you got heifers now is that you couldn't find any steers to buy reasonable. And you're running them like steers, aren't you? Shipping them out as baby beef next fall. Of course, though, if this market should break, you got another shot. You can still breed them and get the calf crop, so you're safe for a while, anyway. And you got your own brand on them all, so that's one good thing."

"Not on all of them, Fred."

"*What?*" He raised up on one elbow, horrified, then tried to reassure me. "Well, you can rely on Matt. He's the most honest man there ever was in the cattle business. Why, he even closed up his own bank to protect his depositors when he figured some cattle loans were sour, even though he was the biggest loser himself and could have gotten out of it if he'd done what Jigger told him to do. Matt will look after your heifers and put your brand on their calves."

"The ones I'm running with Matt are all branded. It's the others that aren't."

"The others?"

"Yes. I only unloaded two hundred at Wyola. The others went up to Lewistown with three hundred and twenty-five head that Skel bought for himself, and they're the ones not branded. Some friend of his, named Langer, is running them for us and making a quick turnover. We've got the bill of sale for them, so we didn't bother to brand."

This time, Fred sat bolt upright on the bed and looked really horrified. "*What?* . . . You're running unbranded stock with some friend of that renegade's up in Lewistown? God, boy! You shouldn't have done that. Why the hell didn't you ask me about it?"

"Why, it's perfectly all right," I answered, as calmly as possible.

"All right, is it? I'll tell you how all right it is. You'll probably never see most of those heifers again. They'll get lost, or they'll die of blackleg, or they'll disappear somehow. Have you got some kind of loss guarantee, like in the Antler contract?"

"You mean, a 2 percent loss clause? No, we don't have a contract yet."

He was outraged enough to get up off the bed and pace the floor, lecturing me. "God! I knowed I shouldn't have let you go off with him alone, but it all happened so sudden. And how do you

know they was all open heifers? How do you know some of them
hadn't been bred already?"

"Oh, Skel didn't make any bones about it. He said some of
them had been bred. He even said he hoped some good bulls
would bust through the fence and breed more of them. What's
the matter with . . ."

"There!" he burst in, furiously. "What did I tell you? That
sonofabitch up in Lewistown is going to try to rustle some of your
calves! They'll hold the heifers over somehow. Maybe say they
couldn't get a good enough price to sell this year. Then they'll
fix it so you won't be around at calving time. They figure Lewistown is too far away for you to be snooping around after them,
seeing how many calves they get. And they'll move the heifers,
so you won't know where to find them. They can always say they
ran out of grass or had a dry year. That's an old racket. And you'll
wind up not knowing where your stock is, or how many calves
you own. In fact, you won't own a goddam thing 'cause you haven't
got a brand on them."

"There's the bill of sale."

"*Where's* the bill of sale? And how do you know it's any good?"

I couldn't answer either question. I hadn't even seen the bill
of sale more closely than ten feet and fluttering in the wind. But
I explained, hopefully, "Skel has it, and I can get it easily enough."

"You'll probably find that easier said than done. And by the time
you get around to locating it, you'll see that they have that brand
in their own name, and they'll be acting as your agents. Then that
brand, or some other, but not yours, will get on those calves, and
you'll never see the bill of sale again, or the calves, either. When
the whole mixup comes to a head, the calves'll be sold, and they'll
make a settlement with you . . . for about half what you got coming. And all the time you won't even know where your stock is,
unless you get after them before there's any time for excuses. I'll
bet you don't even know where them heifers are right now."

"Oh, yes I do . . . more or less. They're right near Lewistown,
where this fellow, Langer has some range."

"Whose range, his own?"

"Well, I guess so, but Skel made the arrangements, so I don't
know all the details, exactly. I know at least some of it's Langer's
own range. But anyway, Fred, there's lots of grass up there, and
Skel seems to know where you can get the best of it. He knows

everybody from Pueblo up to the Canadian line. He even knows outfits over the line in Saskatchewan."

"Who gives a damn about Saskatchewan? I'm talking about Lewistown. Where's all this grass that you're so sure they're putting your cattle on?"

"I told you, this Langer owns some of it, and Skel's got lots more located in case it turns out to be a dry summer or something, and Langer runs low. Just for emergency, so we make absolutely sure. Skel talked to dozens of people up there about grass."

"*Dozens* of people? How long were you up there?"

"Just one night."

"You don't see dozens of people in just one night up in that godforsaken country. There just ain't that many people in that country all in one place, unless there's some special occasion. Where was it, at a poker game in a saloon?"

"No. At a big ranch where we spent the night, somewhere north of Lewistown in Fergus County. They were working a huge herd there. Cattlemen and reps from all over the state. Skel talked to most of them and also went out that night to some other ranch, I don't know where or what for, but I'll bet he scooped up some information on grass. It's a cinch he can line up enough for our little bunch of heifers, with all his connections. Driving home, he talked as if he might even have some lined up right on this big ranch where we were staying."

"What big ranch where you were staying? Where's this spread?"

"I'm not exactly sure, but you drive like hell for about two hours from Lewistown, over dirt roads, in the general direction of the Judith Mountains, as far as I could make out. Nobody seems to have any address up there, and this guy's kind of a recluse, anyway. Somebody called Delane."

"Not old Silent Bill?" Fred gasped, incredulous.

"Yes. That's what they called him."

Fred went around snapping up all the window shades to denote that, because of this emergency, the siesta was over. "He's one of the coldest-blooded killers they ever had in this whole country in the old days. That's why he's holed up. He's scared to open his mouth for fear of getting hung."

"Well, anyway, Fred, there's lots of grass up around there, and I'm sure Skel's got enough lined up for us, come what may. Why the hell should he try to fool me? We shipped four hundred and fifty heifers up there together on the same deal. He bought three hundred and twenty-five himself. His interests are the same as mine. We're in the same boat."

Fred had settled into his paradise chair. "All the same deal, is it? That's what *you* think. But it's not what Jigger thinks. Nor me, either. Let me tell you something, and don't forget it. With lots of these cattle brokers, you never know *what* boat you're in. This renegade might be your partner in the same deal, or he might not. He could be moving the whole bunch up to Lewistown on a previous deal at a lower price. So he'd just be boosting the price along the way, with you throwing in some gravy on part of them."

"I don't believe it. Why, Skel didn't even want to take his commission check from me until I made a profit out of the deal and was satisfied. Doesn't that prove he's in with me?"

"It depends on what you mean by *satisfied.* If I was you, I'd be satisfied to get out of the whole deal right now, if I could get all my money back. He probably figures on making you a small profit and himself a big one that you'll never know about. That way, he can claim you made a profit and ought to be satisfied, so you won't feel gypped in paying him the commission. But he knows that he's going to get the commission anyway in the long run, if he wants to hold out for it. I don't suppose he put his generous commission offer on paper, did he?"

"No, but whoever heard of anyone doing that? It's a gentlemen's agreement."

"These gentlemen's agreements don't always work out just that way in a case like this, 'cause you can't always tell who's a gentleman and who ain't, and there's usually other things you can't tell about either. For instance, he might even own all of them cattle himself, on paper, and just be selling you part at a profit. Jigger thinks he's had them on his books for weeks as a speculation in partnership with this Langer up in Lewistown. He could even be a partner of those dealers you bought them from down in Gillette. But no matter what he is, I'll tell you one thing: you'll never find out. It's not like your deal with Matt Sheardon. Now with Matt you know where you stand. You should have put all your heifers with Matt in the first place."

The swiveled, rocking paradise chair was having its soothing effect, so I hoped he might talk about Matt and something pleasant for a change. He was just beginning to relax, wiping his telescope lens in preparation for the afternoon's observations. As a starter, I asked about Matt's banking troubles.

"It ain't nothing to do with that little bank he's got now in the old Wyola Grocery store that Jigger says he's moving into the brick building on the corner. It's in fine shape, and came through the depression better than lots of them big ones back in eastern cities.

"The one that busted was in Billings, but Matt paid off all its depositors in the end. In the meantime, there was this depositor who thought he was ruined, and nobody could tell him any different. He got drunk for a week and went all around Billings telling everybody how he was going to shoot Matt. Matt's friends all warned him, but old Matt, he never even bothered to carry a gun. Well, sir, one morning, this drunk trails Matt into a restaurant where he was having a real early breakfast, and they was the only customers except Jigger McCabe. The drunk tells Matt he's going to check out of this goddam no-good world, but first, he's going to arrange to take Matt with him. So he sticks a gun in Matt's belly and tells Matt to say when he's ready to die. Old Matt says he's always been ready, but he hates like hell to die on an empty stomach, 'cause he's heard it's mighty painful, so he orders a big breakfast for himself and one for the drunk too. The drunk had been up all night and was hungrier than hell, so he puts down the gun to eat. Seems like he lost his nerve when he smelled the food and was kind of half hoping Matt would grab the gun, so he'd have a good excuse to get out of it. But Matt just keeps right on eating, unconcerned-like, and telling the drunk how he's looking forward to dying, as he's a gambler, and that'd be his biggest gamble yet. Then, when he got all finished eating, he told the drunk to go ahead and shoot. But the drunk just unloaded the gun and asks Jigger, 'How in hell can you shoot a feller like that?' Matt helped him to make a comeback till the bank paid off, and they've been good friends ever since."

This biographical preview of my new partner made me more anxious to rejoin him, so I set about gathering my saddle, bridle and tack for the roundup. There was nothing much I could do about the Lewistown situation until I got back from the wagon, so I tried to dismiss it from my mind with the determination that, somehow or other, I'd get rid of those heifers right away or brand them and bring them back to the Crow Reservation.

Fred eyed my every movement like a hawk. When I asked him if he knew where my seventeen-foot canvas bedsheet was, he rose from the paradise chair pleasantly and got it out of the shed for me, suggesting, "Here, boy, better let me help you. It's so long since you made up a roundup bed. You might get it folded wrong, so the rain could get in."

6

A Glimpse of Sheepherders
and on to the Roundup Camp

THE WAGON HAD BEEN OUT nearly a week when I got back to Shear-don's ranch. That night the supper table was just as full, but now there were only two sittings, cowpunchers being conspicuously absent. Matt himself was away on business . . . some thought, in Denver. But no one seemed to know very much about his movements. "There's only one way to see that man," an irrigator told me. "You can't never catch him. You just got to be in the right place when he whizzes past."

After breakfast next day, the "steadies" disappeared in all directions—by truck, on horseback, and afoot. Suddenly, I realized that I was the only person on the ranch who had nothing to do.

I was standing at the heart of nearly half a million acres of going concern in which I had an interest, infinitely small in proportion to the whole outfit, but important to me. I was completely equipped for work, with my saddle, bridle and tack, and had striven with the details of my personal life for a whole week in order to be there in that particular spot, with lots of time to devote to the work at hand and unlimited enthusiasm. But I had absolutely nothing to do. Yet people around me were all humming with quiet activity. The kitchen crew was cheerfully lashing into mountains of dishes; an old man trudged off to the chicken house with two buckets of cracked corn; women beat rugs outside the little houses; the merry ring of an anvil came from the blacksmith shop. But I had nothing to do.

What was more, I couldn't seem to get any information that might lead to something to do. Everyone I saw had a cordial word or waved gaily from a distance. But not one could enlighten me as to where the roundup wagon was, or how to get to it and see my heifers. Some didn't even know I *had* any heifers. "Heifers . . .?" the old fellow repeated quizzically, as I caught him coming back from the chicken house. "Heifers . . .?" He could not have looked more surprised if I had said "diamonds." One just didn't have heifers on a straight steer outfit.

Finally, I strolled into the ranch office, hungry for information but feeling a little sensitive about having heifers. There was the man in the green eyeshade I had seen on my first visit, still wrestling with his Indian leases. He beamed at me and said jovially, "Well, I'll be damned if it isn't our new partner from Tongue River! I hear you're going to be with the outfit from now on."

"Oh, yes. I've got a few head of stock around here, somewhere, if I can ever find them."

He considered a moment and then smiled knowingly. "I remember. It was you unloaded those two hundred heifers at Wyola about ten days or two weeks ago. Say, they sure were light, weren't they?" He reached for a large book and cracked it at the record of their weights. "Averaged under three hundred pounds. So you got about twelve cents a pound in them. That's three cents too high or about a 30 percent handicap against them. Well, now, that's too bad. We'll have to see if we can't pamper them a little for you to make that back. You'll be surprised how fast they'll gain back that weight on this range. Grass in fine this year, best we ever had, especially on the west side of the river, and I think they're over there. But they might still be on the east side."

He was trying to be helpful like the rest. But it was too obvious that even this man, with all his books and records, didn't know where my two hundred heifers were. Perhaps Matt might know, if I could only locate him.

"When's the boss coming back?" I asked hopefully.

"Oh, the last word we had was, he might blow in tomorrow sometime." He put the weight book back on its rack and added casually, "But, of course, he might not show up for a week or so. He's supposed to be in Denver today. But that don't mean a goddam thing. He'll be wherever there's cattle to buy. We're hoping a message will come in at the Western Union in Sheridan today. There's a hell of a lot of people around here wants to see him."

"Well, let me know if you hear anything."

"Sure will." And he dove back into his Indian leases.

A large, grinning, burly fellow in boots and a well-worn Stetson was coming toward the office as I left. His general appearance gave some hope that he might have just come in from the wagon and would know where my heifers were. "Looking for something?" he asked pleasantly.

"Just looking around. I'm kind of new here."

"Well, make yourself at home. Let me know if there's anything I can do."

He had his hand on the office doorknob before I could say, "By the way, I wonder if you've seen any stock around here branded Reverse RN on the left ribs?" He shook his head thoughtfully.

"No, can't say that I have. I'm just the ranch manager. You want to see the cattle manager for that. He's out with the wagon. I remember having the branding irons made up, though."

"Thanks."

I followed a little path aimlessly, watching the toes of my boots. It led through a small clump of pine trees, on the other side of which was another white house, one I hadn't seen before. The doors were open and I wandered in. A young woman was sitting in the kitchen alone, peeling potatoes. She introduced herself as Matt's daughter, and we settled down to a nice, long talk. She was extremely fond of music, and, although I didn't know much about it, I tried to describe the Metropolitan Opera to her. "I just love listening to the Metropolitan every Saturday afternoon on my new radio," she said. "Ella Feames comes over to sit with me. She loves music too. That's our sheep manager's daughter. Here comes her father now, probably looking for her."

An enormous man came clumping up the porch steps. He was smiling like all the rest, but of different shape, hue and attire. He wore high shoes instead of boots, and his color scheme was fawn. Faded green suspenders curved over his ample anterior, and he wore a much smaller Stetson, which was beaten almost to a pulp but, somehow, looked just right for him. He took the pulpy mass from his head as he entered the kitchen and cracked a broad grin. "Hello, Martha! I see you got company." Then, turn-ing to me jovially, "Well, you must be the feller from over on Tongue River that's got the little RN heifers. How're they doing now? Picked up any?"

"Can't say. I haven't seen them since we branded. I wonder if you'd know where they are?"

"Oh, they're out on the leases somewhere by now. Probably still on the east side of the river. I'm just the sheep manager, so I don't see much of the cattle." He turned to Martha. "Seen any-thing of Ella around here? Her maw's looking for her."

"No, I haven't, Steve."

"Well, I guess I'll be going. Got a lot of sheep camps to stock up with supplies. I don't know what these sheepherders do with all the grub. They must throw it in the crick." Then he turned to me thoughtfully. "Say, maybe you'd like to come along? Give you a chance to look over the range a little. And we might just happen to run across some of your heifers. Maybe we can get a line on where the wagon's camped too. My sheep range goes quite far up."

It went so far up that we drove nearly an hour before we even came to the first sheep wagon. Although the pickup truck was new, I noticed that the speedometer showed a very high mileage. It was loaded to capacity with groceries, canned goods, meat, flour and rock salt, so that it rode easily and silently along the wagon-track roads and across the creek bottoms. Steve blew the horn when we were still a long way from the first camp, and a bearded man poked his head out of the sheep wagon. "This is a spooky old bastard," Steve explained. "He's got a gun in there, and he don't like nobody sneaking up on him. He shot the door handle off one of our trucks last year. Some of these herders sure gets queer from being out here alone so much. Sort of antisocial."

For the spooky bastard we unloaded enough food, I thought, to keep him shooting at least another year without further help. Then we skirted around his band of sheep and went on to the next camp, where the herder was more congenial. He invited us into his wagon. It was neat and clean inside, with a little oil stove and a kitchen table on either side of the door. There was a built-in bunk at the front end, with drawers underneath, where he kept his clothes and meager possessions. He fumbled around in the drawers and finally pulled out a half-pint bottle of whiskey. The label was worn, as if it had been kicking around a lot, yet the seal was intact. He handed the bottle to Steve, who looked it over but said, "No, thanks," and I followed suit. "I don't drink either," he said to me and put the bottle back.

"That herder's a lot more congenial than the other," I suggested. "Looks as if he's had that bottle a long time."

"Oh, yes. He's been offering me that same bottle for years. He knows we don't drink anything on the job in this outfit. That was just a gag for your benefit. Wants to impress you that he don't drink either. He used to be the worst drunk in the country, but he reformed years ago."

"Who reformed him?"

"Nobody. He just reformed himself, and he keeps that bottle as a symbol. He offers it to everybody, but nobody ever accepts, 'cause everybody knows it's his big gag. It's the last bottle he ever bought, and we don't want to see him buy another. He just can't handle the stuff, and he knows it."

"Then what does he have it around for?"

"He keeps it to talk to, when he feels a spell of temptation coming on. I slipped up on him one time when he was having a spell, and it sure was comical. He puts the bottle on his table and shakes his fist at it and says real loud, 'Now, you little brown sonofabitch, you've kicked me around long enough. You knocked me down every Saturday night for twenty years. But now I've got you whipped and, by God, you're a-gonna stay whipped!' Then he puts the bottle away again. Says it makes him feel good inside, and he doesn't have another temptation for a long time."

Steve eyed each band of sheep carefully as we pushed on. There were twelve or fifteen hundred ewes to the band and they grazed about peacefully with the teams, while a quiet old saddle horse was tethered nearby. A few nondescript but cleverly trained dogs lurked around the bands to keep strays from getting too far away, and they would bark at the slightest disturbance.

Our next customer was worried only about his newspapers, though his larder was down to coffee, pork and beans. His wagon was littered with girlie photos. "God, Steve, I thought you'd *never* come with them papers! Why, I've been out of newspapers for a week!" And he pounced ravenously upon a bundle of very old newspapers which Steve dug out of the pickup. I noticed that they were not local papers, but came from California, Florida and other unlikely places. "Why doesn't he read the local papers?" I asked, as we drove away. "Seems to me that his news isn't very fresh."

"He don't care how old the news is," Steve laughed. "He can't even read. Just cuts out the girlie pictures and pins them up in his sheep wagon. He keeps changing his favorites all the time and throws the others away. Runs a regular beauty contest all by himself. It's the only fun he gets. The local papers don't have pinups, so different friends of the outfit send us these old papers from all over."

There were twenty-eight sheep wagons in all, but only about seven of them were on the list for supplies, so we started back to the ranch in midafternoon, our empty pickup now riding high and bouncing. When we got back, I noticed the speedometer again. We had driven nearly a hundred miles and had been over only part of the outfit's sheep range. There was no sign of the roundup camp, and we hadn't seen any cattle at all. But Matt was home, and I thought he would surely know about my heifers.

Matt was not quite sure where the heifers were either because, as he explained at breakfast, "That's up to Jerry Flynn, our wagon boss. But we'll be going up to the wagon today, so we can find out."

"Don't you give him orders where to put the cattle?"

"Oh, no. I just tell him what I want done with them. He figures out the rest and does it."

"Suppose he figures it out wrong?"

A faint smile crept over Matt's face. "If he figured things wrong, he wouldn't be wagon boss."

It answered my question in a way. But still, it didn't tell me where the heifers were. That afternoon, as we sped along headed for the roundup camp atop a mound of supplies in the back of a pickup, surrounded by our beds, saddles and gear, Matt explained more fully. "You see, this job of wagon boss is something that's getting mighty scarce these days. There aren't many outfits left operating on open range that's big enough to need a wagon boss. And there aren't many wagon bosses left big enough to run a spread like we've got here. I can't be my own boss any more, though I used to be. But now that's just impossible. I've got too many other things to do."

"I see it's a ticklish job. Not the kind you can just call up an employment agency to fill, like getting a housemaid."

He smiled. "Not exactly. This wagon boss job is a survival of the old days and carries a lot of pride with it. If Jerry Flynn thought for one moment that I doubted his judgment about handling the herd, he wouldn't respect me for putting him on the job. And he'd quit tonight. That's why it's ticklish giving orders to a wagon boss, even about the smallest thing. You tell him what you want done, but you don't give him orders. You give him the job. He gives the orders. Even when you're on the wagon yourself."

"That's a good system. I wish more people would use it." But I also wished that it weren't quite so secretive. The fate of my heifers on the Crow Reservation was now beginning to look almost as mysterious as the fate of those in Lewistown, although with a less terrifying aspect.

We rolled by the hour over every kind of road: the graveled one to Wyola and the main, tarred highway; the paved streets of little towns and back onto rutted dirt roads of the Reservation; wagon roads branching off from them and petering out on the range; and finally, no road at all. For the last few miles we just bumped over the sagebrush to where the wagon was camped. But we were still on the outfit's range. I marveled at how the driver had made it without a compass.

Sheardon's roundup camp was on the same old time-honored pattern as those I had worked with on Tongue River fourteen years before, except that it was on a greater scale. For where, in my experience, there had formerly been hundreds of cattle to be handled, there were now thousands; where there had been five or six cowpunchers, there were now ten or fifteen, plus a "nighthawk," a livestock inspector, the U.S. Indian Agent, and "reps" from other outfits who were running cattle with us. In all, what with the cook, the wagon boss and ourselves, we were more than twenty souls in camp.

The center of activity was, of course, the mess wagon and tent. This was the standard four-horse roundup wagon I had seen being groomed at the ranch, and the mess tent was pitched a few feet behind it. Between the two was the cook's work space, covered by a canvas fly extending from the mess tent over it, and thence forward over the wagon body on arched wooden hoops, the fly extending well out on each side and being held taut by guy ropes running to pegs in the ground. On the rear end of the wagon was the cook box, its various compartments holding all the most needed

Boys at the Antler camp, shipping from Benteen, Montana, 1958

utensils and supplies, its back being hinged at the bottom to let down and form the cook's worktable. When the back was closed up for travel, this space accommodated the cookstove, which rested on supports protruding from beneath, and was held firmly in place by very heavy straps. Everything folded up or fitted into something else for travel and had a definite place on the wagon, whether traveling or in camp. Water barrel and axe on the left side; butcher's hook for hanging raw meat, on the right; tools, medicine, horseshoe nails and such in the jockey box under the driver's seat; and so on. There was no time to be wasted in hunting for things or in arguing about who misplaced them. Everyone was responsible for what he used and for putting it back where he found it.

We arrived at the wagon in time for supper, unloaded the supplies and turned in at about half-past seven, as did most of the men, except a few whom Jerry sent out to butcher in the cool of the evening and, of course, the nighthawk, whose duty it was to keep the cavvy grazing within a reasonable distance of camp during the night. The cook and a few men slept in the mess tent; some slept around the wagon under the fly; others, off at a little distance. Matt and I rolled out our beds together behind the mess tent, both front and back flaps of which were open. On one side we could see into the tent and on the other we commanded a view of the butchering. There was a last bawl, the crack of a .22 rifle, and the thud of the animal's fall. Then the boys set to in calm, businesslike manner, draining, skinning, opening up the carcass, rolling out the great blue stomach, hacking and sawing. This gory scene didn't take the place of a bedtime story very well, but it was necessary for us to eat and because half a carcass was needed down at the ranch, to be sent back in the pickup. In time, darkness blotted out the scene of slaughter, and stars appeared. A great calmness descended over camp. The atmosphere grew crisper, clearer, cooler, revealing ever more and more stars, until it seemed that they would shortly be crowded for space. Through the clear air there floated occasional bawlings from the herd, which seemed nearby but actually was about half a mile off. Small swift night birds dropped through the sky, diving after insects, with a guttural twang like a low base note on a cello.

At two o'clock camp began to stir again. The cook's alarm clock clicked its warning before ringing, and he grabbed it to prevent

Ed Aspaas, roundup cook, with Antler Ranch over fifty years

the alarm from waking others, a custom of his in which he took great pride. He fumbled for his tobacco sack. A match popped, revealing for an instant his tired face. Then there was just the red glow of his cigarette, as he dressed swiftly, silently, in the dark. Presently another match popped, and he lit the big, plumber-sized candle, held by a long iron rod, one end of which was coiled around to receive it, the other sharpened and spiked into the ground near the stove. He shook down his grates and lighted a few cedar chips, which snapped and popped cheerfully as he put his water pail and kettle on to boil. Then he set about mixing dough for his soda biscuits, those traditional "death-wads" of the range. The nighthawk rode in and woke up the wranglers, whose horses were staked nearby. They seemed to spring from their beds, dress, saddle their horses and mount, with one quick uninterrupted motion lasting but a few moments. All three galloped off, leaving behind them a fading trail of laughter mingled with the beat of their ponies' hoofs. In a little while we could hear them rending the stillness of dawn, vying with each other in piercing shrieks, rounding up the cavvy. Then the faint, but ever-increasing thunder of hoofbeats as a hundred horses galloped into camp, frisking, kicking, whinnying, biting at each other. If one was not awakened by then, the cook's loud and raucous call of "Roll . . . OUT!" would soon remedy the situation.

Breakfast was at three-thirty, but long before then, the men were up and about, rolling and strapping up their beds and loading them into the bed wagon. The hub of one rear wheel of this wagon is the standard anchoring point for one end of a temporary rope enclosure which serves as a corral, into which the wranglers herd the cavvy. The horses are held there behind a "gate rope," which is opened or closed by letting it lie slack on the ground or raising it by bearing back on the loose end.

As the men finished eating, they scraped their plates into the pit dug behind the mess tent, discarded them into the large washtub, and lined up at the gate of the rope corral, ready to go in two at a time and catch their horses for the first circle. It was not yet light enough to distinguish the horses very well, and I didn't know one from another, anyway, never having seen them before. I was never a good roper and years of absence had not improved my skill, so that the problem of what horse I was to ride, and how I was to catch it, began to loom as I took the throw rope off my saddle and got in line, hopefully looking around for Matt whom, to my dismay, I finally spotted at some distance having a conference with Jerry Flynn.

Jerry, however—a quiet man of few words—had his eye on me and came up just as it was my turn to go in. "Here, let's change ropes," he said. He took mine, flipped the loop wide with one flick of his wrist, stepped in among the wildly milling horses and made a sure, swift throw. They dropped the gate rope for him to lead the horse out and up to me. "Better do it this way 'till you get to know the horses a little," he suggested. "This one's hard to saddle, but you can ride him all right. He's gentle. Just watch him when you step up."

The other horses were not so gentle, however, most of them not having been ridden all winter until the week before. Some of them put on a good show of bucking, to the delight of the bronc-twisters who rode them and liked to practice for the Fourth of July rodeos in Sheridan and Billings. So much so that the livestock inspector asked Matt, "What in hell are you running here . . . a roundup or a rodeo?" There were some pretty well-known riders with the outfit that year, and we joked about seeing them ride without having to buy tickets.

Everyone waited politely for the last man to mount and get his horse quieted down, no matter how complicated the process might be. Then the boss shouted, "Everybody caught?" . . . and, "Turn 'em loose!" At which command the gate rope of the corral was dropped and the cavvy thundered out to graze until they were needed again at dinnertime for the second circle. Then we all rode off in groups of four or five, more or less abreast, led by Jerry and Matt, who had a puzzling way of mumbling things to each other which I tried to figure out but couldn't. Nobody had said anything about where we were going or why. We rode on through the main herd as the dawn was beginning to get bright enough to read brands, and I recognized a few fresh ones that I had seen at the ranch. Everywhere, I saw nothing but steers, not a sign of my heifers. Jerry eventually deployed us in groups of two, with individual instructions as to what he wanted done. I was sent off with two others, as I didn't know the country, and was told that if I got separated to come back to camp for dinner at ten-thirty.

The cavvy was wrangled again at dinnertime, and everyone caught a fresh horse. Matt didn't ride the afternooon circle, as he

Part of the 212-horse Antler cavvy on the Little Big Horn River in Montana. *Courtesy Roahen Photos, Billings, Montana*

had a business appointment at the ranch. He went back with the pickup and the half carcass of beef, leaving his bed and saddle at the wagon in anticipation of returning in a few days. All the other riders went out again until suppertime (three-thirty), when we caught more fresh horses. Some were then sent off again, and others, including myself, kept with the main herd for holding it and working out strays. After supper the cook left snacks out for us to eat when we came in, but he himself curled up and was asleep before sundown. Furthermore, nobody was supposed to ask him to do anything or even go near his sacred corner of the tent, bounded by the entrance tent pole, his stove, woodpile and the serving table. If anyone made too much noise in the tent, he would rouse up, cuss them colorfully, threaten to quit the outfit, then drop back to sleep and forget all about it. I went to sleep wondering whether anybody had seen my two hundred heifers. Nobody had said a word about them.

Next morning at breakfast I determined to ask Jerry, who was sitting next to me, somewhat glumly looking into his plate. He hardly ever talked but seemed always to be figuring something out. "By the way," I asked him, "have you seen anything of my heifers?"

"Oh, yes." He looked up without smiling.

"How are they?"

"Oh, fine, I guess."

"I haven't seen anything of them yet."

"You haven't? . . . Here, take a look." He held up a chunk of meat on his fork. His face was dead serious.

"What do you mean? What have you been doing with them?"

"Haven't been doing much with them so far. Just eating them." He shoved another piece of meat into his mouth. "Getting tenderer every day too. The next time we butcher an RN, you'll see the improvement over this one. Then you'll get an idea of what this grass really does for beef. You'll know you're with the right outfit."

For a moment I was stunned, until I saw the stifled smiles around us. Then he explained that he had put them temporarily in a little pasture of thirty thousand acres on the other side of the river to make back their weight, as he didn't want to get them too far from the railroad until he was sure whether or not I had decided to ship them that fall. "I believe I'd double-winter them, if it was me," he advised. "They'll do a lot more for you next year."

Why, you won't even recognize them by then." And I decided on the spot to do just that. Later, in the fall, I actually saw the heifers and had to look twice at the brand to realize they were mine, so improved was their condition.

We were slated to move camp next day, and before I had finished eating, they started knocking down the mess tent. Stout hands and hearts rallied to the job of properly folding and rolling this monstrously heavy piece of canvas and loading it with all the other paraphernalia into the two wagons. The cook then hitched up his four horses, climbed up on the box and, with appropriate curses at the straining team, started off for the location Jerry had picked as our midday stop before moving on to the next campsite. The nighthawk loaded into the bed wagon our bedrolls and the large coil of soft rope which was the corral, hitched up his four horses and pulled out right behind the mess wagon. Day wranglers took charge of the cavvy and loped on ahead with them to keep out of the way. The rest of us rode out to round up the main herd and start it moving on its course toward the mountains and summer range.

Our general course was always upward toward the high, cool mountain range, with its minimum of flies and maximum of moisture; and also toward the Garvin Basin, a great hole in the mountains, two thousand feet down from the rimrock, where some of the outfit's steers would spend a safe winter in a fifty-six-thousand-acre pasture, a part of Matt's leases. The steers could not be pushed too fast, so we would camp a while along the way to let them rest, to pick up others, to work the herds for branding and tallying and to help our neighbors, the grangers on the opposite side of the fence from our range, as we went along.

The grangers—traditionally known to cattlemen as Punkin Rollers—followed our movements with interest, for we helped them work their own herds, brand their calves, repair their fences (sometimes suspiciously weak-looking) and find stray cattle (which, mysteriously enough, occasionally got through the weak spots in the fences to feed on our range). As we moved along with our own cattle, a number of these poachers got mixed in with our herd, causing at one time considerable annoyance, as the Punkin Rollers would suddenly appear and expect us to hold up the herd just to find perhaps a few of their own strayed cattle and cut them out. Considering the fact that Matt's outfit helped them fix their fences each year, it was remarkable how weak the fences were, especially in the right places to let Punkin Roller cattle in on Sheardon grass. After throwing out several head of poaching cattle singly, Jerry Flynn got tired of the nuisance and apparently decided to wait until we reached the end of the Punkin Rollers' domain and then cut out all the poachers at once.

This plan, however, did not fit in with the ideas of a certain Punkin Roller family who wanted us to cut out their cattle immediately, so they wouldn't be inconvenienced by going so far after them. But Jerry turned down the old Punkin Roller's request with the suggestion, "Considering how many years your whole family's been stealing our grass, you ought to be goddam thankful we don't take you to court for it or at least send you a pasture bill."

"Well!" shouted the irate old Punkin Roller, "If it's goin' to be a question of law-ing over this, we'll find out whether you big outfits got the right to gather up everybody else's cattle and run off with them or not. We'll show you who's taking who to court!" With that, he laboriously wheeled his old farm horse around and walked away, violently kicking the horse in the ribs and shaking his fist at us.

The next evening just before sundown, when most of us had turned in, an ancient, battered car bumped into camp, bringing the sizzling old Punkin Roller and three thuggy-looking younger male relatives. All obviously had their dander up as they demanded to speak to the wagon boss. They were told that Jerry was still out with the herd but would be coming into camp shortly, if they cared to wait. "We'll wait, all right!" the old man said ominously. And they sulked in their rattletrap, mumbling among themselves.

Jerry came in from the herd and rode over to them. From his perch on a tall horse, he looked down, expressionless and silent, as the old Punkin Roller raved on about the iniquities of cattle kings and the plight of the little fellow, finally pulling a document from his pocket — his trump card — and holding it up to Jerry, who made no move to take it but said simply, "Not interested."

"Did ya hear that?" the old man cackled to his accomplices. "He ain't interested in a legal pernouncement. They must think they're running the whole goddam State of Montana. They even got their own law! . . . Here!" He shook the paper at Jerry again threateningly. "This'll show you who's who! . . . You are hereby summoned . . ."

Jerry cut him off, explaining patiently, "Look mister. You're not even in the State of Montana. This is the Crow Reservation. It belongs to the U.S. Government in trust for the Indians, and we've got it leased for cattle range . . . *our* cattle, not yours. And anything you got there, unless it comes from Washington, D.C., or Crow Agency, isn't worth the paper it's written on. My instructions are to pick up all the cattle in this pasture, and I'm carrying them out. If some of yours are in here, you're just trespassing on federal property. They might even be confiscated until you pay up for the grass you're stealing. *This* time, we're going to give them back to you again and forget about it. But at our convenience. If you don't like it, take it up with the Agency. As a matter of fact, you don't even have to go that far. We've got Yellowtail right here at the wagon."

Yellowtail, the Indian Agent, was sometimes with us, but happened to be asleep at the time.

Jerry's sudden loquacity was such a rare event that it aroused us all. One by one, faces appeared at the tent flaps or, propped up on elbows, peered over the sagebrush. The Punkin Rollers looked from one to another of us in dismay. When they saw Yellowtail, that decided it. They cranked up their car and drove off.

Matt came out to the wagon from time to time and rode with us for a few days. But he was very busy with his various business deals and was always having to rush back to them. One day in July he brought a message for me. "Skel Baxton sent us word to tell you that he's got a chance to sell fifty of your heifers at fifty dollars a head, and if you're interested, to come down and see him about it."

A great feeling of relief came over me as I loaded my gear into the supply truck. The wagon lay idle during midsummer, with just a skeleton crew, or sometimes came in for repairs until the fall beef roundup started. So there were a lot of us coming back to the ranch, perched about on the load of bedrolls and saddles. I felt happy at the prospect of having a good bath. The best I had been able to do on the Reservation was in the Government irrigation ditch where it crossed a gully in a great, semicircular metal culvert. I had jumped into the culvert and hung onto my throw rope, made fast to a crossbar, letting the waters rush over me. But I had had the opportunity only once. I was even happier, however, at the prospect of escaping from at least part of my heifer deal up in Lewistown and wondered what the details might be. Matt had brought only the simple message.

The next inkling of information I got was from Fred Lauby, who was sitting on the cabin porch with his telescope when I drove up. "I figured you'd be coming back from the wagon just about now," he announced prophetically. "By God, boy! Ain't it wonderful news about selling them heifers? And to the Governor of Montana too! I hear that Skel and that Langer feller up in Lewistown got to scrapping with each other over range fees, and this feller threatened to cut off the grass, so old Skel he ups and pokes him in the eye and sells all his heifers and fifty of yours to the Governor." He slapped his thigh in delight.

I didn't have to wonder whether my elusive guest, Jigger McCabe, had been over for another visit during my absence, but I couldn't help wondering whether he knew what would happen to my other seventy-five unbranded heifers.

7

La Plata Ranch in Chihuahua

FRED'S INFORMATION WAS CORRECT. My first customer was the Governor, all right, and there was his check for $2,500, signed Roy E. Ayres and dated June 13, 1940.

This pretty well vindicated my faith in "the renegade," at least for the time being, but Fred was still skeptical. "It was one chance in a million," he said. "You were just luckier than hell this time, like you were here years ago. . . . Well, what are you going to do with the money? Put it in cows and calves, like any sensible stockman?" he added hopefully, probably thinking that I had learned my lesson.

"Oh, I don't know, Fred. This deal came out so nicely, what with that little profit, that I've been thinking of going into another deal with Skel."

His face dropped. "What kind of a deal?"

"Horses. Wild horses. He has an option on nine thousand head for canning contracts. You know, these European armies live on horsemeat."

"Goddam them European armies! You never can tell which one is going to win, or whether you'll get paid. Stay away from horse deals with Skel Baxton, I tell you. He's got a perfect mania for running down them wild horses and stuffing them into cans. I tell you, it's a mania with him. Lots got fooled that way during the World War."

Of course, I hadn't any idea of stuffing wild horses into cans, but it might be well to let him think he had convinced me against

93

it to humor him along into working on the water system. Actually, I had decided to get into a steer deal with Matt.

While we were riding together with the Antler wagon, Matt had convinced me on the theory of his Mexican steer calves, which, at that point, he was shipping up north by trainloads that had set the whole cattle country to raising eyebrows. His shipments seemed ill timed for cattle from a warm country to the colder climate of Montana in early spring, sometimes so early that they were caught in late snowstorms which were very hard on them. Old-timers shook their heads that one of their fraternity didn't know better. And whenever he was known to have a shipping loss from late storms, or a trainload of his steers came through the country in poor shape, there were always plenty of wagging tongues to exaggerate the sad figures.

But the scenes they painted of the whole operation were not the scenes that Matt showed me from the saddle as we rode with the wagon. "Look," he had explained, sweeping his arm over a great area of range lush with grama grass and dotted with thousands of fat steers, "there's nothing the matter with them except the color. They don't look as pretty as a bunch of native whiteface steers all matched up, but they're making more money. Once in the packing plant with the hides off, the color don't count, and these buyers know it. The weight's what counts. These have been double-wintered here, and by the time we ship them out this fall, they'll have nearly tripled their weight. Sure, we lose a few once in a while when they hit storms in shipping. But results like this more than make up for the losses. You can lose cows and calves too in winter. And they cost more, with the range, hay and labor you've put into them, than a few skinny calves that you've bought by weight at six cents a pound and haven't put anything else into them except a little freight."

"The grass doesn't really amount to much expense at that point, does it?"

"Exactly. This outfit makes money because we get our grass at a reasonable price: around a half million acres for something like seventy thousand dollars a year. That comes to about fifteen cents an acre net, and the range will carry twelve thousand head. Mexican billies don't eat any more grass than native steers, and you can get more of them for your money, because they're lighter, coming from that dry country down there. A little difference in the price of their meat just because of their color doesn't offset those advantages. Not when you can double or triple their weight in eighteen months."

The idea made sense to me, and when Skel Baxton unexpectedly broke the welcome news that he had sold the balance of my Lewis-town heifers in mid-August at seventy dollars a head, I adopted it. Skel had certainly vindicated himself and earned his dollar-a-head commission, even though (as I had learned in the meantime) the standard commission at Eagle Pass, Texas, was half that. But then, the Eagle Pass brokers were inactive lobbyists in cheap hotels, mere spittoon ringers compared with Skel's radius of activities, intensity of operations and general entertainment value.

My deal with Matt was a fifty-fifty proposition on five hundred head. He was then buying his steer calves through a dealer in Albuquerque, New Mexico, who was reported to have made fabu-lous sums by crossing them over the drought-stricken border and selling them to northern cattlemen with plenty of grass and water. But the source of these steers was a closely guarded secret. Matt confided to me that he longed to unlock it, since the dealer's prices were rising with each trainload, and the end of a very pleasant situation was undoubtedly in sight. We took the dealer out on several rounds of strenuous entertainment in Billings but could not pry from him the source of his cattle in Mexico.

The next fall, while we were riding with the wagon on the beef roundup, Matt loped up alongside me and said dolefully, "You know, I don't think we'll ever be able to ship any more steers with the profit these are showing, unless we find out where in hell he's getting them."

The dealer had raised his prices again. Also, there had been some rain along the border, and calves were running heavier. Where we had originally been paying for only three hundred pounds' average weight, our last purchase of two hundred and seventy-two head had averaged three hundred and forty-one pounds.

Matt suggested, "I've just been thinking that, instead of working on the wagon here to ship this year's beef, you and I ought to be down south, locating cattle to ship two years from now."

In November and December we haunted the Mexican border from Nogales, Arizona, to Eagle Pass, Texas. Matt knew a lot of cattle brokers, and we spent countless hours with them on the endless highways between their widely separated ranches, bumping over miles of sagebrush to see their cattle and running back and forth to strange places in Mexico. They seemed to have a web of activity all over the southwest, with its main nerve center located in El Paso. They could always be found in the main hotel's lobby, in their sand-colored pants, their leather jackets, large hats and highly polished boots, a race apart from other races. Nobody knew why, but everybody knew it was so.

We ate and drank with them, worked and played with them, exchanged information with them, and made some deals. But always the cattle prices figured out just about the same as they did with the broker from Albuquerque, and always they were edging a little higher. Matt finally analyzed the situation from our standpoint. "What we need down here is two things: our own source of cattle *in* Mexico and a few thousand acres of holding pasture. Then we could pick our own weather for shipping. The trouble with our present system is, that when a good buy shows up, too often bad shipping weather up north comes along at the same time."

We were spinning along the border highway near Columbus, New Mexico, and suddenly he had a notion to turn south into Mexico. "I've heard of a deserted ranch down here about a hundred and twenty-five miles south of the border that might be just right for us. Two years ago I got down as far as their northern pastures, but I've always wanted to go on down to the headquarters."

At the international port of entry just south of Columbus, the border formalities did not take long. The American officials made a little polite conversation, asked a few discreet questions, scrutinized our identification papers and poked about in our belongings. Then they passed us on to the Mexican officials, where we were greeted by a short, swarthy, dark-skinned individual in a rumpled khaki uniform, who touched the cracked visor of his cap and flashed us a good-natured expectant smile as he eyed Matt's large, gleaming car. He was rewarded with a carton of cigarettes which someone had left in the baggage compartment and snapped to a salute as we passed over the line.

We followed a narrow road along miles of level greasewood and mesquite country, crossing a few dry river beds and going up a long, gentle slope to a much rougher, stony country, gradually rising into the foothills of low, blue mountains. On the far side of the mountains was a bovine paradise of grass. The road petered out into little more than a wagon track and from time to time was crossed by other wagon tracks, with no indication of where any of them came from or led to. We referred to Matt's road map, which had been roughly marked in pencil by one of our cattle broker friends, as to the general location of the ranch. From there on, we went mostly by guesswork, general directions and a few hints from river beds, until we came to what was undoubtedly part of the La Plata Ranch, so-called because it once included a silver mine. Windmills, mostly in dilapidated condition, were scattered about in the distance, only a few of them holding water in their dirt reservoirs. Traces of fence, with wire stripped off and posts knocked down, vaguely outlined the former pastures. Here and there, as we passed by, cattle rose from the tall grass and darted wildly about. They were in uniformly good condition, fat and sleek, but acted as if they had never seen a human being or an automobile before. They were of all ages with various brands. Some cows had slick calves following them, although they were large enough to have been branded long since. It was obvious that no roundup outfit had been in the country for many a moon. There was no sign of human existence anywhere, and for awhile, as the mileage on our speedometer crept upward, we began to wonder whether there even *was* a headquarters.

Then we came upon it: a long, low, adobe wall on the horizon. We passed through the battered gate into a great dusty area about the size of a city block, bordered by huge cottonwood trees. The ground was deep in dead leaves, and our car rustled over them eerily. To the left was the compound, with living quarters for about three hundred peons, tumbled down now and full of leaves. To the right was the *hacienda,* likewise adobe, a squarish, spacious building set around a patio. Beyond it were the shells of several smaller buildings, housing the remains of ancient carriages, rotted harness and broken tools. Their crumbling walls were splattered here and there with clusters of bullet holes. "They tell me that Pancho Villa captured this ranch and made it his headquarters when General Pershing was campaigning against him in 1911," Matt explained. "Some of these walls were where he staged his executions. When he left, he took all the silver from the mine, of course, then dynamited the shaft and flooded it." In the chapel also it was the same. Even the bells had been torn from the belfry for their silver content and then abandoned on the ground beneath, obviously because they were too heavy to cart off in a hurry. From a distance there came the scream of a mountain lion. "I understand the country's full of them. You can't even stake a horse out at night," said Matt. And in the dust of the patio there were the unmistakable tracks. Around the patio boarded windows of the house frowned at us intruders.

We strolled about among the tall weeds, glancing through battered doors and broken windows at the pitiful reminders of long-vanished occupants: a crucifix lying on the floor, a broken, empty bird cage swinging from a porch ceiling, a rusted spur in a cottage yard. Sheds were roofless, their mouldering beams making weird, barred designs against the sky. Only the communal laundry remained fairly intact, with its indestructible scrubbing stones lining a trough through which a stream once ran. It was certainly not a happy place. It reeked of violence, failure and death. But the surrounding grass was still there. About four hundred thousand acres of it. "I've heard that this spread is owned in the United States. A sort of absentee ownership deal." Matt smiled, wistfully. "I wonder just what the owners are getting out of it."

Through the information net in the El Paso lobbies, we got a line on the La Plata owners. It was a corporation in New York, composed mostly of disillusioned businessmen who had long since abandoned any hope of returns from their investment. It was controlled by a childhood schoolmate of mine whom I had not seen in years and who was at the mercy of a ranch manager named Sam Ellery, a native of the border country, with powerful Mexican connections. Since the owners never came near the place, except for occasional quail-shooting parties before the panic of 1929, and had cut Sam's salary drastically since then, it was pretty generally supposed that he ran the La Plata for his own and his friends' benefit. Or rather, he let it run itself and lived a jolly life in El Paso.

A long-distance call to New York put us in touch with the boss, my former old-school-tie classmate, Truxford Harbridge. We offered fifty thousand dollars down for a five-year lease on the whole ranch, although we needed, for our immediate purposes, only a holding pasture of a hundred thousand acres. We wanted the right to sublease the balance and to purchase the whole for an additional fifty thousand dollars after two years. In the meantime, we offered to repair the windmills and fence lines, make the house habitable and pay the owners a percentage of our profits. Such improvements, in fact, would be absolutely necessary in order to carry on any kind of cattle operation Montana style.

No matter how the owners figured it, they couldn't possibly take a loss, since at the time they were not getting anything but headaches from the ranch.

Trux Harbridge called back to his manager, Sam Ellery, ordering him to get in touch with us immediately and give us technical information on the ranch, while the owners considered drawing up a contract.

Sam offered to take us on a tour of inspection, but we had seen enough of the grass to know that it was what we wanted; in fact, it was a great deal more than we wanted. So we contented ourselves with his maps, mentioning that we planned to sublease much of the range and use the lease money to finance improvements on the fences, windmills and water holes.

Naturally, we told Sam as little as possible about our future plans for the La Plata—the importation of our own labor, management and methods—which did not include him. He suspected that they might not and set about making himself indispensable to us. Since he was letting his friends run cattle on the La Plata range for practically nothing, taking favors in return, it occurred to him that this happy state of affairs might suddenly dry up if we took over the ranch before he had been definitely focused into the picture. His personal fifty thousand acres, fenced off around the hacienda, where it was most convenient (and the only really solid fence on the whole outfit) might be used for something else. And his political grazing club of several hundred thousand acres would be (as he saw it, correctly) dissolved.

Little by little the information leaked to us in the bars and lobbies of the El Paso hotels. "How about it, Tom?" one of the web members asked another in an early morning confidential mood, "You've had experience with us on that grass down there. Speak up for the gentlemen from Montana. They think they've got grass on the Crow Reservation. Maybe we should educate them a little."

Tom answered apologetically, "Well, sir, I'm a mighty poor hand at educating anybody. And as for that country down there, why I'm about the smallest outfit on it. Haven't got hardly two thousand head, nor more than twenty-three thousand acres at most. But it seems that they just naturally double the money every year or so."

At eleven acres to the head, that was more than three times what our range would do. As for water, the wells were already dug, and the windmills were standing by, ready for a few repairs to make them pump. There was also an underground river, which appeared and disappeared in different places. And there were no winter problems. All in all, Sam Ellery had good reason to block our deal until he could be sure that he was in on it.

As for Trux of the old school tie at the helm of the La Plata Company, he didn't do so well in the estimation of web members. "He's never even had a meal at the mess wagon," one of them volunteered. "That's what plumb disgusted his cowpokes so they mostly all quit. They just wasn't good enough for him to eat with."

"The chuck wagon grub ain't good enough for him either," another added. "He's got to have his grub put up for him by the chef on his private car and drug down from the railroad in a station wagon to where he wants to shoot quail."

"That's right. Sam Ellery says he ain't never even stepped up on a horse to go out and have a look at the beef herd, when they had one. And it wasn't because he was crippled or couldn't ride. He's husky enough right now to get on a horse up north and chase hell out of them poor, harmless little foxes or beat a polo ball up and down an irrigated flat."

"I've seen a lot of them New York dude fellers visiting around fancy outfits like the Babicora and the Running W," one of their pals chimed in. "They'll hunt foxes and shoot birds and beat polo balls around, but they won't do nothing that makes sense when it comes to running an outfit. They're all the same—useless as tits on a bacon rind."

It was enough to make a born Manhattanite feel rather small.

Up to then Matt had bought forty-six hundred steers along the border, of mixed ages and weights, averaging about nine cents a pound for them. They were mostly snipe-nosed, slab-sided billies; but still, it cost about twelve cents a pound to raise a calf in our own country, while in Mexico at that time it could be done for a nickel. There was ample room in between for all foreseeable overhead and handsome profits besides.

By that time Sam had seen the color of Matt's money and knew that we were in earnest about taking over the La Plata. He redoubled his efforts at making himself indispensable to us. From the top of his baldish, pudding-like head to the toes of his gleaming boots he was at our service by night and by day in both countries and even on the bridge between. He knew all the bridge officials and sped us by them, all the local officials in Juarez and (he could not let us forget) every other official worth knowing right on up the line to the greatest *politicos* in Mexico City. Drinks in the border bars and quail feasts at the Lobby Number Three were all on him, whiling away endless hours of "visiting" with his important friends, attended ever by his two favorite *mariachis,* who strummed softly to him on guitars. "Now, boys," he explained to us, "along the border, the first thing you must learn to do is visit. By visiting, we don't always mean just visiting. But we always call it that. In Mexico you've got to pull strings to get a job done, especially a job like taking over a ranch that some big *politicos* are after for themselves, and that they can confiscate under the agrarian laws any time they want to. In a case like that you got to pull strings. And I'm the one who pulls the strings around here. But I only pull them for somebody who treats me right."

"We'd treat you right," Matt led on. "How much will you take to put the deal through?" He was worth a decent sum just to be rid of once and for all. "We'd like to make a simple proposition to these *politicos.*"

"In Mexico there's no such thing as a simple proposition. You begin with the boss *politicos* in Mexico City. They have to be visited first. And visited *properly,* what I mean. You know . . ." And he made a gesture of peeling bills from a bankroll. "Then — and only then — you get the job done. But that's not the end, it's only the beginning. Afterwards, you have your protection . . ."

"From what?"

"Mostly, the agrarian laws. But they're very flexible, and I don't have any trouble with them. Before I came along, though, it was different. You know how big the La Plata was originally? One million and sixty thousand acres. Now it's just a little over four hundred thousand."

"What happened to the rest?"

"Confiscated by the Mexican Government under the agrarian laws. But that was before my time. Since I've been on the job, not an acre has been confiscated, although they've been talking about it just lately. Then, besides the boys in Mexico City, you have to know the Governor of the State to operate there. That's very important, and, luckily enough, the Governor of Chihuahua is a great friend of mine. Wonderful man . . . if he likes you. Through him, you get your stand-in with the *rurales*. They're the boys who keep the cattle rustlers away from your range. . . . That is, if *they* like you."

"Good God! Do all these people have to be visited?" Matt's voice sank in dismay.

"Yep. All. Every one. But I could save you a world of money on that. And I could save you money all along the line too, even in buying the place. I can chill the juice in those stockholders with a few threats of confiscation, and they'll take a lot less for the outfit than you're offering. . . . In fact, I might be indispensable."

So saying, the man of influence slumped forward in his chair, giving himself up to the oblivion of an alcoholic stupor and the care of his two guitarists.

8

A Trip to Chihuahua City

UP IN NEW YORK that Christmas season I renewed my acquaintance with Truxford Harbridge. The contract was not ready. But that was understandable because of the Christmas rush. Also, there were a few points that the lawyers wished to clear up with Sam Ellery, who was flying from El Paso right after Christmas, at which time we could surely conclude the contract.

With Sam's arrival, however, the complications grew worse instead of better. It seemed that since I left El Paso, questions had arisen concerning *inafectabilidad* on certain titles of the La Plata: their susceptibility to confiscation under the agrarian laws. The acreage we wanted most was desired also by a certain powerful Mexican general. Unfortunately, it did not carry the *inafectabilidad* classification of immunity. This situation was regrettable but not impossible of solution. Luckily, as my old schoolmate explained, we had such an influential man as Sam Ellery with us, who could fly to Mexico City and, in one fell swoop, remove all our difficulties. The old school tie would now come into play. Sam would be sent to Mexico City immediately to protect our interests, so that the contract could be signed. It was all very simple, in fact, bully—just a couple of old schoolmates working together. And, by the way, could Matt fly back east for the final closing of our deal?

As Sam left for La Guardia airport, the last thing he said to me was, "You'll never get anything done unless you play ball with me."

Matt couldn't fly to New York, because the airlines were full, but he arrived by train from Washington, where he had business with the Indian Bureau. When he finally arrived, it was only to be met with the news that the contract would have to be postponed again.

Sam Ellery was back in New York with his report from Mexico City. His negotiations had gone very well down there. But unfortunately, the Governor of Chihuahua had raised questions about two strange Americans taking over a large property in his state, and there were several aspects of the matter which would require further time and consideration if our interests were to be safeguarded. A trip to Chihuahua City to inspect the state archives was in order, but later. Nothing could be done now. It was all a question of an indefinite *mañana*.

In the meantime, I had borrowed money to finance my end of the Mexican deal, and it was lying idle in the bank. I wanted to get on with our plans. Matt (who had brought along a certified check for twenty-five thousand dollars) did too. But there wasn't a chance at the time. The forty-six hundred steers he had bought were ready for delivery on the border, together with nearly three hundred of my own, so we decided to ship them to Montana, even though it was dangerously early in the season.

I went back to El Paso to attend to shipping details and await Sam Ellery, who would soon follow with our contract, ready to be signed. Since Matt was a diabetic and had an appointment at the Mayo Clinic in Minnesota, he would return from there to the ranch to be on hand when our trainload of steers arrived. Then he would meet me on the border to resume his hunt for cattle and pursue the La Plata problem. Sam Ellery stayed on in New York to talk things over with his boss. Truxford and I waved our school ties at each other, and everyone took off in a different direction.

Back at El Paso I was treated to an almost daily long-distance call from New York. Trux, Sam and I, on a three-way hookup, discussed the mounting difficulties of our proposed deal: General Martinez, the big *politico*, had decided, after all, that he wanted the La Plata and was preparing to invoke the agrarian laws. The Governor of Chihuahua was becoming more difficult. And, incidentally, there had been a recent outbreak of cattle rustling in the La Plata area. Trux did not really think that it was a good time to be pressing such a deal, and did I mind if we sort of let the whole thing drop for a while? The old school colors were fading.

I minded very much indeed. So much, that I later elucidated somewhat upon the true nature of his cattle manager and threatened to expose the falsity of his statements if I had to make a trip to Mexico City myself. Actually, at the moment I had no idea of how this could be done. But after several calls to kind friends in New York and Washington, a telephone appointment was arranged for me with the aristocratic Don Francisco de Portal-Mendoza, a banker of pure Spanish descent, with mining interests and complete political connections in Mexico City from President Camacho down, besides being trilingual.

Don Francisco's voice exploded into my life in a rocket-like trilingual telephonic blaze (for which, kindly enough, he insisted upon paying). There were bursts of French, high Castillian and English, cleverly interwoven but almost incomprehensible, though delightful to hear. After we had compromised upon a sort of French-English, it became clear that there was nothing he wouldn't do for me, no government official he couldn't reach, no question to which he couldn't find the answer. And it would all be no trouble whatever for him. I explained briefly the situation at the La Plata ranch and my desire to learn, definitely, whether the property might be leased or sold without danger of interference from or confiscation by, the Mexican Government. That, he assured me, would be one of the simplest feats imaginable. He would, in fact, take me personally to the fountainhead of all *politicos,* who dictated the government policy on this delicate subject, and I could hear the details for myself if I would come to Mexico City. He then offered to send his car to the border at Laredo, Texas, to fetch me (a mere seven hundred and fifty miles). But that I really couldn't accept.

Matt returned to El Paso full of cheerful news. They were having an easy winter of it up north and were scarcely feeding any hay at all. Our trainload of steers had fared well, arriving with a loss of only one. On my own account, two hundred and seventy-two steers had weighed out at an average of three hundred and forty-one pounds, which made them cost me thirty-seven dollars a head laid down at Wyola, Montana, including about one thousand dollars of freight and feeding charges from Eagle Pass, Texas.

They were worth, on the open market, about a cent per pound more than the heifers, for which I had paid nearly the same delivered price (per head) nine months before, with freight only from Gillette, Wyoming, and which weighed but slightly over three hundred. So I had reduced my cost by better than two cents per pound on a commodity worth one cent per pound more, and in the face of a rising market, thanks to having dealt with Matt direct on the border. After that experience I never bought any more cattle through local brokers up north, as it was clear that the process involved too many mysteries. The heifers, however, according to Matt's report, had long since gained back all their handicap in weight, were doing fine in the mild winter, and were way into the black on the books.

We knew that Sam Ellery was back in town. Not that he had called up, but because, from our hotel window, we had seen him being carried across the street from the hotel bar and loaded into a car. Several days after that, he called us up and came over to visit. He was sober, dapper in a freshly pressed sand-colored outfit with large hat and sparkling boots, polite and without any indication of knowing what I had told his boss about him, so I couldn't see any point in mentioning it. There was no immediate talk of the contract, which meant that this was to be an evening of visiting. He invited us to have supper with him across the border at his favorite haunt, the Casita Blanca.

We took a cab to the International Bridge and walked over that long, narrow span with its ever-present hordes of nondescript humanity and antiquated vehicles continually shuffling, for divers obscure reasons, across the Río Grande. Beneath us the great, shallow, murky river writhed its dismal way between those sad, gaunt banks so romantically misrepresented in folklore and on lithographed calendars, while little bare, brown-skinned ragamuffins slithered about in its forbidding ooze, looking up pitifully and waving long poles fitted with small nets, begging one to toss them a coin. They would fight savagely in the muck for the coins that missed their nets.

The long bar at the Casita Blanca was brash and noisy. Half-drunken Mexicans exchanged bawdy remarks with totally drunken tourists to the twanging and singing of meandering *mariachis* done up in sombreros and serapes. They may have been good enough for the tourist trade, but they were not good enough for

Sam, who waved them away, ordering them to send him his two private *mariachis*. These presently arrived, and we settled down at the bar to the strains of Sam's favorite tunes, amid strong alcoholic vapors and a thin haze of blue smoke from cheap tobacco. Beneath us, around the base of the bar, ran a tile gutter in which a stream of water flowed constantly, charged with cigarette butts which bobbed up and down in sad procession toward the sewer. Above us, hanging from the walls and peering down from the top of the bar, was a galaxy of stuffed animals. There were birds from eagles to hummingbirds; beasts from mountain lion to chipmunks; fish from tarpon to trout. They were, for the most part, badly mounted and very dusty.

Here Sam was in his element. He had long since grown accustomed to the harshness, the dustiness, the tawdriness and the foul atmosphere . . . had, in fact, grown up with it. The alcoholic vapors were as perfume to his nostrils; and, if the tile gutter had been a babbling mountain brook, it could not have been a more welcome sight to him. Here he met and backslapped with his friends: Mexicans, Americans and half-bloods. The noise they made, their cursing and drunkenness and sickness were part of the warp and woof of his life. Among them he felt himself to be a big shot — key man for a bunch of New York millionaires — and he strove continually to act every inch of it.

In the casino adjoining the bar the tourist trade was dancing. They were for the most part in that comfortably dizzy state which, oddly enough, is deemed necessary by the great majority of Americans who cross the International Bridge, but which is not conducive to learning the Varsuviana. Nevertheless, a few border Lotharios struggled bravely through the dance with some of the tourist women, while their men sat sheepishly guzzling drinks on the sidelines. Our table had been arranged at the edge of the dance floor. Sam barged toward it noisily, and we sat down to a full meal of soup, jumbo shrimps from Guymas and a main course of quail floated by innumerable icy splits of light Mexican beer. As we ate and drank, the repetitive strains of the Varsuviana gave way to more conventional music and dancing, which got louder and louder, whipped to a frenzy by crashing cymbals and blaring cornets, until it rose to an unbearable crescendo, and then stopped suddenly. The lights went down and dancers returned to their tables. Drums rolled, a spotlight stabbed through the blue haze, making a dazzling oval in the center of the floor. From the surrounding shadows Pepita stepped swiftly and silently into it.

Pepita was tiny, palpitating and lacquered. She stood there, shimmering in a cheap gown of sapphire sequins, daringly low cut and clinging. Within its restricting confines she squirmed and writhed with a natural suggestiveness that seemed inborn more than just a part of the game. One got the idea that she was physically incapable of standing still. She beamed at the circle of drab tourists peering at her from the semidarkness, then got our table in her sights and flashed a pearly smile at Sam. Her large, round, sensual eyes blazed from beneath their mascara-tinged lids and her hair shone an uncanny blue-black in the powerful light. Suddenly she burst into a plaintive, nasal song with a metallic ring to it.

Sam stared at her hungrily. Between songs he led the applause and winked proudly at us. After her act she came over and sat with us.

There was no doubt but that Pepita had a way with her. She was short on English but made a great effort to be polite, then put in a plug for her girls. "Many of my *muchachas,* they speak *ingles* so much more good than Pepita. *Comprende muchachas . . . ?"* She made curves in the air with her hands and then clapped, childishly. *"Muy bonitas . . .* very preety. You will like them. They will like you. It is good, so." She slipped from her chair to Sam's knee and slapped him gently on his ample jowl, while he stared stupidly down her bosom. "You do not call me this afternoon."

"I've called you up every other afternoon, though."

"Not enough, *querido."* She slithered back to her chair, pouting, then beamed at us. "But when he call, he say such nice things to Pepita! . . . *Querido,* why you do not call me in the morning too?"

"Because you're always asleep then."

"Ha, ha!" She pointed an accusing finger at him. "He also. In the morning he is sleep, sleep, like old *lobo . . .* how you say . . . wolf! But tomorrow it is different. Tomorrow in the morning I go on the plane to Chihuahua for my vacation. You will come with me and bring the *señores,* no? I will show them my new house, and I will have some nice *señoritas* for them, and you will take us all to the *teatro,* and afterwards we will sing in the garden. Adios! I must go now. Do not forget." She threw her arms about

Sam's neck, kissed the top of his bald pate, decorating it absurdly with large smears of crimson lipstick, and slipped away.

Sam beamed and called lustily for more drinks. "You know, that reminds me . . . I have to go down to Chihuahua City anyway pretty soon to have a look through the public archives, like I told you in New York. Why don't we make it tomorrow, and you two come along? I'd like to show you the real dope on some of the La Plata titles right from the records in the state capitol."

Next morning Sam's telephone at first did not answer. But later he called to say that there hadn't been any room on the small plane and would we like to drive down with him, it being only a few hours' run? We had made several business appointments for that day that we couldn't cancel and were also expecting an important long-distance call from the ranch in Montana. So we decided to split up. Matt would drive down with Sam and back the next day, while I would stay in El Paso as liaison officer and put a call through to their hotel in Chihuahua City early next morning. Matt hurriedly packed a small bag and went downstairs to meet Sam in the lobby.

At seven the following morning, as I sat down at the writing desk for the long ordeal of the Mexican telephone, with my notes and messages for Matt, I was startled to see his little black diabetic's kit with its hypodermic needle and supply of insulin. He had been particularly careful lately about taking his shots regularly, after two narrow escapes from slipping into a coma from lack of them. I had been schooled by his family on the absolute necessity of his insulin routine and begged to keep a watchful eye on it, which I had promised faithfully to do. He was never to go anywhere without sweets in case of an insulin reaction and his hypodermic kit in case of a sugar reaction.

Waiting for the telephone connection to go through, I counted up the hours since his last injection and shuddered. I had not seen him take his evening injection before leaving, so that he must have missed it, being afterwards on the road to Chihuahua City. And once enmeshed in an evening's sport with Sam and Pepita, it seemed possible that he might have forgotten it, even if the drugstores were open at that hour and had the proper type of insulin on hand. What if he had become separated from Sam (who would, obviously, be staying at Pepita's house) and found himself drifting into a coma, with no knowledge of Spanish by which to

call for help or explain his plight? Was it reasonable to expect
that, in a small Mexican hotel there would be an English-speaking
doctor on hand in the middle of the night? By five-thirty in the
morning he would have missed two injections, and that was an
hour and a half ago. By seven o'clock it seemed impossible that
he could have escaped a coma. And by that time, Sam, even if still
around, would be in his usual morning torpor and completely useless in handling explanations of *materia medica*.

With my Spanish dictionary close at hand, I waited nervously
for results from the shrill conversation of Mexican telephone operators, which took half an hour before a connection with the hotel
was made. There was the usual fuss about identification and
spelling out the name, followed by a long series of unanswered
ringings of the room telephone and then the report, "Señor Sheardon is not awake yet."

Knowing that Matt never got up later than six, I urged the
operator to keep ringing until he awoke.

"It is no use, Señor, he will not wake up."

"Are you sure he's in the room? Send someone up to knock on
the door and wake him. It's very important."

Five minutes later the operator reported, "Señor, they have
bang on the door and they have call at the door and they have
shake the door, but Señor Sheardon will not answer. They have
also climb up and look over the top of the door. He is there in the
bed, but he will not wake up, and he have bolt the door inside.
So maybe he is tired and wish to sleep some more."

"No, no. He is sick . . . *enfermo*. He is *diabetico.*" Here my
phrase book came into violent play. "Call a doctor. Call an ambulance. Say he needs an insulin injection . . . insulin . . . yes. Break
the door in. Shake him, wake him up. Let me know what happens.
I'll hold the line. Don't cut me off!" I put the instrument down on
the desk and called downstairs on the house telephone to inquire
about a doctor, and was told that the management would locate
one and have him call me. Then I rushed back to listen on the
Chihuahua line. Nothing yet. So I started packing a bag, determined to charter a plane and fly to Chihuahua City with an American doctor. Every few minutes I would check up on the Chihuahua
line. It continued to buzz but was otherwise silent for a long time.

Finally, the operator came back again. "Señor, the manager
wishes to speak to you. He is upstairs in the room of Señor Shear-

don with the ambulance doctor. There is trouble. Just one moment, please . . ."

A click on the line ushered in a din of shouting and struggling, above which the manager's voice strained politely, "Señor, your friend, he is very ill. He is resisting the doctor and attendants. They cannot get near him with the needle. What shall we do?"

"He is delirious. Get some help and hold him. He'll quiet down after the innoculation."

There followed a perfect bedlam of scuffling and, as I listened to it carefully, the drunken curses of Sam Ellery came through, interrupted by the manager's voice again. "Señor, he is very strong. The doctor says he cannot be in a coma! Also, he says he is not Señor Sheardon."

"What does he look like?" A vivid description came back. It was Sam, dead drunk. "Where is Mr. Sheardon?"

"I cannot say, Señor. . . . This is his room, but the gentleman in it is not even registered in the hotel. The night hallboy, who is here helping us, say that Señor Sheardon went out of the hotel early this morning . . . he thinks, walking to the Zócalo for a newspaper in English. Shall I have him call you when he comes in?"

"Yes, please do. He'll be glad to pay for the doctor and ambulance."

I hung up in relief and wonder; then, still mystified, canceled the call for the house doctor. How was it possible . . . ?

During my breakfast Matt called back. "I'm all right," he said, "I'll be up on the afternoon plane. There's been a mix-up down here."

"But your insulin kit . . . you forgot it on the desk . . ."

"That's my spare kit. I've got the other one with me. I'm taking the afternoon plane to Juarez."

A storm came up and there were several reports that the flight had been canceled, but I went over to the Juarez airport anyway. The small plane finally made it, scudding in under low clouds, an hour late. It was old, overcrowded and leaky. The pilot was wearing a golf suit and, as he climbed out of the cockpit, he mopped water from about his neck. Matt, who had been jammed into the aisle at the last moment, emerged looking somewhat pale. "Hope I never have another trip to Chihuahua City like *that!*" he gasped.

"What happened down there? I thought you were dead."

"I just went out for a walk around the town about six-thirty and left my door open, I guess. While I was gone, Sam stumbled in, bolts the door from the inside and passes out on my bed. He'd been staying with Pepita, but I guess he got kind of rowdy towards morning and she threw him out. When I got back, they were trying to stick a needle in him, and all hell had busted loose."

"What about the government archives?"

"We never went near them. When we got down there, it was too late, and then Sam discovered that today is a *fiesta*. Tomorrow is Saturday, and I couldn't wait till Monday, even if Sam gets sobered up by then. That's the craziest trip I've ever made, but I wouldn't have missed it for anything. Just to see Sam fighting off that doctor with the needle was worth the price of admission."

9

The Proper Connections

AFTER THE CHIHUAHUA FIASCO we stayed clear of Sam Ellery and went about our business of locating more steers to ship north. Discussion of the La Plata ranch with him went into the doldrums. When Matt returned to Montana to take delivery of his cattle it was the ideal time for me to make my trip to Mexico City on our own personal investigation of the La Plata titles. So one fine spring morning I appeared at the home of Don Francisco de Portal-Mendoza, where I was ushered into his study.

Sitting behind a large desk fitted with several telephones and electric buttons was a smallish, handsome aristocrat. He was of the pale Spanish type, with exceedingly white skin and great, moist, hound-like eyes. He had a sensitive, vibrant, passion-ridden face which seemed to clash with his occupation as a businessman. Here was no flinty-faced banker with a heart of granite or rough-and-ready miner in the traditional American pattern. But he did have a dueling pistol on his desk. He was evidently explaining something about repairing it to his male secretary, as he tapped the pistol violently with a long, delicate finger.

Don Francisco received me with flowery courtesy and sat me down in a large, red leather armchair. He was in a fit of nerves over the pistol, which he had loaned to some friend for an honorable encounter in the Chapultepec forest, and who had dropped it, putting the trigger mechanism out of adjustment. As he talked, one foot pumped lightly under the desk, as if he were playing the piano. After the first polite preliminaries of conversation, he said,

"Now, tell me more about this question of the ranch which you wish to lease."

I explained our proposition and how Sam Ellery was trying to block it with threats that the titles were subject to confiscation: the point Matt and I wished to determine. From time to time, while I was talking, the telephones on his desk would tinkle softly. He would beg my pardon for the interruptions, splutter violent and rapid Spanish with terrific scowls, then slap the instruments back in their cradles and turn to me again, smiling. On the desk there was also a little bronze elephant, curiously blindfolded by a piece of paper held in place by a rubber band. There were other rubber bands around its loins and tail. After one of his telephonic torrents, he gave another twist to the band around the elephant's loins. "What do you do that for?" I couldn't help asking.

"I punish him."

"Why?"

"Because this elephant controls all the luck of my mining ventures. I can assure you that it is actually so. Lately, he has not been looking after my interests very well. Each one of these tortures you see on him is a punishment for some mining venture he has not made successful. The blindfold, it has been on nearly two years now, and I will not take it off until the ore makes more profits. Ah! How he hates that blindfold! The one on the tail is for a very small venture that did not go well. But the other torture—and you see where it is—that is the most terrible of all, for a faux pas on one of my larger claims. Just now, I have more bad news of it, so I give the rubber band another twist, to make it more painful. However, you did not come all this way to talk about mines, did you? Please go on about the ranch."

When I had finished, he turned his brightest smile on me. "My dear sir, it is simple. Very simple." He shrugged his magnificently tailored shoulders and reached for the telephone, which had rung again. "Bueno, bueno!" he barked into it impatiently. "Yes, yes, I want all the lions I can get!" And he slammed the instrument down again, with the explanation, "That is an American circus manager. He is providing some lions for a party I am giving to impress a young lady. But pardon the interruption again. Do not think for a moment that I have lost sight of the mission for which you are here. On the contrary, I have been working on it steadily. Be assured that no mere lawyer will be entrusted with your affairs.

I myself will take you personally to see the highest authority on the matter: he who dictates the agrarian policy to the Government, the greatest lawyer and *politico* in our country, Don Porfirio Ramirez. But . . ." He put his index finger to his lips. "We must be discreet. Don Porfirio lives in seclusion, under guard, for he is in constant danger of assassination. It is often so with power in Mexico. So not a word of this to anyone, remember! Shhhh!"

He led the way up a staircase to the end of a long tiled corridor and his bachelor living quarters: two rooms of old-fashioned, ample proportions, with plum-colored carpets, extraordinarily high ceilings and neatly painted white woodwork. A large dressing-and-bathroom combination adjoined, with ancient but adequate plumbing, in which a small, brown-skinned old man in a white jacket was occupied with the details of Don Francisco's clothing and personal belongings. "Enrique is my valet, born in my grandfather's employ. He is quite deaf from a musket ball caught in the head while defending my grandfather's *hacienda* against the Revolutionists. He lives here with his old sister, Concepción, whose duty it was to look after the moustache cups of my grandfather." Winking at me, he gave the little old man a playful hug. "He cannot hear one word I say, but he knows that I love him." The little valet smiled and bowed. "And here," my host continued, indicating an old-fashioned shaving stand with various unfamiliar objects on it, "are the moustache cups of my grandfather. Also the comb, brush, curling irons and wax, with which Concepción made the toilet of his moustache, and the white linen cloth she tied behind his head until it was ready. And now," he concluded, "I shall make a telephone call from the privacy of my chambers. It is to Don Porfirio himself. You agree with any time tomorrow for a meeting at his villa?"

I agreed and turned my attention to a leather case containing several foils and rapiers, while he telephoned.

"There, it is done! We shall be received tomorrow afternoon at four o'clock in his villa near Coyoacán." He held his fingers to his lips again. "Say nothing of this to anyone. In Mexico there are millions of unseen ears. Aha! I see that you are inspecting my weapons. They are fine indeed, and I love them." He took the leather case and unbuckled it. "Nowadays, unfortunately, dueling is against the law, but one does well not to part with his weapons, as it is occasionally necessary to curb the tongue of

some braggart. Also, we have a fine *Salle d'Armes* here, so there
is fencing practice, and there are tournaments. You see, for instance, what a beautiful blade that is! More than once it has served
me well." He drew out a gleaming rapier and danced nimbly
about the room with it, lunging, parrying and flicking his wrist
so that the supple blade whipped and whistled through the air.
"There is a certain poetry to dueling, which is not well expressed
by firearms. I prefer *armes blanches* always." He threaded his
imaginary foe on the blade and then came to rest, sadly reflecting,
"It is a pity that the custom is passing, like those who practiced
it in the noble days. The noble blood is all leaking out in Mexico.
It is the tragedy of my country." And he relapsed into a morbid
silence, his great moist eyes gazing out the window.

Enrique, sensing his master's mood from the dressing room,
came to him solicitously and put a fresh carnation in his buttonhole, from a supply he apparently always kept on hand. This
seemed to revive Don Francisco, who put away his blades and
said cheerily, "Now we must go to lunch. It is time. Come, I will
take you to the club." And he strode briskly toward the door.
"Let us walk. It is only a few blocks. I am nearly fifty now and it
is becoming necessary for my figure."

He had a trim, well-proportioned figure. His well-cut, obviously
hand-tailored, dark sharkskin suit had ample shoulders without
being unduly padded, and it sloped gracefully to narrow hips.
He wore a starched white collar and black knitted tie over a
starched dickey with a tiny blue horizontal pinstripe on it. He
looked much younger than fifty, so that the dickey had a strangely
out-of-place but pleasant appearance. His highly polished black
shoes were made to order of heavy box calf on a small British
last.

At his club we strolled out onto a tiled roof garden set with
shrubs and comfortable deck chairs under a gaily striped awning
upon which the sun beat fiercely. From this vantage point our
view took in the whole sprawling, growing city, over which soft
breezes seemed incessantly to flow from the two great, snow-
covered volcanoes dominating the horizon.

After an aperitif we went in to lunch, during the course of which
Don Francisco kept up a guarded, running commentary on the
various members and their guests, who from time to time would
wave at us or stop to chat. "There," he would say, "is the presi-

dent of our national bank, lunching with the Minister of Finance," or, "The distinguished old gentleman with the long moustache is the Duc de Bolère. That scar on his face comes from a duel which he fought with the son of the brother of my grandfather, who died with the Emperor Maximilian." Some general, sitting in the corner campaigning against a dozen very large oysters set in a huge platter of shaved ice, was a powerful *politico* who had had more love affairs than anyone else in Mexico. "He has dozens of illegitimate children and is always wishing for more. All of them he maintains in great magnificence at a beautiful country estate in Michoacán. It is said now that he is building another wing to the castle. Unfortunately, he is not well and so may not be able to fill the new wing, but he is trying very hard. With children he is *muy simpatico.* The man with him is his doctor, who has seven bullet holes in the intestine, but he does not suffer. He says they serve to ventilate the evil gases when it stretches from much overeating."

With coffee I got a polite briefing on plans for the morrow. It was a great honor to be received by Don Porfirio Ramirez—who was even sending one of his *pistoleros* to escort us—so we must be punctual. Enrique would drive us in Don Francisco's car, and they would pick me up at my hotel at about three-thirty.

Don Francisco was prompt in calling for me, and we set off in his car with Enrique driving, under guidance of the *pistolero,* who sat in the front seat, his right hand stuck under the left breast of his coat. We drove up the Paseo de la Reforma and out the Insurgentes, until the *pistolero* turned us off it into a long, narrow street and then again into a cobblestone lane where, after a few hundred yards, we stopped between high walls on either side of the lane.

"From here we must walk," Don Francisco explained. "Enrique will wait for us here. Come."

I fell in between Don Francisco and the *pistolero.* We walked a few dozen yards down the lane to a corner of the wall, turned it and found ourselves in an alley. Here the wall was covered with vines. The *pistolero* groped among the vines and knocked on a little wooden panel which opened, revealing a face. After there was an exchange of nods, the panel snapped shut again, and we walked on to an iron gate, where the knocking was repeated. There was a heavy clanking of bolts, and the gate opened slowly on a crack.

Two faces peered through the crack and then the gate opened wider, but just wide enough to admit one person at a time. The *pistolero* slipped through sideways and then motioned to us to follow.

The inside of the gate was reenforced with steel sheets to a height of about seven feet. One of the gate keepers had a large and ferocious dog on a chain. The dog snarled menacingly at us as we slipped through the gate, and his master reared back on the chain, saying, "Bueno, Pedro, bueno!"

In the center of the walled courtyard was a stone house of two stories, with a cupola on top. The house was of no particular architectural design but had the curious look of a cross between the simple squareness of a Mexican hacienda and the formal pompousness of a villa on the Italian Riviera. In the cupola were two men watching us intently.

The *pistolero* led the way up some steps and into the house through a little vestibule which opened into an entrance hall of bare fumed oak paneling, where he motioned us to be seated. Near the door, on the left as we came in, was Don Porfirio's secretary, sitting at a desk littered with papers. Doing duty as paperweight was a handsome, silver-plated, pearl-handled .45-caliber Colt revolver. The secretary was a small, dark-skinned man with great, expressive eyes, the whites of which just missed being white. He sat sullenly nursing a sheaf of papers and from time to time gave us an appraising glance.

"I'm sorry it is not very comfortable here," Don Francisco apologized, glancing at his watch, "but we shall not have to bear it long. I must go in first to prepare the way for your introduction." Then, nodding toward the secretary, "He will let you know when to follow." A buzzer sounded on the secretary's desk and Don Francisco was led off by the *pistolero,* who slid back a panel in the fumed oak through which they both disappeared.

The buzzer sounded again, the door slid open and the secretary nodded at me, saying, *"Pase Vd."* I went inside, and there was the *pistolero,* cautioning me about several wooden steps leading down into a large and somberly furnished room. He walked just behind me as I crossed the room to where Don Francisco and the great politician sat at a long refectory table, on which there was nothing but a dim light and a telephone fitted with a block of push buttons.

After the usual flowery introduction, Don Francisco explained, "Don Porfirio says that he is very glad to meet you and that he regrets being unable to speak English. But I will translate faithfully."

"Please tell him that I am very honored to be here." I smiled at Ramirez and sat down where the *pistolero* indicated, which was in an ugly, squarish, but actually rather comfortably upholstered chair, oddly placed before a fumed oak door with draperies on either side, but affording a good three-quarter face view of our host.

He was of medium height, stocky and very dark-skinned. His head was massive, with straight, rather handsome features, a high forehead, crowned by a luxuriant growth of coarse black hair slightly shot with silver, and kind, smiling eyes. His lips parted amiably to reveal flashing teeth clamped on a long, sweet-smelling Havana cigar. He fastened his gaze on me in a manner altogether kindly but at the same time suggesting that he was a man not to be trifled with. Then he waved the *pistolero* away and transferred his gaze expectantly to Don Francisco.

"I have explained your case to Don Porfirio," the latter began, "and he is sympathetic toward it. He has kindly consented to investigate the matter of the La Plata ranch and this Ellery in your behalf." This was repeated to Ramirez in Spanish.

The politician sat back in his chair stoically, hands folded across his stomach, his keen gaze alternating from one to the other of us, nodding approval as Don Francisco spoke to him, and answering in a few short sentences.

"He now says that he wishes to help you in your difficulties. Of course, you know that Don Porfirio, besides being a great statesman, is the foremost lawyer of Mexico. His services are at a great premium and they are available only to a few people. It is of enormous advantage to have him on your side."

"Please tell him that I greatly appreciate the honor and will be glad to compensate him accordingly."

Another exchange of Spanish followed, during which Ramirez smiled and waved his hand at me in a gesture of dismissal.

"He says that the compensation is not important. He wishes to be your friend because you have come all the way from New York to see him in his home, which is very unusual for an American. He has not had such pleasant relations with other Americans in recent oil disputes, which he handles. None of them has ever come to visit him at his home. You are the only one."

Considering the technicalities of approach to his lair, I could not blame my fellow countrymen for hesitating to rush there en masse, but said only, "Many of us are in too much of a hurry, I know."

These overtures concluded, Don Francisco proceeded to translate a series of what sounded like deliberate, carefully chosen remarks uttered with legal restraint. "He says that he has investigated the titles of the La Plata ranch and that some of them are, indeed, subject to the *agarista* law: that is, confiscation, or nationalization, as it is called here. But many thousands of acres are not subject to the law at present, and no application has been made so far to nationalize any of the particular tract you wish to lease, either by General Martinez or by anyone else. What this Ellery tells your friends in New York is, therefore, a lie."

"I am very glad to have this information and wish to thank Don Porfirio for it. Do you think I should go now?"

"Wait. There is more. . . . He says that he has a report from the secret police concerning this Ellery, who is a great troublemaker in the state of Chihuahua and well known in Chihuahua City as a drunkard. But unfortunately, Ellery is not easily controlled. He has many powerful friends, of whom General Martinez is one. But we know definitely that the General is not interested in this ranch, because Don Porfirio caused him to be ordered to Mexico City for questioning, and he is even now here in one of the principal hotels. If you wish, we can reach him on this telephone right now and you can hear for yourself how he denies the words of Ellery." He tapped the Ericsson instrument violently. "Do you wish to prove this point now?"

"Of course not. I have complete faith in what you say."

"You are welcome to question any part of it, and the proof will be given. It has been arranged that the General will be detained here until you are completely satisfied on this point. Are you satisfied? If so, the General will be returned to his duties."

"Quite satisfied. I really had no intention of causing so much trouble."

"It is no trouble at all, my friend. It is, in fact, rather simple. And as for the General, do not worry. He has probably enjoyed his trip."

At this point, Ramirez took up the conversation and spoke for a few moments. His voice was modulated to quiet, even tones; his face was completely expressionless; his attention was politely divided between us, ignoring the language barrier so as not to make me feel left out. There was about his whole delivery and deportment a quiet, Indian dignity suggestive of the ancient Aztec culture.

"Don Porfirio reminds you that much land has in the past been confiscated from this ranch under the national policy for agrarians. Some two hundred thousand hectares have already been taken, or about half a million of your American acres, to encourage the small farmers. In future, the laws may be changed or differently interpreted. The land might be reclassified and more of it— possibly, all of the La Plata—may be taken."

"On the whole, then, it is not a very bright prospect, is it?"

"For one in your position, it is considerably brighter than for others. By coming to Mexico, you have made a very fortunate friendship. For although Don Porfirio has now retired from public life officially, he still maintains his enormously influential connections in his private affairs. He says that, since you have come such a great distance to see him, he wishes to make your trip worthwhile. You have only to tell him what you want. He is waiting for your instructions. What shall I tell him?"

"Say that I deeply appreciate his friendship and that I am greatly flattered by his offer of help. But as he has already given me the information I wanted, what more is there to ask?"

The subdued staccato of Don Francisco's Spanish rattled softly at the great, tawny statesman who sat bolt upright and still as a statue, except for the massive head which nodded almost imperceptibly from time to time. Presently, he held up the palm of his hand and answered gently in a few clipped sentences.

"He says that, since you now have your information, the time has come to act upon it, for information is useless unless it is followed by action."

"But what action is possible under the circumstances?"

"I will put the question to him." There was another short discussion after which Don Francisco explained, "He wishes to say that, although the process of nationalization cannot be stopped in most cases, still there are a few special cases, such as yours, in which it can be greatly controlled. For instance, the particular tract which you mention can be protected definitely up to four or five years, or long enough for you to make a profitable lease with your friends in New York, regardless of what this Ellery says."

"I shall take this information immediately to my friend, Mr. Harbridge, and it will be most helpful. But I should like to offer something in return for it. Please tell Don Porfirio that I would like him to accept 10 percent of any profits we might make on such a transaction under his protection."

The big, dark man nodded his head and smiled pleasantly as this message was delivered and answered.

"He thanks you for your generosity and accepts the percentage in lieu of charging fees for whatever legal services might prove necessary. He also asks what you will do if your friend still refuses to draw up and execute the leases?"

"In that case, I suppose there will be an end to the matter. A person cannot be forced to lease his property if he doesn't want to."

There followed a rather lengthy discussion between them this time, and Don Francisco resumed, "In case your friend still refuses, or this Ellery gives trouble again, then Don Porfirio has another plan for more drastic action. But in this, to have the sympathy of the proper officials, he could not act only as attorney, for fees or percentages. He would have to be your full partner, equally with Mr. Sheardon. Are you interested to hear such a plan?"

"Indeed, yes. Please explain it." It seemed that there could be no harm in just listening.

"The plan is this. Your friend's ranch, in its present state of mismanagement, is a nuisance to the Government. It pays little in taxes. No one will improve it or even maintain the present improvements, which are falling to ruins. Of the little income it produces, most goes to Ellery, none to the owners and not enough to our government."

"That is pretty much the way my partner and I had it figured out."

"Well, then, to proceed . . . This . . . shall we say, this sore spot on the face of our country, would be cured if you and Mr. Sheardon took over management, would it not?"

"You can assure Don Porfirio that we'd do our very best in every way."

"Exactly. Now, that is the point. Therefore, if your friend and this Ellery still refuse you the leases, Don Porfirio suggests that the entire property—or, by far the greater part of it—be confiscated now in the interests of the Government. Actual division of the land into small farms need not take place immediately. Reasons can be made to develop as to why this might be inadvisable. Investigations can be postponed almost indefinitely. You know that here in Mexico many things take a long time. Who knows, perhaps this might be one of them? The question could be drawn out into a matter of several years. In the meantime, someone will have to be put in charge of the property to protect the Government's interests. You and Mr. Sheardon will be selected for this, and there you can run your cattle for perhaps longer than you could under an arrangement with the present stockholders. In our plan they will be entirely dispossessed, receiving the regular 8 percent net for their claims. You will pay nominal taxes on your cattle operations, nothing for the land. You may export your beef steers at any time but no cows or heifers, as this country wishes to build up and improve its breeding herds. Thus you can stock your Montana ranges cheaply, which, as I understand, is the object, and eventually sell your cows and heifers here. You may also import, but not export, fine bulls, if you wish. Then you will have a good breeding ranch, far from the clutches of your northern winters and, with Don Porfirio as your partner, it will be a long time before you are seriously molested. In the meantime, you will have made a small fortune. And since you do not put up anything in the beginning, you cannot lose anything in the end. Do you not think this is a good retaliation to offer in case of further trouble with your friend and this Ellery?"

"I think, of course, that it would be most effective, but I hope there will be no need for such extreme measures."

There was a pause in the conversation. For a while it seemed that the interview might be at an end. And so, rising, I suggested that perhaps I should be going. But Don Francisco held up the palm of his hand.

"Not yet," he deterred me. "There is more. He says that, since you have such great interest in this business and have come so far to see him . . . than, why wait? Why do we not confiscate the La Plata immediately? You have given these people their chance, and they have not taken it. They have treated you meanly. Your friend is not acting like a friend. He is not *simpatico* but stupid and greedy. He prefers to believe this Ellery, a subordinate, rather than one of his own kind. Now it is your chance. Why do you not take it? You have but to speak, and the ranch is yours. What do you say?"

"You are both very kind and obliging. But I did not come down here to dispossess a friend of his property. I came only to learn whether it would be practical to lease or buy from him. I still want to lease, if he will be reasonable. If not, then is the time to consider what had best be done next."

Don Francisco held up a warning finger. "Consider a moment," he pleaded. "This is an opportunity which does not come to everyone, even in this country. For you, it is the chance of a lifetime and may never come again. You think too kindly of your supposed friend, who does not deserve your kindness, as he would not show the same to you. So think well before you speak, and reconsider. Your friend will not be getting any less from the ranch than he is getting now, which is nothing, because Ellery steals all; and surely, you can have no sympathy for a common thief. He will be the only one to suffer, which he deserves. Your friend will not suffer, he will still get the same—nothing. And he will save a lot of headaches. If you wish and feel kindly toward him, you can even pay him a little something from your profits. In the long run you will be doing him a favor, because eventually he will lose the property anyway. Don Porfirio is waiting for your answer. I suggest that you ask him to confiscate."

"Really, I must think about it a little longer. I appreciate your advice and your kindness. But the idea conflicts with my purpose in coming here, and it is so different from the way we think in the United States. Thank Don Porfirio again and say that I shall have to let him know more of this later. Shouldn't we leave now?"

"Yes, perhaps the interview is at an end." We all arose and Ramirez smilingly extended his hand to each of us. Then he nodded pleasantly to the *pistolero,* who emerged from the obscure nether regions of the room and escorted us out.

10

La Plata, a Closer Look

OUR SUDDEN AND UNEXPECTED POTENTIAL with regard to operating on the La Plata ranch, though most satisfactory to the ego, was something of a puzzle. Should American citizens take advantage of foreign dictatorial power and use it against their fellow citizens in a show of what could only be considered brash confiscation? Was not this the principle against which we Americans railed when our oil companies operating in Mexico were nationalized?

Aside from the patriotic angle, there was the question of personal friendships and business ethics. Does one suddenly throw overboard one's established, ingrained life pattern of American business integrity and frankness to join with recently met foreigners in a whirlwind scheme against a long-established friend? The exact quality of the Harbridge friendship in the present instance seemed to me beside the point and not an excuse for an American aggression.

Confiscation of the La Plata would have to be immediate, as Ramirez had suggested, and was a nonrecurring opportunity, as Portal-Mendoza had confirmed. Nevertheless, it seemed certain that a lightning decision on the principle of confiscation would not mean any blitzkrieg in actually getting our cattle on the La Plata range to start pumping profits into our treasury. According to Mexican tradition there would be many delays.

There was also the certainty that considerable sums would have to be laid out for the inevitable *mordida*, or bite, extending from the hallowed halls of political power in Mexico City down through the usual chain of command—the generals, governors and minor local officials, to the *rurales* in the saddle on the range. Then, of course, there was always Sam Ellery, who would not speed things up a bit.

These were my thoughts on emerging from the meeting with Don Porfirio Ramirez. They had been building up during my comfortable, but somehow strangely uneasy tenure of that ugly, squarish chair with its ghastly background. I had later mentioned the odd-looking setup to Don Francisco. "Ah," he had explained, "you had no reason to fear, for you were never in any danger. But I will tell you confidentially that behind the door was a man with a machine gun and beside him an electric bell, which would command him to fire at the touch of a button on Don Porfirio's desk." It had been the bliss of ignorance.

After a short stay in New York and a very unsatisfactory attempt to get good old Trux on the dotted line, I took the puzzle out to Montana, where the facts of a cattle ranching life always seem clearer and more easily discussed. In Mexico they are mysterious, always draped in a somewhat voodoo-like veil, sometimes even terrifying. In New York they seem terribly distant in the stultifying, alien atmosphere so utterly disconnected with the ranching concept as to make one feel like a still, small voice crying in the wilderness.

With the feel of saddle leather under one, however, in the clear, sage-scented air of the high Montana ranges, where I soon found myself riding beside Matt in a wonderfully pinkish dawn on the spring roundup, our situation seemed clear as the atmosphere as we jogged along, discussing it.

Matt, always the conservationist with his feeling for unspoiled nature, suddenly broke off the discussion and drew up his horse at the edge of a canyon. "Look," he said, quietly. "There's something you may never see again after a few years. Most of the wild horses in Montana were rounded up for canneries in the World War, and a lot migrated up into Canada. Now the horse hunters are starting up again to meet the market for this war. They think we're going to get into it any day."

Far away across the canyon, against an incredibly beautiful background of rangeland and distant, snow-capped mountains under the pale morning sky, with its pink, puffy clouds hanging about, was a small wild horse herd. The white stud was poised on a rock formation, head up, sniffing the breeze, looking for more mares, while his harem grazed peacefully around him. Alarmed by our presence even at that distance, he whinnied and whirled, rounding up his mares in short order, hurrying some by nipping at their flanks. Soon he had them, a few with their foals, strung out ahead of him, streaking across the mesa and out of sight.

Matt loped off on a little detour to bend some straying steers back into the line of march and then returned to our discussion. "Heard anything lately from your friend, Trux? It's away past our deadline for action, and we still don't know whether the La Plata deal's on or off."

"Haven't heard a thing, and my guess is that we're not going to hear anything worth listening to till we either move in, on the Ramirez plan, or do it the American way. And that means having an understanding with Sam Ellery first. Sam wants to know exactly what he's going to get out of it if we take over. He's afraid we might disrupt his political grazing club for rustlers, and Trux seems to be scared of him, his own manager, mind you."

"God knows what Sam's cut is on the rustling." Matt fell silent for a moment, then turned sideways in his saddle and asked, "Say, do you suppose your friend Harbridge knows about the rustled stock?"

"If he does, he's no friend of mine. But actually, I don't think he does."

"How dumb can a guy get?"

"In his case the sky's the limit."

"Perhaps conveniently dumb. Maybe he gets a cut from Sam that the other stockholders don't know about."

"No. Trux isn't smart enough for that. To be in with rustlers, you've got to be smart like them. You're in the Protective Association, and I'll bet you've never seen a big-scale rustler who wasn't smart and usually good company too. Well, he isn't either. He's just not in with them. They wouldn't have him. He doesn't know a thing, because Sam doesn't tell him anything, and Trux never goes down there to look around for himself. And even if he did look over the range once in awhile, he wouldn't know rustled stock if he saw it. Not even if he saw a cow and calf mothered up, with different brands on them.

Matt shook his head hopelessly. "A man that dumb needs help. I feel plumb sorry for him. Maybe we ought to put him wise, before Sam implicates him. Maybe it'd sort of break Sam's hold on him."

"Who, us? Meddle in a rustling mix-up? Without proof? . . . and in Mexico? What for? We're not down there to play detective. All we're interested in is getting a lease and option on the La Plata. Besides, tattling would never get Sam fired or get our deal through."

"It'd be better to buy Sam off, if we had to. Just subsidize him for his nuisance value, so he'll work with us to help us push the deal through in New York. Once that's over, we could drop him."

"Could we, though?"

We were taking a string of young, new steers to summer range and had been gathering others from Matt's home winter pastures closer to headquarters along the way. Day by day the growing herd plodded on toward the high summer ranges. Crawling along the divide, convoying them, were the outfit's wagons, their four-horse teams lathered and straining at the tugs. Occasionally, we could see the wranglers far in the lead, easing the cavvy along.

Now the wagon boss squeezed lengthening daylight hours to their limit. A fourteen-hour working day was his standard on spring roundup, and occasionally on the lonelier parts of the Reservation he would add night guard. That meant pairs of riders slowly circling the herd in opposite directions, for two-hour shifts from eight in the evening till four in the morning, keeping the cattle from drifting away from a more or less manageable area. We all took turns.

The range was changing from spring to summer mood. Frail prairie lilies furled their petals and gave way to a timid procession of color—Indian paintbrush, lupine, bitterroot, Dutchman's breeches—in its daily retreat from the lower grasslands up the mountain slopes. Grama range grass began to cure, losing its greenish look, and cattlemen knew that nature was beginning to change the feeding formula for her creatures, with fewer chemicals for milk production, more for the building of bone and muscle.

The season for rain ended, so that the cloud banks, except for short and scarce flash storms, often carrying hail in destructive proportions, would not pay off again until they tucked the range away in its protective white winter blanket, when cattle would bunch together in the brakes and under cut banks, hunching their backs, turning their tails to the storm, hanging their heads bleakly.

But by then the herds would have left the high country, and the beef would have been shipped to market, leaving a minimum number to be carried through the winter in pastures close to headquarters, with plenty of hay available.

Finally, one day, after we had turned loose in the farthest summer pasture, a group of cowpunchers cantered by, waving at me to fall in with them. "Orders are to go back to camp," one of them yelled. "We're pulling out in the morning."

11

A Flash of Life
on the Roundup Wagon

THERE IS NO SATISFACTORY WAY of recording the activities of a round-up outfit as they occur. The very nature and spirit of the strictly professional roundup precludes the use of cameras, sound recorders or writing materials. I know this because I tried it for a stay of nineteen days at the wagon. The yellowed notebook pages, written on both sides and numbered to eleven, were never continued. They represent just a short, flash exposure, but at least they are genuine and record a glimpse of the period accurately. The brands are here given in words instead of symbols.

ANTLER WAGON

Near Hungerford Ranch, Rottengrass (Creek)
1941. June.
June 24.   Arrived with Matt 11 A.M. — Tuesday. Worked small herd cows and calves in P.M. (Brand: Lazy H, Lazy K, Hungerford.)

Men at Wagon:
1. Frank Greenough
2. Bill Greenough (came 25th)
3. Ross Rountree — cook
4. Garnet Lee Roberts (1 day)
5. Alvie Boomer (struck by lightning)
6. Barry Roberts, Jr. (broncs)
7. Barry Roberts, Sr. (came & left 25th. stock inspector)
8. Philip Newton (broncs)

    9. Dike Thomas (broncs)
  10. Sam McDowell (rep. for Porter R. Crone outfit, Soap Creek)
  11. Albert Newman (boot powder), repping for Charlie Long
  12. Hungerford
  13. Junior Smith (wrangler)
  14. Eddie Boomer (son of Alvie)
  15. Cecil Wham
  16. Fat Montgomery (brand FAT)
  17. Lyle Leming (drives bed wagon) nighthawk
  18. Happy Roberts
  19. Fred Starina
  20. Broadie Sadler (line rider)
  21. Herbert Loukes
  22. Matt
  23. Self

Brands worked: Antler, Reverse RN, Diamond A, W Diamond, L Lazy S, Lazy H, Lazy K, Reverse C, BS (Starina). Last reading doubtful.

June 25. Wed. Morning circle westward. P.M. circle, Ash Coulee. Worked cattle P.M. & evening. Day: 4 A.M.–8 P.M. Horses (ridden): 1. Smoky, speckled gray gld. 2. Skunk, app. gld. 3. Socks.

26. Thurs. A.M. circle. Shamrock, br. gld. Off 11 A.M.–3 P.M. Eve., worked cows & calves near camp. Socks.

27. Fri. A.M. circle, Cottonwood Creek. Worked Diamond A steers. All off 11 A.M.–2:45 P.M. Heat. Worked grangers' cows & calves till 8:30 P.M. Horses: Smoky, Skunk. 17-hr. day. Crone, Jr. came over from Soap Creek.

28. Sat. Worked grangers' calves and branded till 11 A.M. Broke camp 12:15 and moved up Rottengrass 8 miles to Milt Eychaner ranch. No work after supper. Supposed to move 12 miles more in A.M. Horses: Skunk, Socks. Matt left for Antler noon. Ran across 40 mustangs.

29. Sun. Broke camp 4:20 A.M. Moved thru St. Xavier to Big Horn ditch. Rode circle 10:12 to 4 P.M. Very few cattle. Some fat RN heifers. No work after supper. Bed 7:30. Horses: Streak, A.M., sorrel gld., 2 white feet (hind). P.M., Smoky. Sent letter to B.G.R. by Barry Roberts.

30. Mon. A.M. circle. Branded A Down, H Bar calves. Moved southward few miles to Ford Davis ranch on Big Horn (river). Rain all morning. Finished evening circle 8 P.M.

Antler roundup camp at shipping time. *Courtesy Roahen Photos, Billings, Montana*

Horses: Shamrock, Blue Monday (steel gray gld.) Socks (branded F Lazy D, right side).

July 1. Tues. A.M. circle. Moved camp from Ford Davis' back to Broadie Sadler's on Rotten Grass. Off at 5 P.M. Matt came up with Yellowtail (Crow Indian Agent) to see about range dispute with Blackburn (S Lazy J Bar) yesterday, then left. Brought mail from E.A.R. & Burke re: (La Plata) lawyers. Bath in flume. Horses: Skunk, Smoky.

  2. Wed. A.M., circle. Best catch yet—ca. 1,500 hd. (head). P.M., worked cattle near camp, cutting out Diamond A 2's, beef (steers ready to ship in fall, 2-year-olds). P.M., moved camp back to Eichner's ranch, near Hungerford's, on Rotten Grass. Took cavvy with Junior Smith. Saw 2 herds wild horses on A.M. circle. Bed 8 P.M. Horses: Shamrock, Blue Monday, Streak (went lame).

  3. Thurs. A.M., circle. P.M., circle to Big Horn. Eve., moved cattle Big Horn to Rotten Grass. Worked herd near camp. Horses: Smoky, Skunk, Brockie (small bay, 4 black feet, left flank brand YL, and G, left neck).

  4. Friday A.M. & P.M. circles. Eve., worked cattle near camp & held night guard. Horses: Shamrock, Blue Monday, Skunk.

  5. Sat. A.M. Moved herd & camp to Lone Tree spring near Hungerford ranch. P.M., worked herd. Sarpy Sam McDowell & Porter Crone Jr. left. Matt & Bert arrived. Horses: Smoky, Brockie.

  6. Sun. A.M., circle. P.M., moved camp up Ash Creek, 11 mi. from water. Eve., moved herd to new campsite. Night guard 8–10 with Alvie and Newt. Day 19 hrs.— 3:15 A.M. to 10:15 P.M. Horses: Shamrock, Skunk & Gray Boy (night horse).

  7. Mon. Roll out 2:45 A.M.—½ hr. earlier. Herd on the move 3:40. Moved up Ash Creek 11 mi. to dinner campsite at P. Spear ranch (Rafter, Cross, Bar, vertical), arriving 11 A.M. Time off till after supper. Drove down to Antler with Matt & Bert (who apparently had arranged a rendezvous at Phil Spear's). Heard of C. Henry's death. Matt & Bert to Billings to catch 4 P.M. plane to L.A. Letter from B.G.R. Supper at Antler. Returned to roundup at Big John pasture (good water) with Bub after supper. Sent B.G.R. $550. "Smoky."

  8. Circle in A.M. Held herd in Big John Coulee all day.

Moved camp and herd at 4:30 P.M., 3 hrs. toward mountains. Dry camp. Horses: Brockie, Skunk. Night-guarded
herd. (No guard duty E.R.)

9. Wed. Moved herd 4 A.M. Dinner camp at Red Spring.
Along Black Canyon to Garvin Basin. Good water. Cor-
raled cattle after supper near Bull Elk Divide. Quit
8 P.M. Horses: Shamrock, Smoky, Streak.

10. Thurs. Up 3 A.M. Moved cattle from corral to buffalo
range between Black Canyon & Bull Elk Divide—14
(?) mi. Turned loose 11 A.M. (1528 steers out of 1692
started with). Truck brought dinner. Returned to camp
4 P.M. Supper & laid off. Rode Blue Monday.

11. Fri. Frank Greenough and few men went down to ranch
with truck early. Thin layer of ice on water bucket.
Spent day shoeing horses at corrals near Matt's hunting
cabin, preparing for trip into Garvin Basin tomorrow
after RN heifers. Shod Shamrock. Back to camp for
dinner 11 A.M. Corrals again & back for supper 5:30,
then laid off. Frank & men expected back tomorrow P.M.

12. Sat. Rode circle G . . . Basin 4 A.M.–2 P.M. Picked up
103 RN heifers & put in lower Bull Elk Divide pasture.
Saw about 12 others. Dinner at camp 3 P.M., then returned to Antler with Cecil in truck. Left Antler 6 P.M.
for Sheridan.

If any of these former range-riding companions of mine come
across this writing, I hope they will forgive me for using their
real names without permission. I also hope they may realize that
I have not forgotten their good comradeship.

Happy-go-lucky professional riders like these contributed greatly
to the remarkably low incidence of broken bones or serious injury
on the roundup, where being bucked off and possibly dragged or
otherwise seriously injured was far more dangerous than at a
rodeo, where the arena is a confined space with plenty of help
and with an ambulance always at hand. Out on the range at that
time there was no practical way of getting a seriously injured man
to town, which might be seventy-five miles away; no means of
communication by which to call for help, no road map to direct
an ambulance to the spot; not even a road to put *on* a map. It was
just a matter of manpower, horseflesh, common sense and trust-
to-God. Somehow or other that mode of life seemed to instill

among the men a great feeling of trust in each other; a feeling of concern born of their mutual involvement in an enterprise which was obviously not the world's easiest or the most beloved of insurance companies, but it was in all a very warm, human feeling, and a rewarding one. It was a feeling that all our men were in the healthiest form of competition; not, as in the business world, against each other for gain; but rather in competition *with* each other against any threat to the well-being of the outfit.

12

Negotiating Crow Indian Leases:
Esther Birdhat's Letter

JULY WAS SLIPPING BY, and now the wagons were gone from the range, where cattle were left to graze undisturbed on a silent, broiling Reservation, with plenty of water and grass to put the tallow on them until they reached a thousand pounds or more and could be classified as two-year-olds ready for the beef market. For wintering they would be herded by tortuous trail down nearly 2,000 feet from the rimrock into the Garvin Basin, a protective bowl of 56,000 acres, which provided an incredibly mild winter holding pasture, where the Antler maintained a hay ranch.

For Matt Sheardon the summer doldrums were about the only season when he could enjoy any home life around ranch headquarters and follow his doctor's orders to take an occasional hour's siesta in the hammock slung between two shade trees. There he would catch up on his reading and watch the fat robins hopping about on his lush emerald lawn.

Coming down from the roundup, I found a packet of mail awaiting me at the ranch office. It yielded a clipping from the *New York Times*, describing the sudden death from heart failure of Truxton Harbridge. I strolled across the lawn with it toward Matt's hammock. There he was, snoozing peacefully, a carefree expression on his pinched, foreign-looking face, which seemed striking for one of his age, responsibilities and position in life. Fifty-seven years had left him with an almost childlike composure in sleep, without a gray hair or a wrinkle on his face. A delicate, almost

dainty man who, somehow or other, seemed to exude an aura of
quiet, rugged strength from somewhere within.

As I watched, he awoke instinctively, knuckling his eyes and
swinging his feet to the ground. Seeing my packet of mail, he
asked sleepily, "Any news from Harbridge?" I handed him the
clipping, which he read completely through before saying, "Too
bad. I feel real sorry. Well, I guess we'd better forget about the
whole deal. We can't wait for all the delays of settling an estate.
We'll just get along as we are. Maybe something else will turn up
in Mexico. At least we can always depend on my leases here."

"Are you always sure about them?"

"Yes. There's a very simple way to handle that. I just keep a
little ahead of the expiration dates. I keep the leases overlapping
into the future. That way, you've always got your hold on the
grass."

"Overlapping? . . ."

"Yes. You see, the nature of the Indians themselves makes that
just happen naturally, because they always want prepayment on
their leases as far ahead as they can get it, but the government
sets a limit on that. You can pay them for only two years ahead,
because otherwise they'd just squander it. And their affairs are
always so complicated that you'd never know where you stood
anyway. So the law kind of protects both sides of the deal. I'll
show you an example of the type of mixed-up proposition I'm up
against all the time."

He fumbled under the hammock in a pile of his own mail which
he had glanced through and then dropped on the lawn. Finally,
he found an almost illegibly scrawled letter and handed it to me.
"Here, take a look at this and see what you can make of it."

It was almost impossible to make anything out of the hideously
primitive writing on the crumpled sheet addressed simply "mat,"
aside from the vague idea that some widowed squaw named
Esther Birdhat wanted three years' payment in advance for some
land.

"This," I said at length, "is a most remarkable document. Do
you mind if I make a copy of it?"

"What in hell for?"

"It's sort of fascinating, like a crossword puzzle. Maybe if I
study it a while and can make out some sort of punctuation for it,
I might be able to decipher some meaning."

"The only meaning is that she wants to be paid three years ahead, and that's against the law. . . . Sure, copy it. As far as I'm concerned, you can keep it. You know me and letters. The less I see of them, the better."

Here is Esther Birdhat's letter:

"I would like ask you can you made new lease for me out of that 160 acres over at East Fork. You remember I made new lease last 3 years ago in April that starts in 194(?) it wasnt on them other lease. I like to ask you to let me have some money let me know right away please.

"From Esther Birdhat also I had lots lands on you leases that is belong to my husband hes dead. they is 5 of us in his hiers also I had 3 kids all out to that is you lease to I ask the Agent some time ago he told me I can lease them 194(?) that is lease up in 1950 he told me I could lease myself when the lease up so I dont have to go to Crow Agency this is all lease following names

Breath Flat Mouth
Maud Flat Mouth
Leo Flat Mouth

Flat Mouth have 80 acres over at some place at East Fork to also he had 300 acres over at Wood Ck. we trade a land that belong to Dahlia Emma Anderson. this is numbers of land . . . this land belong to Flat Mouth. that was 15 yrs ago it was proved by Washington that the land belongs to Flat Mouth. When leases all up I'll willing to sign for you so please let me know about three years paying. Answer this letter for me. I'll go over if it is OK."

I handed him back the letter. "This is an RSVP deal. She wants to know if it's OK for her to come over here for three years' paying. I'd like to learn how you make an overlapping lease with someone like Esther."

Matt waved the letter away and sank back into his hammock. "When you've copied it, turn it in at the office and they'll let her know what she's got coming. Don't worry, she'll be coming over anyway without any RSVP. I just wanted to show you how they're always asking for money years ahead of time. Esther's already talking up to 1950."

"Well, what do you do about it?"

"I just read the law to them: Uncle Sam says no more advance pay beyond this point on this lease. Then I make a simple proposition. I say, 'If you want to, we can just tear up this lease and make another lease starting from now for another five years, and I can pay you now for two years on that.' I pay them for two more years, and I have a new five-year lease overlapping into the future."

With our La Plata aspirations now suddenly wiped off the slate and Matt recasting his plans accordingly, shipping more steers to Montana and planning to take on more range if necessary, I thought it about time to take stock of my own position. I was jolted into action by a check arriving from Roberts Brothers & Rose, the Omaha cattle brokers, for a single RN heifer which had been sold on the market there, apparently after having somehow strayed into the herd of someone who had shipped in September. Since she bore my brand, the check was drawn and mailed to me. This little animal which, according to the ranch bookkeeper, was decidely skinny for the $36 per head price I had paid through Skel Baxton, weighing only 276 pounds (the average for that shipment) had sold 490 days later at 850 pounds, for a gain of 574 pounds after shipping shrink. She sold at 7½ cents per pound for a value of $63.75. The broker's commission was $6, making my check come to $57.75. This spoke pretty well for the grass on the Crow Reservation.

So my heifers were doing all right, both the branded ones on the Antler range and, somewhat to my surprise, the unbranded ones shipped to Lewistown. I decided to clean up the heifer deal and go over to straight steer deals with Matt. At conservative market values this figured out to $9,800 profits on sales and would leave me with a half interest in 500 steers, free and clear, with feed paid for, and worth $30,000.

I had also made a quick, sly speculation in a few of Matt's sheep, which turned out well, but which I kept a dark secret from old Fred Lauby because I knew that if either he or his cronies Jigger McCabe and Jack Hart ever got wind ot it, I would become an object of shame among the cattlemen of Tongue River. Actually, this bit of luck turned out to be a curse in disguise, because it temporarily whetted my appetite for fast sheep money with its two payoffs a year (wool and mutton) and later led me into a larger sheep deal with less happy results.

Matt and I quit the beef roundup early that fall and headed south, in the continuing hunt for more light, cheap steers along the border, and with some vain hopes of locating a southern holding pasture in Mexico or some reasonable facsimile in the U.S.A. as far south as possible. We tried the Featherstone Ranch on the Big Bend of the Río Grande in Texas, the Santo Domingo and another Mexican property near San Rafael. We met with Mexican ranch operators, sometimes at their cool haciendas, where we were served deliciously light Mexican beer in their patios as part of the visiting process. At one of these Mexican ranches there was a whole tribe of peons who looked after the family's livestock and lived at the bottom of Pulpito Canyon, a deep cleft in the rocks in which large caves abounded, affording them comfortable, well-protected homes, some with large entrances admitting the sunlight. One cave was so huge and light that it was used as a corral for horses and cattle.

One of the most delightful people we met was young Alfredo Terrazas of the Old Chihuahua cattle dynasty founded in the time of Porfirio Díaz by the patriarch, Don Luis Terrazas, and still living in the grand hacienda style. The original Terrazas ranch extended to something over 6,177,000 acres, and Don Luis had so many cattle that he couldn't count them and didn't really care how many there were. One story has it that, on calf roundup, his wagon boss reported that the vaqueros had branded 100,000 calves and were still nowhere near finished. "Don't bother with them all," Don Luis ordered. "Just tell me when you get to a quarter million, and we'll let the rest go. After that it really doesn't matter."

Another Terrazas story turns on the point of nicely matched cattle. It tells of several big northern U.S. cattle buyers who had formed a pool to buy 50,000 Mexican calves, and who approached Don Luis with some doubt as to whether his ranch could fill such a huge order. The courtly answer they got was, "Señores, of course, with pleasure. But tell me, what color would you like them?"

Don Alfredo did not ask us what color we were looking for, and we did not buy anything from him. The famous Terrazas brand, however, is sometimes seen vented (canceled by a sloping bar) on northern ranges. It is a distinctive, odd combination of the letters T, H and S, all connected, so that it can be applied with a single (or stamp) iron.

One of the most horrifying subjects we interviewed was a Mexican general to whom we were introduced by a cattle broker in some border town in order to verify the heartless efficiency of the *rurales*. This body of state police, corresponding roughly to our Texas Rangers, would give a cattle rustler one warning only. If, after that, he was caught butchering an animal with a brand not his own, he was forced at gunpoint to get down on his knees and say his prayers. Then, often while weeping and pleading for one more chance, he was shot through the head. The general highly recommended this efficient system as a matter of course, patting his .45-caliber automatic, but he admitted somewhat sheepishly that he was softhearted enough to employ more civilized corrective methods on those of his acquaintances who might dare to rouse his ire.

As an example of lenient punishment, he cited the case of some unfortunate man in town who had unwisely ridiculed him. The man was forthwith arrested. The general sent for a long leather thong which he caused to be tied around his victim's genitals and then passed through the fly of his trousers. Using this as a leash, the general then led his victim all around town, stopping for drinks at his favorite *cantinas* and lecturing his friends on the folly of belittling him. He claimed, quite believably, that none of his audience missed the point.

13

War, Sheep-lined Helmets and Wild, Wild Texas Wethers

WHEN WE RETURNED FROM OUR southern trip that fall of 1941, the range had turned from honey color to silver and from silver to white. The beef roundup was nearly over, but the Antler wagons were still out on the range, lumbering and groaning along, though on a more leisurely schedule, as beef steers must be moved very slowly on their way to market to avoid their losing weight. "Don't knock the pennies off them," was an admonition often heard if a rider were seen running a steer.

Now in the shortening days there was only one circle to ride. Occasionally, there would be a day with no riding at all, when snow reduced visibility to nearly zero. Such a day would be declared a "poker day," and there would be a run on the cook's supply of kitchen matches for use as poker chips. No money was involved.

Throw ropes developed their early morning winter stiffness, and saddles sparkled with an uninviting frost. Ponies seemed foxier at ducking flying nooses and fought against taking the icy bits, which froze to their tongues momentarily. The goosier ones threw kinks in their backs as the saddles clumped down, blew up their bellies against the tightening cinches and pranced about, snorting puffs of vapor, daring their riders to mount. Old hands, though somewhat clumsy in sheepskin jackets, well-worn chaps and boot overshoes, took their dare easily and soon had the gimp out of them.

At day's end the cook would have his stove crackling, drafts open, its firebox glowing a deep red. The men would crowd around for steak and coffee, turning this way and that to get their bodies evenly warmed. Then, balancing tin plates and cups, they would sit on their bed rolls or cross-legged on the trampled grass or would squat on their heels to eat.

Down from the high ranges the beef herd pushed slowly toward the railroad: sleek, fat, stocky two-year-olds of a thousand pounds or more, the erstwhile skinny Mexican calves of only two summers ago, now rippling with muscle and tallow. Eyeing them, one realized that the yearly replacement problem was almost at hand again.

When the market returns from the beef shipments were nearly all in, and we knew pretty well where we stood for the year, I went back east for the winter, and within a month, on that fatal December 7, the whole world heard President Roosevelt's ghastly announcement about that "day of infamy" and the declaration of war.

I was not eligible for the draft but felt that I could surely serve some purpose somewhere so made the rounds of the Army, Navy and Marine recruiting centers, volunteering for, and being turned down by, all branches of the service. It seemed that I had been too young for World War I and too old for World War II. It irked me that no member of my family had fired a shot to defend our country since the Civil War, although one of my ancestors had done pretty well in the Revolution. We were just not a military family, and at age thirty-eight I had never had any military training. There was only one gate left open: the narrow one of voluntary induction into the armed forces.

The New York draft board was not encouraging. "Over draft age and no prior military service? . . . Not even ROTC training at college?" The official frowned as he ticked off my inadequacies. "Engaged in meat production? That's war effort, you know, and releases younger men. They're the ones we're taking first. In your case the facts just don't add up."

Months later, after several attempts, and when I was fortified with letters of recommendation from former Army and Navy officers, the draft board finally relented unenthusiastically. "We'll consider you for officer training," they told me, "the V.O.C. program. But the final decision will take some time. Then, if it's favorable, understand that you've got to go in as a private, and the best you can come out as is Second Lieutenant. If you don't make it, back to civilian life. And if you do make it, by the time you're commissioned the war may be over."

I was ordered to take my physical examination at an army medical center somewhere up near Columbia University. Apparently I was all right all over. Then, when it came to the point of final acceptance or rejection, I was somewhat disillusioned by the doctor's attitude. He looked at me meaningfully and said, "You know, you don't have to pass this physical if you don't want to," from which I inferred that some sort of consideration would be acceptable from a man who wished to shirk the service though perfectly healthy, as I was. I told him, "Doctor, I'm trying to get into service, not out of it," and he passed me. That must have been sometime in the spring of 1942, but it was not until the following September that I got my orders to report for training.

In the meantime, the draft board had told me that, so far as my usefulness to the war effort was concerned, the best thing I could do was go back out to Montana and raise some more beef. The message I got from our talks was that they were glad to see the last of me. Incidentally, the Navy had long since written me a curt note, telling me not to send in any more letters of recommendation. Clearly the war did not need me.

By June I was back at the Antler with Matt Sheardon, who had a new idea. He was a member of the principal livestock associations, both cattle and sheep, and from them had gleaned some interesting news. It seemed that the government was in the market for huge amounts of a certain kind of wool to be used for lining aviators' helmets. The most desirable grade was that produced by wethers (gelded male sheep) of which there were great numbers available in Texas, and it was rumored that a prestigious packinghouse in Chicago had agents down there bidding on them. Matt's idea was for us to get into the act.

To evaluate his idea before committing ourselves to this completely new type of deal, so different from the usual ewe-and-lamb deal with which he was familiar, he went up to Helena, the state capital, where he had some government connections. There we corroborated the information, returning to the ranch in high spirits.

The next day we went to the little Wyola bank, which was a sort of outgrowth of the Antler Ranch, controlled and mostly owned by the Sheardon family. The bank's president, Tidd Ketton, was the once-despondent sufferer from the bank closing in Billings, whom Matt had talked out of his murder-suicide ravings and had rescued from the slough of despair, so this meeting had unusually friendly and cozy vibrations.

The bank's capital was then less than a million dollars, and so the amount it could pay out on any one risk was necessarily limited and much less than what was required to pay for our sheep, which were to be delivered in Wyola during our absence. Matt had therefore made arrangements with the Stockyards National Bank—where the president was also a friend of his and where he had arranged a line of credit—to cover the Wyola bank's operations. The arrangement required both Matt's and my signatures, which it was understood that we would supply somewhere along our route to Texas and back, as we had to start for Big Spring, Texas, right away.

Our plan was to drive to Denver, stopping at a big sheep ranch in Wyoming on the way to pick up some technical information on wether sheep, leave the car in Denver and fly from there. We met with the seller of the wethers in some desolate country near Big Spring, where he arrived in his own plane. He was a large, jolly man wearing a proportionately large diamond ring, and his wife also had on two or three diamond rings. We inspected the wethers and arranged with this gentleman and his satellites to have the shipment made to Wyola for delivery in about two weeks, which figured out to around July 16.

Matt wanted the extra time to attend to some business in El Paso and Pueblo, Colorado. There we happened to run into Russ Wilkins, head of a large livestock agency in Denver and a great authority on sheep, whom we already knew and had consulted on the wether deal. He had a car there and offered to drive us to Denver, which seemed to us not only a pleasant idea but also a chance to talk wethers. We arrived at his country home north of Denver on a Friday and thought it a good idea to call the Stockyards National president in Omaha regarding plans for a meeting to sign the credit papers.

We found our friend the bank president disturbed. He had been trying vainly to locate us as a result of terrified pleas from Tidd Ketton in Wyola, who was frantic, because, on account of some fluctuating railroad requirements, the sheep had been shipped sooner than expected, were already arriving at Wyola, and the little bank was up to its credit limit in paying for them. To make matters worse, the state bank examiner was due to arrive for a checkup on Monday, and poor, nervous Tidd was conjuring up nightmares of another banking crisis in his future.

The result was that we had to take the night train to Omaha, and our banker friend there had to give up his weekend in order to be at the bank on Saturday for us to sign the papers.

In the meantime, the Antler office had been besieged by telephone calls inquiring as to our whereabouts. The ranch could not supply any definite information but was at least able to calm the shattering nerves of poor Tidd Ketton. Someone there had the bright idea to take him on a fishing trip up in the mountains, from which he could not return to the bank until late Monday afternoon or Tuesday morning. An appropriate message was sent to the bank examiner, and by the time the two finally got together at the bank, the credit had arrived, and the crisis was over, at least, for Tidd Ketton.

Our own trials, however, were just beginning. Some form of shipping sickness overtook the sheep and laid them low by the hundreds. These had to be hospitalized at various loading points in Colorado and Wyoming, as unfit to travel farther. The ranch sent veterinarians up and down the line to look after them, but there was a shortage of the required medication in the area, and the nearest available supply in quantity was in Jersey City, from where it had to be specially flown. About half the hospital bunch died, and the other half were barely able to survive the railroad trip. Among them there were further losses after arrival.

Once the sheep were on the range, other difficulties arose. These Texas sheep were not broken to open-range herding. They had been raised in fenced pastures and so knew nothing about herders and dogs. The dogs, especially, terrified them. They would not obey the dogs but instead would run in panic from them and wear themselves out. They spread all over the range instead of keeping in a close-knit band, and the herders, with their pokey old saddle horses, couldn't round them up, since one man alone can't round up anything, even on a good horse, and there was only one herder to a wagon. So they got lost in thickets or gullies, out of sight and often far from water.

The sheep manager was in a quandary. He reported that herders were getting discouraged and quitting, saying that they wouldn't be responsible for losing these crazy, wild Texas creatures. Matt doubled the herders and doubled the dogs, but the wild, wild wethers persisted in their nightmarish behavior. Then someone suggested trying out Basque herders. The Basque people have a way with sheep, and there were many Basque herders as well as Basque owners of successful sheep outfits in Wyoming. Basques are quite musical, and some have been said to play the guitar of a lonely evening around the sheep wagon, claiming that it has a quieting effect on sheep. So Matt made the experiment of importing a Basque herder with his guitar.

This caused a minor disaster. At the sound of the first chord of the guitar, a hundred or more sheep broke into a dead run and were never seen again.

At this point, the government changed its idea about the sheep-lined helmets and withdrew from the market for this particular type of wool, which nobody else seemed to want, and the price for wethers crashed.

This was bad enough, but then came the worms. It seems that there are some thirty-three different kinds of worms that attack sheep. Of this number, probably thirty-two kinds attacked ours. They developed strange and expensive illnesses. The lush Montana range did not seem to do them any good; apparently they longed for the dry, prickly pear ranges of Texas. They put on practically no weight and had intestinal and hoof troubles. There was virtually no market for them, so they had to be held over through the winter, during which they consumed great quantities of feed without showing any marked improvement—only a high mortality rate.

Sheep have the most alarming way of dying without any advance notice. A cow or a horse will show sickness long before it becomes fatal. A sick horse just looks sick; its coat, its mouth, its general posture and movements are all indications. A cow will show her general condition by skinniness or sleekness, a full udder or a lack of milk for her calf. But a sheep is just a mass of wool that stands around and looks the same whether sick or not. It has a dumb expression and no real face. Horses and cattle have faces, and horses have general characteristics of behavior that soon become discernible to anyone constantly around the same cavvy. Horses also have vibrations, and they discern vibrations in a person. A horse will know whether you like him or are afraid of him.

He will buck with one person and not buck with another. Good cowpunchers are known to be able to recognize cattle by their faces and have a canny instinct for knowing which calves belong to which cows when they get mixed up, as in a cattle drive. But a sheep's face is just a total loss.

Nobody ever thinks of a sheep as being cold, with all that wool. But a long, cold, wet spring will get them down. A sheep might have pneumonia and stand around on the verge of death for days, even weeks, without showing any discomfort. Suddenly it keels over, dead. There are sheep sheds and windbreaks on a ranch but no indoor quarters. It would take a Madison Square Garden to shelter them all. Even with these aids, sick sheep, such as ours, have a hard time making it through the winter.

I was leading my eastern, family life when most of our winter and spring losses occurred, blissfully but only partially ignorant of them because of the difficulty of persuading Matt to answer my letters, although common sense and weather reports told me that things must be going very badly out there.

We finally got out of that deal in early summer, shipping the balance of our ill-fated sheep, which were classified in the next to lowest grade. Some lost their teeth and actually hit the bottom grade, known as gummers.

Our losses were very bad news, but at least we had the wool returns from one shearing. Most of the losses were Matt's, as I had not gone in very deeply, but our percentages were the same, most disappointing, and the whole experience was a great lesson to us. At least, to me it meant: stay away from fast sheep deals, even if you have a little success at first; stay particularly far away from wethers and any deal that hinges upon the whims of a government contract and the fickleness of Montana weather.

Fortunately, we had a rather soft cushion to land on, as the steers had made plenty of money that year, keeping us comfortably away from the red-ink pot. Matt sold five head during late summer to test their weights and the market. They were two-year-olds from Mexico, which we had bought at 10 cents per pound, when they weighed 341 pounds. Counting range expenses, feed, freight, shrink and all overhead, we had less than $46 invested in each animal after eighteen months. They gained 621 pounds for an average of 962 pounds pay weight and sold at 10½ cents, returning us $101 per head, brokerage commissions paid, at that early date. Later shipments did better, showing more weight in a slightly higher market. So Lady Luck had not completely deserted me that year.

Neither had the draft board. At last, on September 17, they passed me for Volunteer Officer Corps and ordered me to report on November 1 for training at Camp Dix, New York. I returned to New York on October 27.

In my mail was a communication from the draft board canceling my orders. The government had passed a regulation that no one over age thirty-nine could be accepted for army service. The regulation was to take effect on December 5. My thirty-ninth birthday was coming up on December 3. So I was forty-eight hours too old.

14

The von Thurnwalds:
A Ranch Gains, Hitler Loses

WINTER ACTIVITIES ON AN AVERAGE cattle ranch are concerned mostly with feeding out the hay that is put up in the summer. On a cow-and-calf outfit there is also considerable riding to be done to keep tabs on the stock. Some cows drop their calves in bad weather, when without proper care they would not survive. There is a certain amount of "rawhiding," or riding the range to rescue stranded animals that have been missed by the fall roundup.

A straight steer operation bypasses the cow-and-calf complications and goes through the winter with a minimum of steers, since all the animals fit for the beef market have been shipped in the fall. Then too, a steer requires much less hay than a cow with her calf. He can usually forage for himself pretty well with less hay and labor.

This situation made my presence at the ranch superfluous in winter, as even during wartime there were always plenty of men for the feeding operation, since Matt seemed to get along well enough on a feeding labor ratio of two men per thousand head of steers. Thus, during the winter months I was enabled to lead my eastern life of looking after my family and personal affairs, the only difficulty being the near impossibility of keeping in touch with ranch news through letters that were seldom answered and then only with the skimpiest of information.

The fortunes of war, with their uprooting and shuffling of people, often give rise to strange acquaintances. I happened to be mixed up in such a case during that winter following my parting company with the draft board, and it eventually had an odd bearing on the Antler Ranch.

A fellow member in a New York club had, on several occasions, told me about the sudden uprooting of an Austrian noble family who had defied Hitler, refused to join the Third Reich or to turn over the titles to their lands. As a consequence, they had been forced at gunpoint to abandon their palace in Vienna and flee in exile to Portugal, the immediate haven of so many noble and royal families.

I was to meet the head of this Austrian family, by the name and title of His Serene Highness Prince Friedrich von Thurnwald, through one Felix, a mutual friend of my fellow club member, who briefed me on the family's situation.

The Prince was widely considered to be the greatest single landowner in central Europe, with properties in several countries there plus holdings in Mozambique and Haiti. He had always been an extremely active and successful businessman in managing his properties but now was stranded with his wife, Sophie (a royal princess in her own right), in a New York hotel, where he was highly frustrated by idleness, a consuming hatred for the Nazi regime and the bitterness of having his lands occupied by the enemy, who had demanded that he turn over their titles to the Third Reich. He made a brave show of his irate refusal to do so and haughtily declined to sign over a single title. Odds were against him, however, for in his hurried exit he was forced to leave most of his titles in the palace vaults, which would surely be blown open by the Nazis. Foresight, however, had prompted him to sneak out some titles and a small part of his other assets to neutral Portugal. He had also managed to smuggle some works of art through Hitler's lines to safety in Canada.

Being a great agriculturalist and having had much experience with livestock, he was now seeking an investment in Montana cattle ranching, among other New World projects buzzing through his brain. His great drawback was his health. The abrupt turn of events in his life had brought on a cardiac condition, and he was a semi-invalid. Inquiries and investigations had led him to me.

On our way to the von Thurnwalds' Park Avenue hotel, Felix explained, "You must not be surprised to hear Friedrich call me Gu-gu. We are somewhat distantly related by marriage, and it is a childhood nickname which amuses him. Also, he is in a wheelchair, but actually this is only a ruse of the doctor to keep him quiet, for otherwise they cannot keep him in the hotel. He is always trying to get out for business deals. I must also mention that he and Princess Sophie do not use their titles in public, as they are traveling incognito with Swiss passports. She, however, being royal, has the diplomatic status of extraterritoriality, though she does not use it. To the general public they are now Dr. and Mrs. Thurnwald."

"He's a medical man, then?"

"No. The prefix is purely academic. He has several doctorate degrees from European universities. A very scholarly man, though one might at first not realize this from his language when he is excited. At present he is studying for a Ph.D. degree from Columbia University. It is one of his ambitions."

The elevator stopped near the top floor and we were let into the Prince's apartment by a nurse, who showed us into a little anteroom, since Friedrich's heart specialist was examining him.

When the examination was over and the doctor had left, Friedrich appeared, propelling himself vigorously into the living room and calling out, "Nurse! Where have you put my guests?" He looked wildly about him. "What have you done with them? Gu-gu! . . . Oh, there you are!" He spotted us through the half-open door. "Come out, come quickly. What is all this delay? . . . These miserable doctors! Will they never let me alone long enough to attend to my business?" His rotund, fiftyish face was pink with excitement, setting off penetrating brown eyes and crowned by a luxurious growth of dark chestnut hair, slightly dishevelled. He waved away the approaching nurse, who was making signs to him not to wheel so fast and protesting that she should have pushed him. "Never mind, never mind!" He dismissed her pleadings. "Let us get down to business. Gu-gu, introduce me."

During the introduction, I felt the Prince's keen eyes sweeping over me appraisingly. Then His Serene Highness leaned back in the wheelchair and relaxed, smiling and smoothing a stray lock of hair. "Well . . . so, you're the cattle rancher I've been waiting for so long! It is very kind of you to come, Mr. Randolph, to see an old cripple. Very kind indeed. I'm glad to see you finally, for I feared that I would not last long enough, what with the threats of these damned doctors and all this electrical nonsense." He waved disgustedly at some apparatus at the far end of the room.

"They wire me up like a bomb every day. Some day, I shall explode, surely. Then, I shall be rid of all this rot, and also of all their enormous bills, and they will have killed the goose that lays the golden eggs, which will serve them right . . . fiends that they are!" He shook a fine malacca cane at the door through which the doctor had just departed and announced, "Now that he has gone to electrocute some other poor devil, we shall have champagne to celebrate this occasion."

The nurse gave signs of opposition to the champagne but ceased when her patient rapped the spokes of his wheelchair loudly with the malacca cane, lowered his voice to an even, threatening tone and commanded sternly, "Champagne, I tell you! Call the *sommelier* at once!" Then she picked up the telephone and called for room service, while the Prince added warmly, "Miss Elliott is a wonderful nurse. She has only one fault. Like all nurses, she has been too much around doctors." He smiled affectionately at Miss Elliott, who seemed somewhat relieved as she beat a hasty retreat from the living room. "Doctors . . . bah!" the Prince called after her.

"But I hear you're a doctor yourself," I said, jokingly.

"Yes, but not that kind. He . . ." shaking his cane at the door again . . . "is a doctor of the body. I am a philosophical doctor, a doctor of the soul. One needs much philosophy to survive in the world these days. God damn Hitler! Yes, much philosophy. I am studying now for a degree from Columbia University. Since I hope to be an American cowboy, is it not fitting that I should have an American degree?"

"Not just to be a cowpuncher. But it helps."

"Yes, it helps everywhere," he reflected. "It is always likely to be a benefit. One never knows. Especially when one is about to enter among the cowboys. They are, I am told, excellent philosophers themselves."

"Not all, but many, more or less, yes." I didn't have the heart to disillusion my host.

"Pardon me while I clear my head for the bouquet of the champagne, which now is here," he explained, as the door opened and two waiters wheeled in a table of glittering array, amid which two bottles of vintage champagne nestled in buckets of shaved ice. Then from the vest pocket of his well-valeted British suit he drew a small jeweled box of brown powder, taking two pinches and sniffing one up each nostril. Next, he broke out a huge silk hand-kerchief which, as it unfurled, showed a minute coronet em-broidered in one corner and gave off a faint trace of cologne. He waved the handkerchief in a gesture of "time out," gasped several times, then sneezed into it four violent sneezes. "God damn Hit-ler!" he exclaimed on emerging tearfully from the silken folds. And, "Ah . . . that is better!" relaxing from the strain of the sneez-ing and dabbing at his eyes. "Now, let us enjoy our champagne!"

There was a violent knocking on one of the doors, followed by stern-sounding words in German, which I could not understand, and which the Prince answered curtly. Then, in English, "Quickly, Gu-gu, open the window. Quickly, quickly!"

No sooner had Gu-gu thrown the sash wide, than Miss Elliott reappeared, agitated. "The doctor has said *no snuff*, sir!" she ad-monished severely.

"Merely the draft, my dear," came the smiling reply from His Serene Highness. "Please shut the window." His eyes followed her threateningly as she did so and until she had left the room again.

I noticed that there were glasses and canapés for six.

"We are not alone, as you have just heard," the Prince ex-plained, impishly jerking his thumb over his shoulder at the door whence the German scolding had come. "But perhaps we had better begin to pour the wine, Gu-gu. What with my wife in there and these nurses ever on guard, we are well spied upon. I never know when they may descend on me and waft away the last of my innocent pleasures." When our glasses were filled, he raised his high and declaimed loudly, "Against Hitler!" Then he mo-tioned Gu-gu to refill.

But before this was possible, the library door opened, admitting a tall, spare, plainly dressed woman of middle age and a plump, dapper, graying man with a red carnation in his buttonhole. They advanced toward the wheelchair, exuding admonition.

The Prince swung his chair toward them. "My wife, Sophie," he announced simply. "This is Mr. Randolph, who has come to take me to Montana . . . without, I hope, any doctors or wires attached!"

The Princess extended her hand smilingly, with the simple graciousness of true royalty. "We are so glad you have come at last," she said warmly and then shook a warning finger at her husband. "And you, Friedrich!" she scolded, noting the few golden drops remaining in the bottom of his glass, "If you take more than one glass of champagne, you will not be allowed to have your whiskey tonight!"

"Bah!" he answered, shaking the malacca stick at her playfully and then turned to me, with a gesture toward the dapper gentleman. "And this is my banker, Baron Rathville. They both have noses like bloodhounds for champagne and always come running to where it is. Perhaps you had better pour out some more all around, Gu-gu."

The Princess removed her husband's glass and placed it on the mantel.

"It is a pity that I am not allowed to celebrate the beginning of my new business with Mr. Randolph!" Friedrich wailed.

"Your new business, Friedrich?" the banker asked solicitously.

"Yes. I thought I told you about it. I am going into business with Mr. Randolph and his partner in Montana. I want you to give him a hundred thousand dollars. I am going to be a cowboy."

"A cowboy? A hundred thousand dollars, Friedrich?" The Baron scanned his client, eyebrows slightly raised.

"Yes, yes. A hundred thousand dollars. You see, I am going to be a financial cowboy. And I want you to give him a hundred thousand dollars. Do you think we can spare it?"

"So soon after your last investment, Friedrich? . . . That depends. I shall cable Lisbon to see if the latest shipment of securities was safely delivered." He turned to me and explained, "Friedrich is a thief and smuggler you know, Mr. Randolph. I feel duty bound to warn you, now that you are apparently going to be in business together. He plays a running game with Hitler . . ."

"*Against* Hitler, you idiot! Get it straight for Mr. Randolph, before he thinks you a stupid banker," Friedrich corrected, rapping the spokes of the wheelchair.

"Very well, then, against Hitler. Anyway, they are both thieves. Hitler has stolen most of the contents of Friedrich's palace in Vienna, also his castle near Prague and other residences, to say nothing of the estates themselves—hundreds of thousands of acres. But Friedrich, here, he has stolen many of the movable objects back again from Hitler, which requires a skill that only a real thief could possess. Now he is engaged in smuggling these restolen goods—including some very desirable securities—right through

Hitler's lines into neutral countries, Switzerland and Portugal. From there, he is distributing them to various far lands . . . Haiti, Canada and the United States, where they will be tolerably safe."

"We've been pretty smart fooling Hitler so far, haven't we?" The Prince brightened up, fingering his close-cropped moustache. "I must say, though, Mr. Randolph, in all fairness, that it has been entirely through this fellow's machinations. . . . Gu-gu, pour him another sip of wine to give him more inspiration." Then he turned to his banker, "Now, get on the telephone to Lisbon and find out what is happening at the bank. Let us not bother waiting for cables. I am anxious to conclude this cattle business with Mr. Randolph."

While the banker was on the telephone in an adjoining room, I supplied answers to my prospective partner's barrage of questions about the ranching business. Presently, Rathville returned to us, his face drawn with disappointment, his tongue fumbling for words.

"Well, what's wrong? Don't stand there looking like a goat!" Friedrich roared.

"Now, Friedrich, please don't get excited. You know what the doctor said."

"To hell with what the doctor said! What does the bank say?"

"The bank says that, although the securities have arrived and are in your vault there, unfortunately, some envoy of Hitler is also there, demanding them on the grounds that the bank is illegally harboring property belonging to the Third Reich. What shall I tell them?"

"Tell them to kick the Nazi messenger boy in the ass!"

"Friedrich!" his wife intervened, "Miss Elliott is in the next room, with the door open."

"Tell them to kick him out and send him back to Berlin with the information that Portugal is a neutral country. Don't they know at the bank they're not obliged to take Nazi orders? Idiots!"

"It is not just a messenger boy, Friedrich. It is a high-ranking officer, a personal aide of Hitler. There is a diplomatic side to consider. And the bank's president is a friend of yours. Surely you wouldn't embarrass him after all his help to you?"

The Prince seized his cane again. "The lily-livered fools! . . . Tell them . . . Tell them . . . Here, I'll tell them myself. You bankers never know what to tell each other." He started wheeling his chair violently toward the telephone.

"Friedrich, no! You mustn't exert yourself!" the Princess pleaded, stepping into his path.

Miss Elliott rushed from the adjoining room to cooperate. "It is really much better for you to let Baron Rathville speak for you," she said sweetly.

"All right," Friedrich capitulated. He had also agreed not to oppose Miss Elliott on pain of losing his evening jigger of bourbon. "But tell him . . ." He panted from his exertions while Rathville filled in.

"I shall give him your compliments, of course."

"Yes, yes, of course. Then tell him that I have foreseen this situation and provided for it. He need fear no embarrassment. He may open my vault. There is no German property in it, confiscated or otherwise. He may even show that swine of an envoy. The swine may look, but he may not touch, after which he should be started back to Berlin with a kick in the . . ."

"Friedrich! Remember where you are. Not in the barracks!" his wife reminded him again.

When Rathville returned from the telephone, his features were relaxed and normal again. He was happy to see that his client showed the same signs. "I think everything will be all right, now that the securities are there and, as you say, cannot be confiscated," he announced reassuringly. "They will send us a cable definitely tonight. It was too long to hold the telephone while your vault is opened."

"The securities are safe," Friedrich smiled confidently. "Because, you see, I have played another trick on Hitler. Before leaving Europe, I secretly reorganized that company, which was incorporated under Austrian law. It is now incorporated under the laws of Portugal, as the swine will see when they open the vault, and it is, therefore, immune from Nazi clutches. Tell me, my friend, don't you think this is one more rather good kick . . ." he indicated his bottom . . . "I have given to Hitler?" He smiled sweetly toward Miss Elliott.

"I think, Friedrich," the Baron humored him, "that you are a genius. I think also, that we can now arrange the credit you ask for Mr. Randolph."

Friedrich smiled and said to me, "I look forward now to my venture with you in Montana as a proper balance to my similar investment in the east, which is a farm in Vermont. But somehow the Vermont venture is not much of a success. The land is old and worn-out, as in Europe. The people are narrow-minded toward foreigners, especially German-speaking ones like me. The automobile highways are closing in everywhere, bringing with them the unattractive things of life. But in Montana I feel it will be different — a freer life. So we shall have a toast to our business future together there, and I shall gladly forfeit my drink of whiskey tonight."

15

Getting to Know Them: New Steer Venture

A FIRST-NAME INTIMACY soon flourished between Thurnwald and myself, and long before spring we were on a Fred-and-Ned basis as we enjoyed an occasional "whiskey time" together in his apartment.

Apparently, he had been very much the active, outdoor man of unlimited means, accustomed to traveling widely between his far-flung interests and to having his own way by reason of his wealth and the respect accorded to his family's noble status then in its third century. He was highly educated and had military training which, together with his Germanic background and upbringing, imbued him with a natural love for the exact, the meticulous and the orderly.

Friedrich seemed to be reaching out for friendship, a slightly lonely man having few acquaintances in New York (which he was visiting for the first time) other than a small circle of fellow expatriates, Baron Rathville and some of his banking fraternity. He never mentioned being very close to any native-born Americans and seemed to be groping for some foothold among us, rather cautiously feeling his way, as if fearing that he might not be welcome because of his Germanic extraction and the American tendency to draw no line between Germans and Austrians, especially in wartime. Thus he may have looked upon me as a sort of lighthouse to show him the way to a safe harbor where, for the obviously limited time left to him, he might at least taste the freedom of life that Europe had never known.

Princess Sophie would usually join us at "whiskey time," but she stayed in a relatively minor part, more or less as a charming guardian, to see that doctor's orders were obeyed. She was always elegantly but very simply dressed and usually wore magnificent strings of pearls in the most peculiarly unostentatious manner, so that they were visible only above her dress, the main length plunging down into it. Sometimes a scarf concealed even those exposed around her neck. The pearls seemed to vary in size from day to day, and also the clasps were different, suggesting that she had several strings which, for some reason, she wished to wear but not to show, a singularly unfeminine trait.

Sophie's face was somewhat sad, possibly because so many of her male relatives had been killed in the war, as her husband explained, and she dwelt on these bereavements in frequent praying. They were both deeply religious and devout Catholics. However, occasionally bright bursts of sunshine would light up her features in response to some humorous situation, and at times she would register an impish delight in telling jokes.

I did not go into many details about the Thurnwalds with Matt Sheardon, knowing that I would be out west again soon, and that explaining things to him personally was much more satisfactory than writing letters which he surely would never answer. I mentioned only the business end of the deal, asking if he would be willing to take on a contract with Friedrich similar to mine and providing his own personal brand. Matt's answer was that he would if I would vouch for the integrity of the parties, produce the money and relieve him of all correspondence. He proposed to make a special trip to Helena for the purpose of visiting his friend, the Recorder of Marks and Brands, to arrange a personal brand for Friedrich.

Matt later reported that one of the most favorable brands available for immediate registration was an "Open AO," "Open" meaning simply that the "A" has no bar, a right ribs brand. It was highly legible and easily applied with irons already on hand. If acceptable, he wanted to know the exact name and address in which it should be registered.

Friedrich was delighted with the idea of having his very own brand, so that checks for sales of his cattle could be made payable directly to him under government brand inspection, but he hesitated at supplying his own name and address for the registration.

This, I thought glumly, might be because of the possibility of his sudden death at any moment. Then he began to lead me into the outer edges of his complicated financial setup, evidently based, in part, upon some fear that, if Hitler won the war, all his tangible personal assets might be claimed by the Third Reich.

With his Swiss passport, all his business affairs were safely centered in one of the large Zurich banks. He also used the bank in Lisbon and Baron Rathville's international banking house, which had branches all over Europe and an office in New York.

His legal setup was less developed, but he had been referred to a very high-toned international lawyer in Washington and was considering several legal firms in New York. I connected him up with my family lawyers in New York, and he immediately loaded them with work. He also had an employee of a large Wall Street bank, whom he paid to do his nonlegal correspondence chores in off hours. From this man, a Mr. Erlander, and my family lawyers, I gradually came to realize what a complicated life Friedrich led and the heavy load of work involved. My end of it started out to be just the proposed steer operation but later was broadened.

Friedrich had already bought two adjoining farms in Vermont, one as a possible future home for Sophie and himself, and the other for some royal relatives of Sophie's who wished to remove their children from Europe during the war. Sophie had numerous relatives with children, but she and Friedrich were childless.

He did not want to take these properties in his own name, and so had incorporated them into a sort of holding company known as Green Mountain Estates, Inc., the stock of which was all owned by the families involved. He had planned on acquiring other American properties and throwing them into the corporation also. Therefore, when the question of the cattle brand came up, he wanted the Open AO registered in the name of Green Mountain Estates.

This was done, the papers sent back to Helena, and Friedrich was at last a full-fledged financial cowboy, probably the most unusual one ever recorded on the Montana brand books. He then gave me a power of attorney over the brand, which my New York lawyers, evidently thinking that I might need maximum protection from strange foreigners, drew up in such broad form that it is a wonder he signed it at all. But he did, in very good faith, later admitting that he realized I could have "bought him out for a

song and sold him to the nearest butcher" before he knew anything about it.

I transferred the money to Matt Sheardon, who wrote back that
he was just starting south on another steer-buying trip and would
"cut the Prince in on it" for as many head as his cash would cover
according to the final delivered cost. The price of southern steers
was steadily climbing, but he thought that, with good luck and
shipping weather, the ranch might be able to brand two thousand
Open AO's. He then disappeared into the limbo of Texas, and as
usual I heard nothing more from him for weeks.

When I did hear from him, the news was not good. He had
bought a big string of steers in Texas, and they were already on
the rails in bad weather, which was moving north with them. It
would take them five or six days to reach Wyola, and the Montana
weather forecast was terrible, with wet snow turning to rain predicted. He was short of hands at the ranch because of the drafting
and volunteering of his men but would do the best he could and
write me about the condition of the steers on arrival and what
the shipping loss might be.

Of course, I never heard, but nationwide weather reports were
terrifying, and newspapers were full of the woes of livestock men
in the west. Perhaps it was just as well that I didn't have any
further definite news to report to Friedrich, to whose questions I
tried to give the most heartening answers possible to spare him
anxiety. Not satisfied with generalities, however, he had been
writing Matt also, but his letters met with the same fate as mine.

By the time I arrived at the ranch, our steer deal had gotten
off to a bad start. We had a 10 percent shipping loss and, on top of
that, an obviously terrific shrink in the weight of the steers, some
of which were so weak that they could not be trailed from the railroad to the ranch and had to be kept in a shipping pasture until
they could gather strength. Wet snow, rain and sleet had persisted
day after day, flooding the pasture into a bog, which claimed
many animals before they could be rescued, especially during the
freezing nights.

Matt himself was out there on a rope horse, working with his
men, trying to free as many as they could from the icy mud of an
aspen grove, where they were difficult to get at. "Now you see
what I mean by having a Mexican ranch," he explained between
chattering teeth. "Those cattlemen may have other problems down

there, but at least they don't have to stay up all night, jerking billies out of a swamp. I've even lost count of the dead ones."

"I dread having to make up the figures and report them to Thurnwald."

"What have you been telling him so far?"

"As little as possible. Considering his condition, I didn't have the heart to jolt him with too much bad news at once right at the start. And anyway, you didn't write me too many details."

"You know me and writing letters. I've been pretty busy here. The Prince has been writing me, too, but I couldn't answer him either. Actually, we haven't got the full figures yet."

"What do you think they'll be?"

"Perhaps 15 percent. That'll raise the average price of what we've got quite a bit, but I don't think it'll go above fifty dollars per head."

"Maybe it won't be that much. There's no use rushing bad news when it might get better."

"I'm not so sure about that." Matt shook his head doubtfully. "I never saw a shipment of steers run into so much bad weather or pick a more awkward place to bog down in. The railroad didn't do a very good job either. They should have unloaded them when the weather began to get too tough and let them rest up for a day and given them another feeding, but they're shorthanded too and full of wartime excuses. I couldn't even spare a man to go along with the shipment and look after them. Just had to sign the regular railroad release. Glad I don't have to write our new partner about this."

"Oh, he understands business risks, but it'll be a big disappointment for him to get off to such a bad start. He's really keen about being what he calls a financial cowboy. I can just see him sitting in his wheelchair back there, in his big Stetson hat and cowboy boots, pounding away at his little typewriter, writing this bank president in Lisbon all about his new venture."

Matt shot me a sly side-glance under the soggy brim of his little Borsalino. "Say, you don't think this Friedrich guy could have a wire down, do you? They say those noble families over there get kind of silly from intermarrying."

"No. He's all there. He just talked about getting the hat and boots for fun."

"I was just thinking that we ought to tell him something, but we don't want to shock him into a heart attack."

"I won't tell him too much until after these steers have been out on the range a while, and we can honestly say they're on their way to making him some money."

"Weather reports now sound like it might be dry enough to brand soon and get them out on the range. You'll be with the wagon, won't you?"

"Yes."

"That'll give you a good excuse for not writing him too much."

Matt grinned, flipped a loop in his throw rope and sloshed his horse off toward the aspen grove, saying, "There's one I think we can save."

16

Fred, Jack Hart and Jigger McCabe Pronounce Judgment

JACK HART AND JIGGER MCCABE had been visiting old Fred with all the gossip, which he interpreted, as usual, with dire forebodings. "They tell me that everybody up there on the Reservation says Matt's likely to have the pins knocked out from under him. All he needs is a few more trainloads of them slab-sided billies caught in a storm like this last one at the prices he's going to have to pay for them from now on. And what's he getting? Half dead, little spotted critters, all colors of the rainbow, with crooked legs, and snipe-nosed enough so they could eat beans out of a jug. Why, they say this last shipment of steers was all just bones sticking out all over. Jigger says you can hang your hat on them anywhere."

"Well, I've just come from looking some of them over, and they're not quite that bad. We took a big shipping loss on them, but they'll make it up in weight. Once they get on that good grass, it's surprising what these Mexicans can do."

"Mexican, Mexican! That's all he can think about!"

"Just the same, no matter how much you run them down, they made the ranch over two hundred thousand dollars last year, and they've posted quite a record up to now."

"He'll get stuck with them one of these days. You'll see. That's no place for you and Matt to be doing business, down there in a country without law and order. Of course, I don't wish you any bad luck, but I'm kind of glad you didn't get that big Platter ranch down there, or whatever you call it, in a place where you buy land and don't own it, and full of them bastards that even General Pershing had hell with, and you don't know what people are talking about. I hear that Mexican lingo on the radio, and it just don't mean nothing."

"What's wrong with Spanish? You said you have some Spanish ancestors yourself. It's not a hard language to learn."

"Maybe not for you with your edjercation in them fancy schools. But how about Matt? He don't know nothing but English and Crow Indian."

"Matt can figure it out if he has to, don't worry."

"Some day there'll be something he can't figure out. I can't figure out what sense it makes to haul your stock fifteen hundred miles to summer range up here and another thousand to market. That means twenty-five hundred miles of freight bills, and the damn critters have been sightseeing all over the Union." He shook his head in dismay. What's the matter with Montana cattle, any-way? They always made money in the old days."

There was no use arguing with him, going over the same old ground, so I sat down at my typewriter and started a letter to Friedrich.

On and off, Fred eyed me surreptitiously over the top of his *Pathfinder* magazine. "You'll wear that damn thing out," he said finally. "Who're you writing to now?"

"Just a business letter. We've got a new partner coming in. A cowboy with a hundred thousand dollars."

"Never been no cowboy with a hundred thousand dollars. At least, not around this country."

"There's going to be one pretty soon. It's something new we're introducing on the Reservation, only this time it's human: a finan-cial cowboy. Besides the hundred thousand dollars he's got a handle to his name and speaks seven languages including Spanish. What do you think of that?"

"I got to see it first. And, pussonally, I don't like them foreigners. What's this financial cowboy's name?"

"Thurnwald."

"I thought you said he had a handle to it."

"He has, but he doesn't use it in this country. He's a prince, but he calls himself Doctor."

"I'll bet the sonofabitch is a German spy. That's what they all were in the last war. Well, if he's a spy, Jigger will find it out, you'll see."

"Jigger will have his chance pretty soon."

"How's that?"

"The Doctor's coming out here this summer, I hope."

"Where? here? to the cabin? We won't have enough water."

"No, not here. To the Antler. That is, I hope he's coming. It all depends on his health. He has a doctor back there in New York who's trying to keep him in a wheelchair. Heart trouble. He's in with us for a couple of thousand or so of these new steer calves, and he wants to have a look at his investment."

"He'd better not take too close a look, if he's got heart trouble. Maybe you could pick out just one and fatten it up in the meantime to show him. Then tell him the rest is away the hell and gone up in the mountains, where you can't get to them except on horseback. I don't suppose he can ride if he's got heart trouble."

"He won't be able to ride, but Matt can have him flown low over the range."

"If it was me had an investment like that, I wouldn't be satisfied with just looking at my cattle from a flying machine. I'd want to be down there on horseback, where I could read the brands and tell which was mine."

"He'll believe what we tell him. He wouldn't know much more about it anyway, even if he did see the brands."

"It's lucky for him that he's in with you and Matt instead of Skel Baxton."

"What's wrong with Skel Baxton? He made me a good profit, didn't he? Bought those heifers for thirty-six dollars and sold them for seventy in about four months."

"Say, what happened about that stud you and he brought up from Colorado Springs?"

"I never heard any more about it. I suppose he sent *Louis d'Or* back to Pete Drake, the owner, when he got all the mares bred the way he planned."

"He sent the stud back a lot sooner than that according to Jack Hart and Jigger. They found out all about it. When the boss got home and his stud was missing, he sent a telegram to Skel. It said, 'Ship him back tomorrow, or you'll have a visit from the sheriff.' Jigger says old Skel turned white when he got it and sure didn't lose no time getting that horse loaded into a fancy van the same day. Skel sure hates to have anybody kid him about it. They say he just looks down his nose, sheep-like."

It was about time for the mail stage to go by, so I finished my letter, took it up to the mail post and returned, contemplating a good, hot bath.

The hot-water tank of the old coal stove was uncomfortably hot nearly all the way down, and it was a relief to find that, this time, the bathtub contained neither oats nor groceries. So I just dusted a few cobwebs out of it and turned on the taps.

I cut the cabin life short in order to get back to this new steer enterprise as soon as the balmy spring weather returned, since it is impossible to brand in wet weather.

Matt and his now sadly reduced crew were already at work when I got there. Dried out, rested up from their long rail trip, and with some hay in them, the steer calves now showed cheerful signs of recuperation. Some sort of intuition seemed to discourage us both from talking about losses. We dwelt more on the prospects of a good grass year as a result of all that rain; the certainty that our Mexican billies had seen their worst; that only the weakest of them had been lost; that nature's "survival of the fittest" rule had left us with a remainder that would gain the most weight on the least grass; and that, after all, they had eighteen months ahead of them in which to do it.

They were branding in one of the big corrals back of the machine shop, where there was a branding chute. The job was too big, and the hands were too few for time-honored roping and "wrestling" as on the range. Two boys ran the cattle through the chute and into the squeeze gate. One man was on the end gate and also kept the tally book, while Matt and I took turns with the branding irons and working the Johnson bar: that long pole controlling the squeeze gate. We started at dawn, had food brought to us, and worked until dark. We put the Open AO on roughly two thousand head, and the Antler brand on most of the rest, although I branded some three hundred head more RN's in the deal, and some individual members of Matt's family had various interests. Matt and I branded an average of over four hundred head a day before he could scrape up some extra hands, and it took about a week to get the whole job done.

Knocking off at day's end, we felt that we had deserved our jiggers of bonded bourbon, a good supper and a sound night's sleep. There was little conversation, which was dampened by a curious sort of fatigue: the exhaustion of standing in the same place hour after hour, going through the same motions with squeeze gate and branding irons, breathing the acrid blue smoke and gazing at the sea of still unbranded animals which diminished so slowly was greater than the fatigue of being in the saddle all day on roundup. What little conversation we could muster in the evenings was seldom without reference to the Thurnwalds.

Friedrich's letters kept on flowing to me, and they were not all examples of his former ebullient mood. He was beginning to fret over the drop in correspondence, asking all sorts of unanswerable questions about his steers. He considered them as shares in the stock market, which should have more or less actively changing values almost every day, and was terribly interested in knowing exactly what profit they would bring him eighteen months later. He couldn't wait to see them, but his doctor was taking a dim view of allowing him to venture into western altitudes. He was also fretting about his other business affairs: two apartment houses he had bought in New York; the evacuation of works of art from Nazi occupied territories; the personal safety of family members, some of whom were smuggling uninsured crown jewels out of Europe. One of his main worries seemed to be finding a home for a large painting to which, for some dim reason, he was particularly devoted.

These personal matters were wished off, for the most part, on the unfortunate Mr. Erlander, his Man Friday in New York, who labored after hours in the Bank of Manhattan. They got the crown jewels safely tucked away in a vault there, but the wandering agents in charge of the art works seemed to be in a constant turmoil, which Mr. Erlander was supposed to handle. These matters finally became so complicated and time-consuming, that Mr. Erlander had to work during evenings at home and was practically robbed of his family life. He advanced mild, polite objections, whereupon his salary was increased and also his work load. He was then told that my broad power of attorney covered everything he did, and that any important actions he planned to take would have to be approved by me.

This precipitated a flood of correspondence from Erlander to me about matters not even remotely connected with my main specialty, the cattle, and which I did not appreciate very much after a hard day's work and a lungful of branding smoke.

The large painting was one particular item which seemed to cause poor Friedrich more anguish than anything else. This painting apparently measured something like eighteen by twenty-six feet and represented a battle scene painted by some English artist named Hamilton, on commission from Friedrich's favorite grandfather, as a present to the latter's favorite mistress to fill a large empty space in one of her favorite castles. The grandfather and the mistress being long since dead, I could not understand the romantic attachment Friedrich had for the whereabouts and safety of this painting, but the subject was apparently very dear to him.

The painting had finally reached Montreal, where hardworking agents had found for it a series of temporary hanging spaces, in museums, art exhibits and other public places. Nobody, however, wanted to provide a permanent home for such an unwieldy expanse of canvas, so it had finally come to rest in a storage warehouse. Friedrich's concern was with the possible damage to, and present storage conditions of, the painting. Moving and storage bills annoyed him, and he wanted to know what he was getting for his money; whether an art expert could evaluate the condition of the painting and pass on the humidity and other technical aspects of the warehouse. The warehouse, on the other hand, wanted proofs of ownership, guarantee of financial responsibility, insurance coverage and other items to protect itself in the natural course of business. The subject was endless, and, being charged mainly with the success of the cattle, I riveted my energies mostly on that and only slightly on the romantic aspects of Friedrich's grandfather's mistress.

Matt occasionally asked me about the painting to point up the uselessness of a lot of correspondence and to uphold his position on letter writing. "Let him send it here," he suggested. "There's plenty of room on the Crow Reservation. Or we can find a place for it in the machine shop or the hangar."

It was indeed, as Matt had suggested, a relief to be back on the roundup, where mail could not follow, and where we had a perfectly good excuse not to write letters.

Riding along with the wagon one day, he told me of a new turn of events regarding the buffalo herd.

17

The Hollywood Touch:
Filming the Buffalo Herd

BY THE TIME WE GOT the new string of steers up on summer range, they looked a lot less disastrous, and I could truthfully report to the twittering Friedrich that his investment was progressing hopefully, as he could see for himself when he and Sophie arrived for their expected summer visit. The answer was a sad letter stating that he was afraid his doctor would not allow him to make the trip because he had imposed a 1,500-foot altitude limit. I had to report that the Antler country ranged from about three to eight thousand feet. This was a terrible blow to the Thurnwalds, but they immediately set about making plans to join Matt and me in lower country along the border on our next scouting expedition many months in the future.

"Too bad," said Matt, "because we could offer them a special surprise this summer. I'd hoped to pop their eyes out with a buffalo hunt."

"How could you possibly work a buffalo hunt? Get permission from the Crows?"

"I wouldn't be working it. That's the surprise. You know, I've always said you never can tell what you might be getting into in this business. Every once in a while, something peculiar happens. This time, it's damn peculiar. It seems we've been discovered by Hollywood. They're making a film on the life of Buffalo Bill, and they've been scouting around in planes, looking for a herd of buffalo to photograph. They found out we have the only herd in the U.S.A. big enough to make a good hunting scene, so they've been talking with the Crows."

"Who's been talking with the Crows?"

"Twentieth Century–Fox directors. They've made a deal with the Crows and are all ready to start shooting."

"When?"

"Well, that's the trouble. They want some cowpunchers in the picture and cattle and a wagon camp in the background, and they just can't find any except us. Of course, Jerry Flynn won't hear of having a movie outfit around when we're working with the cattle, and he's dead right."

It did seem quite unthinkable to have lots of photographic paraphernalia around, together with actors, actresses and people shouting through megaphones. Jerry Flynn had once bawled me out for getting in front of the herd just trying to take a snapshot from several hundred yards. I wondered how he would like coping with a big, noisy crowd from Hollywood. "So you turned them down?" I suggested.

"On their proposition to hire our outfit for the movies, yes. But I told them, if they want to wait till we get finished working with the cattle in July, they can shoot pictures around the wagon for nothing, and we'll be glad to send some men to help round up the buffalo for this hunting scene they want to make."

In the 1940s, Hollywood still believed that beautiful pictures could be made from romantic American historical episodes in the original types of settings; and of course, the saga of "Buffalo Bill" Cody was rooted partly in this Montana-Wyoming country. The Colonel provided buffalo meat for railroad construction crews along the Yellowstone, was a part owner of the Sheridan Inn and built a home for his daughter Arta on Hanging Woman Creek, a tributary of Tongue River.

It was also for the Indians (hired at unaccustomed Hollywood wages) the first good news they had received in their dealing with the white man since Custer's battle, which took place just over the hill. Yes, said college-educated anthropologist Bob Yellowtail, hereditary chief of the Crows and U.S. Indian Agent at the Reservation, the Indians would allow their buffalo to be photographed, and many of them would undoubtedly like to be photographed themselves, all for a price. This price—it turned out later, according to the film director—was set and reset by one little "medicine man" who kept to his tepee, communicating through its flap by sign language, who had the whole question of wages well under control, a one-man labor union.

Our part of the filming schedule had been set for after the first week in July, when we would be finished working the cattle and could turn over our outfit to help in the big hunting scene. To the disappointment of the boys on the wagon the heroine, Linda Darnell, was not in that part of the script, nor would she even appear. Joel McCrea, the male lead, would be represented by a double, a stunt man named Cliff. Even the hero's horse was kept at home by the insurance company and had to have a faked-up Antler ranch double, concocted from colored photographs.

The idea of the hunting scene was tied into historical fact, in that the Grand Duke Alexis of Russia had paid a state visit to this country in 1872 and, being a great sportsman, was promised a buffalo hunt by President Grant, whose friend, Colonel William F. "Buffalo Bill" Cody, was to organize it. The imperial hunting party, including several playboy guests of Alexis, was a very grand affair, accompanied by luscious supplies of special food and wines carried about in hampers, and with champagne broken out as each buffalo was downed.

The Hollywood invasion began to move in: some sixty in personnel, exclusively male and mostly technicians. They and their equipment were huffed and puffed up the Big Horn Mountains over the rough grade specially prepared for them by the Crow Agency and the Antler Ranch. Tractors pulled buses over creek crossings. Four-wheel-drive pickups yanked at dressing-room, costume-department and makeup-studio trailers. Trucks groaned under the weight of three technicolor cameras, their crews, lighting equipment, batteries, generating plants, food supplies, camping needs and just general "props."

Their camp was set up a few days before the cowpunchers were finished with the cattle, and the Californians obviously enjoyed the respite as a chance to look over the vast "location" and acclimate themselves to the 7,000-foot altitude. In pickups they poked around to gasp at the edge of thousand-foot straight-down canyon walls, or look out over the great, peculiarly pinkish-blue void of the Garvin Basin, with the Pryor Mountains beyond and an unobstructed view for almost a hundred miles toward Yellowstone Park. They looked down into the timbered depths of the Black Canyon, with sides so steep that you have to dismount from a horse to negotiate them. They were shown a cave with a hidden entrance and a depth beyond range of the most powerful flashlight beam, with the unexplained sound of rushing water so far below that a stone thrown into this hole would never be heard to splash but simply to bounce from side to side until its sound petered out.

It was sad to think of all the material Dr. and Mrs. Thurnwald were missing for their records.

Our roundup campsite was at what we used to call Hunter's Cabin, not far from the Californians' headquarters near the top of summer range. As the cowpunchers' work tapered off, visiting began between the two camps; timidly at first, as if each facet of civilization were sizing up the other, then more freely. The cowpunchers' down-to-earth surroundings were a source of wonder to the cameramen and vice versa. Cameramen ventured astride some of the gentle horses in the cavvy, cheered by shouts of "Ride 'em, cowboy!" And Antler men began to learn about operating a movie camera.

Meals at the wagon introduced our visitors to tin cups and plates; washing with a few dipperfuls of water in a small, cracked enamel basin, and the technique of making up a standard roundup bedroll on a canvas "tarp" seventeen feet by six. They noted discreetly the plain, monotonous diet, the lack of distractions, creature comforts, newspapers, liquor and gambling.

Cowpunchers' visits to the camera camp were by comparison a delightful revelation of modern comforts on the range. Tents were less primitive, more Abercrombie and Fitchy. There were tables to eat from and camp stools to sit on. The cook had a gas range. The executives' tent even had its own portable electric light plant, which also powered a refrigerator. There was ice for the drinks, of which the cowpunchers partook sparingly. Radios blared the news, and a phonograph whined music that made cowpunchers with memories of dance halls in Billings or Miles City tap the curled-up toes of their dusty boots.

By then, Indians had appeared from Crow Agency to help round up and handle the buffalo, and they too were happy at getting the traditional meat for their annual Sun Dance: the main fact that made the killing of buffalo at all possible. Everything had been thought of and arranged. The limit of buffalo to be shot was set at five, deemed just enough to supply meat for the Sun Dance. Yellowtail and a Crow expert on the herd, Takes-the-Gun, were on hand. The actors were to have period guns loaded with Phillips shells that flashed and smoked photogenically, but were blanks.

The actual shooting was to be done swiftly and humanely by crack marksmen with high-powered rifles, stationed at advantageous points just beyond camera range. A humane society agent had been sent out from the east coast to see that no animals were abused, either buffalo or horses, and that any possible cripples would be mercifully dispatched.

When the filming operation finally got into gear, our outfit included a camera truck, a property truck complete with makeup artist, the roundup mess wagon, driven by a buckskin-jacketed youth wearing an 1870 vintage beaver cap, and a small truckload of film bosses. Colonel Cody was with us too, all decked out in realistic goatee and an old frontier getup, ancient single-action Colt .45 at one side of his belt and murderous hunting knife at the other. He sat his horse with graceful unconcern, listening to the technical men. With us also was a sprinkling of seminude, befeathered Crows, mounted bareback on flashy ponies, some of which also showed the makeup artist's touch.

That first morning we were unable to get within camera shot of any buffalo, and it was announced that some montage scenes and still pictures for promotional purposes would be taken instead. Anyone could get into the act by submitting to a trip through the makeup and costume unit. Emerging, one passed a tall mirror and had a good laugh at oneself. My reflection showed a well-turned-out period costume of a guest on the Grand Duke's hunt, in startling color scheme: hunters' green tailcoat with a flowered silk, rather purplish, double-breasted vest; light fawn riding breeches of a remarkably lucky fit; black, buff-topped boots, a chocolate-colored silk top hat and perfectly fitting, expensive, brown calfskin gloves. Attached under the back of the hat was a hairpiece, called a "fall," which brought my hairline down to the appropriate shaggy shoulder length required. I was handed an unloaded, beautifully polished percussion cap rifle and placed in a group of similarly gotten-up extras.

In the afternoon a few scattered groups of buffalo were located, but not enough to make a big hunting scene. Our boys, however, did manage to cut out a few cows with their calves and rope the calves for close-up shots, with one man roping, while two others kept the enraged cows at a safe distance. Then some riders came in with news of where the main herd was. They were sent back with orders to get as many as possible together and hold them at

Edmund Randolph in costume for W. F. Cody film. *Courtesy 20th Century–Fox*

a distance, while we moved all equipment to another part of the range about seven miles away and set up camp there.

Buffalo are ticklish to move and, once stampeded, are almost impossible to stop, but the men knew their job. Slowly and carefully they rode the range, deciding which groups could be thrown together for the biggest showing and best background. The film boss was particularly anxious to have as many buffalo as possible run past the cameras at close range, and Matt promised a plan that would have such a result, by using a deep canyon to contain the herd on one side, thus freeing more riders to handle them on the other.

Three cameras were finally set up in the vicinity of two hills rather close together. Between these hills we were to run the buffalo in a direction that would give them very little chance to avoid passing at least one camera close by.

With the cameras all set to roll, our most buffalo-minded authorities, Yellowtail and Takes-the-Gun, gave us the strategy. We were to ease around the herd quietly, join the other riders who were holding them just out of sight in a slight depression, and then, at a given signal, start pushing them gently toward the cameras, letting them gather their own speed at will but crowding them to a dead run at the end; meantime, keeping ourselves out of camera range and, particularly, out of rifle range.

As we closed in, the buffalo, led by an old bull sniffing our wind, ambled out of the depression onto a flat. We followed carefully, trying not to frighten them, but knowing that sooner or later they were bound to make a break for freedom. Then there was a signal from one of the Crows, and down the line of riders came the call, "Start them off!" We closed in further, and they broke in the right direction on a nice, slow trot. We let them jog along quietly for a mile or so, until they began to string out too far, with danger of breaking up into separate groups and scattering. Then Takes-the-Gun rode ahead to check the leaders, sending his young son back with orders to crowd the drag, so as to bunch the herd together more.

As the herd bunched, we could see the leaders away up ahead, breaking from their quiet trot into that lumbering, determined gallop, seemingly so awkward, but yet so practical in getting them over the ground. Our point riders were unable to check the lead, and were finding it no easy task to hem in the herd between the canyon and other riders who were lurking behind cover of timber and rocks along the way, ready to gallop out and correct any breaks away from the intended course. Soon orders came down the line for us to crowd the drag still more and then to push them for all we were worth. Suddenly, there was a whirling sea of brown wool, dust and horns. It was headed straight for the cameras just around the two low hills, which were now quite near. Then rifle fire broke out and we checked our horses.

The herd thundered past the cameras much closer than planned, providing some excellent footage but striking terror into the hearts of the operators. Some men jumped up on one of the camera platforms, mounted on a flatbed truck, thus rocking it in defiance of the "Keep Off" signs and spoiling some of the film.

Dashing about in the melee was Buffalo Bill, the stunt man, on Spec, the beautiful Antler-raised gelding made up to double for Joel McCrea's horse, which was safe in Hollywood. Cliff's period rifle was harmlessly belching puffs of smoke as he fired his Phillips shells, each, by camera trickery, to account for a buffalo on the screen, while two sharpshooters, just out of camera range, filled the meat quota of five head for the Sun Dance.

Unfortunately, there were two wounded buffalo, probably because of the unavoidable alignment of animals in such a close-packed herd, moving in such a cloud of dust. One was a neck shot on a fine bull, the other a leg shot on a cow with a calf.

Cliff saw the wounded bull cut out of the herd and head uphill, as wounded animals often do, and reported to the humane society officer, saying he would be glad to track it down and kill it if he had a real gun. The film boss was standing nearby, holding a very handsome, custom-built .30-'06 sporting rifle with telescope sight, which he gave to Cliff, who started off after the bull. Then Cliff saw the cow, limping out of the herd and taking off in a different direction, and suggested sending someone else after her, so he could keep his eye on the bull, which was running.

Seeing that I had a .30-30 Winchester carbine in my saddle scabbard, the humane society agent asked me to go after the crippled cow. Cliff and I loped off together, he looking very much like a pioneer, galloping along Buffalo Bill style with the rifle in the crook of his left arm, since in those days saddle scabbards were not much in use and his costume getup did not include one. His horse was very handsome, and mine was a beautiful golden palomino with flax mane and tail. This horse, named Sunny, belonged to a well-known exotic dancer in New York, who had married a former Antler employee and world champion bronctwister. She was often a guest of the ranch, and Matt had kindly offered to keep Sunny for her, so he was on temporary loan with the Antler cavvy, though not much of a cow pony. Apparently, she had bought him on looks and then didn't feel safe on him, for he always wanted to run and was very hard to hold down because he had a cold mouth. He was more of a showy parade pony.

Cliff and I soon parted company, he swerving off to the right and easing into a full gallop as his quarry was disappearing around the hill. I slowed down to a walk, because I was by then fairly close to the wounded cow and feeling a twinge of pity for her, since she had spotted us and was making a pathetic attempt to escape. She couldn't get out of a hobbling walk, however, for her right forefoot was all but shot off below the knee and dangling by a piece of the hide. Every time she tried to trot, she would stumble and then look back, as if to see how much I was gaining on her. After her exertions of the last hour or so and under the added strain of limping, she was puffing and blowing, as the July sun beat down. There was no need to run her any more. She had swerved off to the left and was heading for a rocky pinnacle on the end of a hogback formation jutting out into a deep canyon. Obviously, once out on this rocky ledge she could not possibly escape and would present the surest and most merciful coup de grace shot. If I pushed her too hard, she might panic and stumble off the precipitous ledge down into the rocky, inaccessible canyon for a lingering, agonizing death.

In a short time I heard two high-powered rifle shots. Sunny jumped around a bit, as he had during the hunting scene, reminding me that he was extremely gun-shy. I thought Cliff had fulfilled his mission. Soon, however, he reappeared on the gallop, which, if this had been the case, would have been hardly necessary. Thinking that something might be wrong, I loped over to meet him. It turned out that the film director's fancy gun had only two shells in it. Cliff had missed with his first shot and downed the bull with his second. The bull was not dead, was trying to get up and, of course, was in a nasty mood. Apparently, Cliff thought it wiser not to finish him off with his hunting knife. So I gave him my rifle, while I held his, and he was off again on a high lope. There were two more shots, which he put through the bull's head. Sunny gave me a lot of trouble staying aboard at this much closer range, while I had to hold the heavy sporting rifle in one hand, since its barrel was too long and its telescope sight too bulky to fit into my scabbard. For a tense moment I thought Sunny would surely unload me.

"Thanks," said Cliff, riding back to exchange guns. "Now, if you don't need me, I've got to report to my boss in a hurry."

With only my pathetic cow to account for and four shells left in the Winchester, I certainly didn't need any help from a man with an empty gun. In addition, that morning, I had strapped on my .38 Colt, fully loaded, which a cowpuncher had borrowed for a little practice plinking at a "rock dog." As Cliff rode off, I drew the old Police Positive from its holster and swung open the cylinder. There were three spent shells in it and three live ones, for a total firepower of seven rounds in both guns, far more than enough, I thought, replacing it in the holster, as I jogged back to check up on the cow.

She was standing still, turned around, looking toward camp, and bawling. That meant she had a calf somewhere back there. As I approached, she started hobbling back toward camp, and I could see that she had milk so knew there must be a calf around, and that she would be on the prod, especially since enraged by her wound, for buffalo cows are fiercely protective of their young. Only the day before, two expert Antler cowpunchers, both mounted on top-notch cutting horses, really had their hands full riding off a cow long enough for a roper to catch her calf.

I circled around carefully and hazed her back toward the rocky ledge. Before going out on it, she turned around once and weakly but bravely challenged me, then thought better of it and went out on the ledge. To my surprise, she went out all the way then turned around again.

Now there was no question of marksmanship, but there was a considerable question of what to do with gun-shy Sunny, for he would surely run off at the boom of a .30-30 so close and, once running, would never stop till he got back to camp, presenting me with the prospect of a hot, three-mile walk in heavy, batwing chaps.

Since one never ties a western horse fast to anything solid—

Roping out a buffalo calf for a close-up. *Courtesy 20th Century-Fox*

merely lapping the lines loosely two or three times around, perhaps, a tree branch — and since there was not even a tree in sight,
I had no choice but to lap the lines around the stem of a stout
sagebrush. I had decided not to use the rifle, which was not really
necessary now, as the poor cow could go no farther. Perhaps also,
since Sunny would be upwind of the shot and I would have to be
at some distance from him to come within reasonable pistol range
of the cow, the wind might muffle my firing enough not to bother
him.

Thinking of that three-mile walk, I advanced stealthily toward
the cow, feeling that each step increased my chances of riding
back to camp. The hogback formation got narrower and narrower,
until it was not more than six feet wide, with a terrifying drop
on either side. I did not want to get caught out there on it any
closer to that enraged cow, in case the poor thing did decide to
charge me in one last, desperate effort to find her calf. She had
her head down and was weaving it from side to side. The bloody
remains of her right forefoot waved sickeningly in the wind and
she gave the impression that, had it been whole, it would have
been pawing the ground, threatening a charge which even a mata-
dor could not have ducked for lack of space. There was nothing
to hide behind or grab onto. Going much farther, I thought, might
result in her hooking me over the edge to be heard from no more.

It was, however, not an impossible shot, except that I was no
marksman; but I thought of William Tell splitting the apple in
his just cause and knew mine was a good one too. Shakily I cocked
the hammer for less trigger effort, took a bead on that great
shaggy mass against the gorgeous pink background of the canyon
rim beyond, spoiled only by the front sight of the revolver, and
fired. But I was not William Tell. The shot, apparently, was too
high.

This encouraged (or scared) me into advancing a few more
paces to what I considered the absolute limit of safety. Because
the cow's head was now up again, squarely facing me and holding still, I had not only a shorter range but more of a target, from
the brisket (which might possibly reach the heart with a steel-
nosed bullet) to a brain shot. I aimed somewhere in between and
pulled. The brave old mother dropped without a quiver and with
such a thud that it seemed as if her three feet had all snapped
up under her simultaneously, as she fell on her left side. A brain

shot? I could find no bullet mark on her head or anywhere else, and not a drop of blood except from the foot. To certify the end of her misery, I sent the third bullet point-blank through her brain. Then I stepped off the distance back to my firing point, which was just twenty-nine paces.

My next problem was Sunny. He was nowhere to be seen. The uprooted sagebrush where I had tethered him was bleak evidence.

It was late afternoon of July 14 and hot, even at that altitude. My chaps were too cumbersome to walk that distance, so I took them off and laid them on a rock, with my holster belt and the Police Positive underneath in case of rain. Then I struck out for camp on a rough sun bearing.

After walking about a mile, I heard a horn honking away off to my right, and there was a pickup truck heading for me. In it were some of the Antler boys, who picked me up and described how Sunny had come running back to camp, with his bridle but no saddle. They suspected some kind of accident and had been circling around looking for me. I directed them to the dead buffalo, so they could show the Indian skinners where to find it, then picked up my property, and we headed back to camp. Next day we returned to scout the area, picking up my saddle with a broken cinch, then the saddle blanket and scabbard, which had been kicked loose, with a broken strap, all some distance apart, but no rifle. Several of the boys and I combed the area again on horseback, but we never found it.

18

Winter Quarters
in the Arizona Desert

FRIEDRICH THURNWALD'S CORRESPONDENCE kept increasing ominously during the summer and fall until, toward the end of September I was completely swamped and felt that I would have to do something about it. My power of attorney having been originally aimed at handling the cattle situation, it seemed a bit farfetched that this should now include Manhattan real estate, which he was buying.

I made a trip back to New York and had an understanding with him which put an end to paperwork unrelated to the ranching operations. I could by then also give him a fairly cheerful report about his two thousand steers. He was further cheered by his doctor's prediction that a trip to Montana might be feasible in the spring. We also agreed that my compensation was to be one quarter of his net profit on the steers. Thus I left him in a happy mood toward the end of October, assuring him that I would be back in New York for Christmas.

That was my driving winter.

After barely three weeks in New York over the Christmas holidays, I had to take to the highway again. The Thurnwalds were at last going out west.

Friedrich's doctor had ordered him out of New York for six weeks during the foul weather of February and March. The desert climate of Arizona was considered ideal, and, after much poring over maps, we decided upon a headquarters at Tucson, because Dr. Schmidt had located a good heart specialist there.

The effect upon them was as if they had both suddenly been given a new lease on life, since their tastes ran more to the outdoors than to the urban existence. They viewed their coming trip as a winter safari into unknown, sunny lands where as yet unseen flora and fauna abounded, from which they could gather specimens for their private museum in Kenya and a wealth of material for Friedrich's thesis.

Besides being a large town where excellent medical facilities existed, Tucson was not far from the Mexican border, about which Friedrich had heard so much in connection with our cattle venture. He wanted to stay in the little border town of Nogales, but Dr. Schmidt had insisted that it was too far from sophisticated medical facilities. Nogales has a namesake town just across the Mexican border in the state of Sonora, which appealed to Friedrich's imagination as he saw himself and Sophie tripping back and forth between the two countries, thus investigating Mexico also. Furthermore, Nogales was a cattle-crossing point which Matt Sheardon had often used, and which he could conveniently visit sometime in February on his next buying trip, so that Friedrich would have a good chance of meeting his new business partner. Business was always on Friedrich's mind and, as he suggested, "Who knows but what there might exist some marvelous business opportunity in Mexico?"

The Thurnwalds had also learned from their biological research that a certain species of tarantula not yet represented in Sophie's Kenya collection existed in the desert between Tucson and Nogales. They had studied up on this species, and Sophie was very keen on capturing some specimens. Then, of course, Mexico itself conjured up the sad story of the Emperor Maximilian, for whom no Austrian nobleman could avoid some twinge of pity, though he be as far separated from it as Nogales is from the execution spot of Querétaro. But as far as Nogales was concerned, Dr. Schmidt said definitely, "No!" This, however, did not keep Friedrich and Sophie from hoping. Nothing ever did.

The date for their arrival in Tucson by rail was set for February 7. Since we were already in the first week of January, that didn't leave too much time for an excursion of this highly specialized type, and I shuddered to think of the preparations to be made, to say nothing of the mileage that lay ahead of me before I could meet that train in Tucson, having first prepared a soft landing for the Thurnwalds.

The Packard station wagon would need a complete inspection and possibly some mechanical work before undertaking such a journey in midwinter. A breakdown on the then infrequently traveled roads to be covered was not to be risked; nor was subsequent trouble after the Thurnwalds' arrival in view of a possible coronary attack at any moment.

Then there was the trip itself to be considered: a long pull, with no clemency of weather to be expected north of Raton Pass, over the Colorado–New Mexico boundary, and some mighty lonely, high stretches through the Sangre de Cristo mountain country thereafter.

A blizzard and cold spell featured that southward trek. Somewhere in the bleak wastes of Colorado's Pueblo County on my second night out I had to sleep on the roadside at twenty degrees below zero. But I was well prepared with food and furs, an arctic explorer's sleeping bag and plenty of hot tea and slept soundly until a snowplow crew dug me out next morning. It wasn't far to New Mexico's 7,800-foot altitude at Raton Pass, which tipped me down into fair weather, and I arrived that evening at Santa Fe. From there I called the Antler office, which was acting as a clearing house for information on Matt's movements and my own. He was in El Paso, and we arranged to meet up at the little town of Truth or Consequences, New Mexico, two days later.

Matt had been driving along the usual border route on his annual steer calf hunt and with him was Jerry Flynn, his cattle manager–wagon boss. They were headed for Nogales to inspect a prospective buy. After our meeting Jerry headed north, Matt and I southwest for the U.S. Customs yards on the Nogales border, where the cattle were to be held. Upon our arrival we learned of a three-day delay in their delivery.

To fill in this time, we decided to scout the living conditions between Nogales and Tucson, with a view toward locating a possible headquarters for the Thurnwalds that would come within reasonable range of medical safety and yet satisfy Friedrich's longing to be in the desert near the Mexican border.

"One cannot please everybody," Friedrich had written. "There must be a middle ground somewhere reasonably close to the Tucson doctor. Find it. Dr. Schmidt will never know."

I showed this to Matt, briefing him again on the Prince's general health situation, and we went over the latest sheet of pronouncements, stumblingly typed on legal-sized paper under the title, REQUIRED ACCOMMODATIONS, HEADQUARTERS.

The accommodations were to consist of four rooms: three with bath and one a baggage room. They must be adjoining, as Friedrich could not have a stranger, possibly noisy, beside him to interfere with his strictly prescribed rest periods. Sophie could not have a stranger next to her, either, for "security reasons" (probably involving the pearls, I thought).

Therefore, the first room was to be mine and Matt's (when he could be with us). The second was to be Sophie's, connecting with Friedrich's. The fourth room would be a sort of combination baggage room, a study for Friedrich and a makeshift laboratory for Sophie's scientific activities, and it must be at the end of the corridor or building. These rooms were to be taken in my name, with the others as my guests, the Thurnwalds being registered as "Dr. and Mrs."

Matt adjusted his little pearl gray Borsalino from time to time as I went over the conditions, as if trying to figure out what all this had to do with the cattle business. "He sure as hell knows what he wants. I'll say that for him. What gets me is that he also knows his days are numbered, and how cheerful he is about it. We ought to do everything we can to make it easy for him. He's so damn interested in this business that it's almost pathetic."

"And that's not all, either. We're collecting flora and fauna, too . . ."

"What in hell's that?"

"Flower and animal specimens, just some of the Latin he and Sophie use so much. It's the way scientists talk. Also, we're writing a thesis for Columbia University, shipping cactus to East Africa and carrying on correspondence with the State Department in Washington. I'll bet you didn't figure on being part of such a worldwide educational scheme when you took on this deal."

Matt shoved the Borsalino to the back of his head. "When did you say they're coming?" he asked almost fearfully.

"Their train's due in Tucson on the seventh. They're keen on seeing you."

"After all you've told me about them, I'm getting kind of scared. That Latin's harder to savvy than Crow Indian."

We found the accommodations we wanted at the Border Bungalows, a few miles of the main highway from Tucson to Nogales, and about thirty-five miles from each. Our main difficulty was trying to make the management admit that they had tarantulas around there. The boss seemed skeptical about our interest in them.

As the Thurnwalds' train ground to a stop at the Tucson station, it was easy to tell which Pullman car they were in before they even appeared, by the baggage being unloaded onto the platform, since nobody else traveled any more with those old-fashioned, heavy leather cases, canvas-covered and strapped up, or with hatboxes, shooting sticks and hampers. On the princely luggage were scratched-out labels from foreign lands. Here and there a coronet showed, or a faded tag with the letters S.A.R. and the address Palais Grand Ducal. It brought to mind how sensible was Friedrich's stipulation about the baggage room.

Suddenly, there was Friedrich's large Stetson hat waving frantically from the Pullman step as the porter handed the couple to the platform and beamed at his folded bank note. Sophie, tall and spare, her hair just turning pepper-and-salt, in a simple traveling suit and with a well-maided air about her, followed meekly behind her boisterous husband, grinning and carrying his malacca cane. His finely tailored plaid suit, with the little extra outside coat pocket, Edwardian style, and the double-breasted vest clashed oddly with his hat and the large yellow butterflies on his cowboy boots.

"Here we are, at last, my dear Ned. . . . How glad we are to see you! Sophie has been looking out the window watching for you this last hour."

"And Mr. Sheardon!" Sophie added, enthusiastically shaking our hands in the firm grip of her long, bony, well-manicured fingers. "It is too, too marvelous!" she tittered, looking from one to the other of us. "We have had such an interesting trip!" Then she peered around inquisitively, and turned to her husband. "Have you seen the rest of our luggage, Friedrich?"

"The *rest*? . . ." Matt mumbled.

"Oh, I see it's mostly all here, Mr. Sheardon, don't worry. Only, I am watching out for my little *picure* case. . . . Ah, there it is!"

Friedrich suggested, "We can return later for my case of books, which has been checked through in the baggage car. . . . Come, now, let us be off! Where is this shooting brake of yours? I hope we have not brought too much luggage to fit into it."

What with the baggage rack on the roof, we got the load aboard nicely and headed for the Santa Rita Hotel.

"Have you arranged for the permanent headquarters?" Friedrich asked eagerly.

"I should say we have," Matt answered him. "The Border Bungalows, out in the desert."

Sophie giggled toward her husband, "It will be like being back in the Sahara again, Friedrich, only without the Pyramids."

"How far?" Friedrich asked.

"Only thirty-five miles from the doctor here. About halfway to Nogales."

"Not a bit too far. Yet far enough so that he will not be dropping in on me all the time to run up huge bills." Friedrich glanced at his watch. "I telegraphed ahead for an appointment tomorrow morning at eleven. In the meantime, let us drive about the city now and make some notes."

Matt handed him some Chamber of Commerce booklets. "Here, Doctor. We picked up some literature for you."

"Very thoughtful of you, Mr. Sheardon. . . . Sophie, take care of these. We shall read them tonight. Then file them."

"Yes, Friedrich." She stuffed the literature into a satchel, suggesting, "We must find out first what is the meaning of the name Tucson."

"Yes, it is such a strange name. Do you know the answer?" he asked me.

"Frankly, no. But I think it's an old Indian name."

"Sophie, do you hear that?" Friedrich called over his shoulder to her, in the backseat. "Name of Indian derivation. Make a note of it."

"Yes, Friedrich. . . . Have you seen my binoculars?"

"You don't need your binoculars now, Sophie."

"I thought we would be coming to the desert soon."

"I'm sure I put them under the coats in the back," I reassured her. "Shall I stop and get them for you?"

"No, no. Drive on," Friedrich commanded. "She doesn't need her binoculars now. She is always thinking that she needs something. . . . Tell me, do you have the accommodations according to my list of specifications?"

"Yes, but it was a good day's hard work to find them, with all those conditions you imposed. Even without them rooms are scarce in wartime."

"Yes, yes. I apologize for all those specifications. It is my military training. But you got them?"

"Almost to the last specification. The best I could do. Accommodations are limited around here. There's not much choice."

"It is definitely not a hotel or a home, then, like this one we are approaching on the right? Going through these western towns, I have seen so many of this type, with the elaborate planting and the neon signs. Tell me, why are the lights always blue? Is it a law or just a custom?"

"That's not a hotel or a home to live in. It's a funeral home."

"A what?"

"A mortuary. There are very few hotels in the small towns. Mostly tourist courts."

"Ah, I see," he said, eyeing the building, "A hotel for the dead. But they are always there, whenever one looks from the railway carriage window. So there must be many people dying. Yet they say the country is so healthful. It would be interesting to find the explanation."

"The explanation probably is that it's a good business."

"How good, I wonder? . . . " His voice trailed off, then rose again to a sharp, commanding pitch as he called over his shoulder, "Sophie, make a note of that. Everywhere hotels for the dead, but nowhere hotels for the living, and it is a good business."

"Yes, Friedrich." Sophie reached for her little notebook again.

"Your American tourist courts . . . tell me, where are they? So far, I have seen three hotels for the dead, nothing more."

"They are mostly on the edge of the desert."

"Undoubtedly, we'll see some tomorrow, when we'll be on our way to the Border Bungalows and an end to this city life for, I hope, many weeks."

"Many weeks!" Sophie sounded horror-stricken. "You must keep up your regime and come here to town to be examined by the doctor every week. You know what I promised Dr. Schmidt. If he doesn't get a weekly report from out here, I will take away your whiskey."

"Weekly reports . . . bah!" Friedrich grumbled, then added, grudgingly, "Well, perhaps every other week. We shall see."

"If you obey your regime strictly all this year, you know the promise: you may have back your snuff next year."

"Ach! For the third year now, I hear this! These doctors! They prolong my life only to torture me. They take away my bad habits, and I have no good ones to fall back on," he said to me. "And Sophie, she is in league with them. I shall have to punish you," he teased. "I shall cast a spell on your tarantulas and forbid them to come out of their holes."

"His family inherits the power to cast spells," Sophie explained. "But not over animals, only people. Therefore, my tarantulas will laugh at him."

"We shall see, we shall see." Friedrich's voice had the tone of a parent disciplining a child. "Perhaps I shall cast a spell on this Tucson doctor, so he will send his weekly reports by remote control."

19

Thurnwald Maps a Campaign

"WHISKEY TIME AT THIS HEADQUARTERS," Friedrich announced with military precision, "occurs every day except Thursday. It is always at five o'clock, and it lasts for one-half hour, no longer."

"What happens on Thursday?" Matt asked.

"Nothing. Thursday is . . ." The princely voice sank to a mock seriousness. ". . . the Day of Atonement! It is the day when we appreciate whiskey time the most, by not having it. Doctor's orders. But of course, they don't apply to you two."

Matt poured an unmeasured, Montana-styled drink for Friedrich.

"No, no, Mr. Sheardon!" Sophie objected, holding up a little silver measure. "Dr. Schmidt says two of these, one at a time."

Friedrich rolled his eyes dejectedly. "You see how they are torturing me to death? I have been captive for so long in a wheelchair that I have learned to submit like a caged beast. So now I intend to do a little . . . what you call in this country, freewheeling. . . . Well, let us get to more pleasant subjects . . . first, business. I understand that my steers on your ranch in Montana are doing very well. So?"

"Yes, they're making you money, all right."

"How much? Remember, you guaranteed me 5 percent per annum. Are they making more than that?"

"Considerably. I'd say, at least 15 percent at the moment. Ned, here, has seen more of them on the roundup than I have." He turned inquiringly to me.

"Splendid, splendid!" Friedrich reached for a ledger, opened it and, with fountain pen poised, looked at me expectantly. "How about it? Do you agree to 15 percent?"

"The wagon boss and I guessed them even higher, based on their condition as they went into the winter, and the market then looked more like 17 percent."

"Excellent! Superb! Bravo!"

He wrote in the ledger with a slow, deliberate hand:

Cattle Venture No. 1

Nogales, Arizona, U.S.A. — Feb. 7, 1944
Two Thousand (2,000) steers.
Capital earning 17%.

Blotting this with a flourish, he returned the ledger to his leather traveling file, while Matt and I heaved sighs of relief at escaping from the shipping details and losses.

"Of course, a clear 17 percent profit is not definitely in the bag yet," I warned. "That's only as of last fall. We don't ship and wind up the deal until this coming fall."

"Yes, yes, of course. I understand. But in the meantime, there's nothing more I can record about Venture No. 1, is there? . . . And so . . ." He took a block of legal-sized foolscap at his elbow and made a careful heading on it:

Venture No. 2

I noticed that he omitted the word "Cattle."

"Well, gentlemen, what shall it be?" The financial cowboy included us both in a benign gaze of expectancy.

"It's a little early now to count our chickens before they're hatched," Matt suggested. "Of course, there's no reason to believe you *won't* make that much return, but we can't actually rely on it to reinvest in another venture before the shipping money comes in. However, you could borrow on the steers."

"At what rate of interest?"

"Five percent."

Friedrich considered it a moment, then wrote down on the pad:

1. Interest rate, 5% per annum

"Not bad. Yes, I could borrow. Or, I could begin an entirely new venture with new capital. I have just recaptured some more of my funds from Hitler—a comfortable amount. However, that's neither here nor there. Let's get on with the details." He fingered the writing tablet impatiently and drew a firm, straight line under what he had written, then looked up, "Mexico, land of opportunity and romance!" he announced, confidently.

"Of course, in Mexico you run greater risks."

"Yes, yes, Ned. Naturally . . . but then, conversely, there are greater rewards. Remember: nothing ventured, nothing gained. As for me, I wish diversification in many countries for my investments. In these times one in my position never knows in what country he may have to live. So I must make preparations. I have already prepared in Kenya, Mozambique, Haiti, Canada, Portugal, the United States. And now . . . Mexico! We must go to Mexico City and investigate the possibilities for investment there."

"Why Mexico, particularly?" Matt asked. "You know, Ned and I've had a lot of hell down there."

"I know, I know. But your experiences can all be turned to good account. You have connections and powerful friends there."

"They didn't seem to do us much good in getting the La Plata ranch, though," I reminded him.

"But only because the owner died. Without that, you could have made a magnificent killing. Never mind. It's all experience, valuable experience. We can perhaps use it in another venture which might be fruitful. Yes, I feel that, with you help, I can make a killing in Mexico. Perhaps with an oil well or a mine?"

"You know how they expropriated the American oil properties recently? And I can tell you what happened to a silver mine owned by the Harbridge family on the La Plata ranch," I suggested. "It's not very encouraging."

"Well, then, how about real estate in Mexico City? Perhaps a hotel? Couldn't I, with the influence of your friends down there, make a killing somewhere? Because, you see, I have a special reason, a personal reason. . . . I want to make a killing in the land that killed my kinsman, their Emperor Maximilian. What an appropriate revenge that would be! Magnificent!" His eyes glinted with the expectation of both revenge and profit at the same time, and his breath began to come in short puffs.

"Friedrich!" his wife sought to calm him, "You must *not* get so excited. You have forgotten your second drink."

"Here, pour it out." He gave Sophie his empty glass. "I am all right. Let us get back to this business about avenging the Emperor."

"I can think of one complication already," I began. "If you're related to the Hapsburg Dynasty, the less said about it down in Mexico, the better. After all, as history goes, the Querétaro affair wasn't so very long ago."

"Oh," Friedrich laughed, "If that would interfere with business, we could keep it a secret. You know, Sophie and I are incognito."

"It's hard to keep that kind of history a secret. You could, of course, change your name to Smith. Perhaps nobody would suspect."

"My kinship with Maximilian is rather distant, as a matter of fact." He sounded almost as if he were sorry he had mentioned it.

"Personally, Friedrich, I think it's rather nice to be related to an emperor even distantly. Maximilian was a very lovable fellow, and he had a rough deal. He still has faithful secret admirers among the aristocracy in Mexico. I know one of them very well."

"Who is that?"

"Don Francisco de Portal-Mendoza. The man we dealt with on the La Plata ranch matter, as I told you. His grandfather was the Emperor's aide-de-camp and great friend in Mexico and died with him at Querétaro. The family has many imperial mementoes."

"Very interesting. One more motive for our trip to Mexico City." Under the first entry he put down "2," then handed the writing block to me. "Do you mind noting his full name and address here?" He put down "3," then sat back in his chair and beamed at us. "Very well. So far, so good! Next. Do you ever hear from this gentleman, nowadays?"

"Yes. I have quite a correspondence with him. Since our deal for the La Plata fell through, he has been sending us lists of other properties near the border to consider for a breeding ranch."

"Other properties, eh?" Friedrich reached for his pad again and, after "3," wrote "Properties for Consideration."

"Oh, yes," said Matt. "We have the names of several I'm going to look into in the next few weeks."

I had fished out my notebook and was reading from it. "Well, there's a possible forty thousand acres available on the two-million-acre Palomas outfit. Then, there are parts of the Babícora. There's the Tepehuanes: three hundred thousand acres, with *inafectabilidad.* There's General Ortiz's ranch, and the La Zarca, near Torreón and the Soto right here near Nogales. Also . . ."

"Wait, wait!" Friedrich interrupted. "Not so fast!" Under "Properties for Consideration," he was tabulating frantically, "(a) Palomas, 2,000,000 acres, (b) . . . , (c) . . . , (d) . . . ." He handed me the pad. "Would you please fill in the names? And the number of acres in each case, if possible? We shall investigate these thoroughly and make complete notes to form, more or less, the intelligence phase of our Mexican campaign. Then we shall plan our tactics. The first step is to open up correspondence with Portal-Mendoza who is, obviously, the fount of information."

"When it comes to correspondence," Matt announced, "I'll leave that up to you two. I've got cattle brokers waiting for me up and down the border from here to Eagle Pass, and that's a lot of border. There's been a little dip in prices lately, and I want to take advantage of it."

"Do you think it will be a serious recession, likely to affect my profits, Matt?" Friedrich inquired, obviously worried.

"No, Friedrich. Just on these local calves. After all, the livestock market hit a seventeen-year high in January last year, and it's been holding up to that level ever since. We're due for some backtracking."

Friedrich jotted down, "N.B. Livestock prices, 17-year peak, January, 1943," then tore off the sheet, placed it in a manila folder marked, "Prospective Business" and put it in his traveling file. "Now, gentlemen, whiskey time is over. Let us freshen up and go across the border for supper."

20

Of Tarantulas, Napoleonic Pearls, Franz Liszt and Hog Wire

"YOU MAY LEAVE ME NOW for two hours," Sophie instructed Friedrich, her face beaming. "I have several promising burrows in this vicinity, and I feel that luck will be better today. This time I shall capture one surely. I know it!" She looked hopefully about the desert, pointing to stakes with little ribbons fluttering from them, which she had set out on a previous trip.

"Now, I think you have everything, dear: your *picure* case, notebook, binoculars, . . . are you sure you won't need us sooner?" Friedrich asked solicitously, laying her paraphernalia on the sand.

"No, no. I shall not need you. I shall be all right, quite. My *hentzi* do not like to have people around. They are not like our European *Lycosa*. I think this has been our main trouble."

"Dear Sophie, we shall keep watch on you through the glass and not get too far away. If we see you dancing madly, we shall return at once for the victorious moment, but anyway in two hours."

Sophie then opened her kit and from it removed a small packet of broomstraws. "See what I have for my *hentzi* today, each straw differently treated. Surely, they will find one delicious, and their little hands will cling to it irresistibly. When I find which one, I shall draw my *hentzi* out. Then later, I shall go again over the desert with Ned and search for other specimens."

Friedrich and I got into the station wagon and started off.

"Do you mind if I ask a stupid question, Friedrich? What is this *hentzi* business, and why should Sophie be dancing suddenly?"

199

"*Eurypelma hentzi.* That is the desert tarantula which now, since nearly two weeks, Sophie has been trying to catch for our collection. We have the European *Lycosa* tarantula, but she is very anxious to have some specimens of *Eurypelma hentzi.* She will, however," he confided in a stage aside, "not get them, I'm sure, although she is now trying every possible bait on broomstraws, which she pokes down the holes."

"How do you know she won't get them?"

Friedrich chuckled and readjusted his Stetson, which he was beginning to learn how to do. "Of that I make a joke. I tell Sophie that it is because I cast a spell on them. She does not know that actually it is because their hibernating habits are different from those of the *Lycosa,* the one in southern Italy whose bite is supposed to cause tarantism, an uncontrollable habit of dancing."

"I see. Does the local tarantula cause uncontrollable dancing, too?"

"Nonsense! That's just an old Italian superstition."

"Suppose she gets one on the broomstraw, what then?"

"She gives it a *picure* with her hypodermic needle. Then it becomes quiet and harmless, in a state of suspended animation, so she may examine it alive without danger. After that she gives it another *picure,* producing instant, painless death. Then she mounts it for the collection, and we'll ship it to our museum in Kenya Colony along with some of these other specimens." He indicated the back of the car, in which several kinds of cactus bounced about. "Those are fine young specimens of *Cereus giganteus* and *Opuntia vulgaris.*"

"They're just good old giant cactus and prickly pear to me. But I'm trying to learn those Latin names, from the easiest one up, starting with our *Yucca gloriosa* back there. The animal ones too. I get a kick out of working them off on Matt. I say, 'Look, Matt, there goes *Canis latrans* chasing hell out of *Cynomys ludovicianus!* . . . But Matt says they'll always be just a coyote and a prairie dog to him . . . *Felis concolor* too. They have a lot of them down in Mexico. Those big old cats come right into headquarters at the La Plata. We saw their tracks in the courtyard."

"Tell me more about Mexico." Friedrich's gaze searched the desert intently as he spoke. "Do you think there is any chance of ever getting that La Plata ranch?"

"Not any more, with the heirs all battling the Mexican Government, as I hear."

"Or any of these others we've been looking at?"

"The ones we've looked at nearby haven't been any too good. But all this border stuff in Chihuahua and Sonora is difficult. Maybe Matt might bring us some better news from down in Durango. He ought to be back any day now."

"But Durango is more difficult for a foreigner like me, because I understand there's a wartime limit for foreigners, except Americans, restricting us to a certain distance south of the border. And Durango is beyond that limit."

"We'll see what can be done about that in Mexico City. Look! There goes a coral snake."

"Stop, quickly!" Friedrich jumped out and with his cane jabbed about under a clump of sagebrush where we had seen the flashing red, yellow and black. Finally, he clamped the stick down on the bit of squirming color and leaned over it curiously.

"Watch out, Friedrich! That thing's fatal if it strikes you."

But Friedrich was picking it up by its tail. "I think not. My fancy little friend, you would try to fool everyone, wouldn't you? But you're not really *Elaps fulvius* at all, are you? You're the false coral snake! Ned, get out one of those jars."

I set the jar on the running board of the car and stood off at a respectful distance. "Friedrich, . . . are you sure?"

"Yes, yes. This is the false coral snake. Enough like the real one to fool anybody, but harmless, though he will bite, so we'll stay clear of him and put him safely in here." He screwed the top on the jar. "You see . . . the same red, black and yellow bands but in a different order. Our deadly *Elaps fulvius* ends up with the *black* on his nose."

"I wouldn't get close enough to see *what* he had on his nose."

"Now, to go back to Mexico," Friedrich resumed, seating himself, unruffled, in the car again. "I'm beginning to understand what you say about the complications of dealing in that country. So far, in the properties we have seen close to the border here, there's always a drawback. Either it's no railroad for shipping the cattle or no adequate headquarters to live in or else the owners make unreasonable demands. Today," he added darkly, "I have further bad news . . . from the State Department in Washington, with whom, as you know, I am in constant contact through my Washington lawyers."

"I noticed a fat letter from Washington when I went to get your mail this morning."

202

"Now it seems that there may soon be a new restriction, preventing anyone except American citizens from crossing the border into Mexico."

"It would just be a wartime security measure, Friedrich. I'm sure we could get a ruling making an exception in your case."

"I'm not so sure. Why should they make an exception?"

"Because you're engaged in the war effort. You're helping to produce food as a partner of an American corporation in a top priority bracket."

"I was producing food before in Vermont on my farm there. I asked for a much simpler favor: the right to buy a little hog wire. I filled out all sorts of forms. I waited for months. My neighbors got everything they needed and sometimes more. But did I get the permit for hog wire? No. Then in desperation I telegraphed the state ration board. They answered that they had referred the matter to Washington for a thorough processing."

"What happened then? Hog wire?"

"My God, no!" He raised his pudgy hands heavenward. "Guess . . . no, you couldn't guess! I'll tell you. It is true. The answer came at three o'clock in the morning of a blizzard the following winter, when I had no longer any use for the hog wire, because my hogs had all escaped by then. My servant roused me from bed with the news of an urgent call from Washington, which I must answer." He took off his Stetson and fingered its brim agonizingly.

"Yes, Friedrich, no need to get excited at this late date. It's all over now. Tell me calmly what they said about the hog wire."

"Well . . ." He gulped. "They asked if I had applied for a hog wire permit. I said, yes, and where is it? They said, 'Will you spell your name, please?' So I spelled it, and they said, 'Are you the man who was the benefactor of Franz Liszt?' And I said, 'No, that was my grandfather. Franz Liszt died in 1886, and what has he got to do with my hog wire?' . . . 'Well,' they said, 'we have been processing your file, and it seems that Franz Liszt gave your family some of his unpublished music scores. Do you have them?' . . . 'No,' I said, 'do you have my hog wire?' And that, dear Ned, was the last I heard of the matter. The next thing I knew, I was back in bed, with Sophie and the valet bathing my head. . . . That was all the cooperation I got from Washington. . . . Oh, let's get out of this jouncing car for a moment and sun ourselves."

We drove up onto a little butte in the desert and sat on the sand.

"We'll be able to see better from up here, Friedrich. I thought perhaps we might have a look back at Sophie."

"Yes, from here we can spy her, and it is very peaceful. There's really no place like the desert for meditation. That's why Sophie likes it out here. She's very religious, you know."

"I gathered that from our strict church schedule."

Friedrich removed his telescope from its leather case and extended it. "You should be able to see her clearly with this. Perhaps you can see if she's caught any tarantulas."

I laid the powerful telescope across the hood of the car and focused carefully. "She's sitting very still. Looks as if she's reading something."

"That's her prayer book. She prays continuously for the souls of the men in her family. Every single one of them was killed by the Nazis. Seven in all. It is what makes her so quiet. She used to be gay, but now she is always sad."

"Perhaps she has caught some tarantulas, at last, and that will make her happy. She has a white cloth spread out beside her."

"Let me have a look." He scrambled to his feet, removed his large, horn-rimmed spectacles and squinted through the glass. "Aha! I see what you mean. She is sunning her pearls. You know, that is very good for them."

"Pearls? You mean, she has brought pearls out *here*? . . . *Real pearls?*"

"Oh yes, very definitely real."

"But she mustn't keep real pearls around a tourist court. She should leave them with the bank in Nogales."

"This is one thing I meant to discuss with you. Come, let us sit down again. I will explain." Friedrich folded the telescope with an air of resignation. "If you could persuade her to put these pearls in a bank vault, I should be very happy. I have tried and failed. She would not leave them in New York with the other jewels."

"But she doesn't really need them for tarantula hunting in the desert, does she?"

"Need them, no. But it is one reason why she goes to the desert: to sun them. These particular pearls have been locked up too many years in Europe. They are very old—part of some former crown jewels she has inherited—and she is afraid they will die. Pearls are not like other jewels, you know. They are alive. If they stay in vaults too long, they lose their luster. They need sun and must be worn, but only by someone whose skin is chemically suitable, as hers is. So she wears them all the time and suns them every day in the desert. Of course it is a risk, but she insists upon it."

"I suppose they are insured?"

"No. Frankly, I wish to avoid the insurance companies. Their premiums are ruinous. They take advantage of the fact that no one can prove the value of these pearls, because they have never been bought or sold, always inherited, since Napoleonic times."

"In New York there are several good professional appraisers."

"We have tried all and they do not agree. My patience is exhausted with them. We have found out nothing, except that the cost of insurance would be intolerable. We think the best insurance is care and secrecy. So Sophie never wears the pearls openly —always under her clothes, next to her skin. This is why I made so many specifications about the accommodations, and why I asked you to have a gun along."

"I'll try to persuade her about the bank vault. Really, she must see that the Mexican border is not the place to wear uninsured oriental pearls."

Friedrich again trained his telescope in her direction. "She must be ready to leave, as she is stuffing the pearls down the front of her dress. Remember, you're not supposed to know about them yet. But she will tell you in time."

Rolling down the gentle slope I considered this new facet in my life as a cattleman. I had not planned on being a guardian of court jewels. "Suppose we take Sophie to the bank in Nogales this afternoon and get her a safe-deposit box?"

Friedrich held his index finger to his lips. "Hush. Say nothing for the moment. I had words with her on this only last night. She is violently opposed to banks. She will not go near one. It is one of the few remaining little peculiarities of royalty which she still hasn't overcome. She's old-fashioned about having direct commercial contacts or even carrying money. Strictly speaking, you know, royal personages never do."

Sophie's gear was all packed, the pearls were out of sight and she was waving gaily as we drove up.

"Any *hentzi*, dear?"

She made a long, sad face and shook her head, "No. But tomorrow, surely!"

That night the blow came, as we sought to cross the border for supper at their favorite Mexican restaurant.

"Sorry, sir," said the immigration official, who had developed a speaking acquaintance with our trio. "I can't pass foreigners into Mexico any more without reentry permits. Orders from Washington today."

21

A Session with the Pearls

MATT DREW OFF HIS alkali-caked boots, started a bath running and stretched out on the bed. "Chroust, it's good to be out of Durango!" he sighed. "I haven't been able to talk to anybody for a week except through these cattle brokers."

"Do any good?"

"On the cattle front, a little. Contracted another twelve hundred calves that look pretty light and cheap. Just a drop in the bucket, though. I don't know what we're going to do for the rest. This situation's getting really tight."

"And on the rancho grande front?"

"Nothing definite. A lot of talk back and forth, all in Mex, and I don't savvy anything these bastards are talking about. But I have a feeling we don't want to get that far into the country. Too far from the border and too far from a railroad in case of trouble. That was the main thing about the La Plata. It's close to the railroad."

"Yes. The La Plata was just too good to be true."

"How about your end, here at the G.H.Q.?"

"Oh, quiet enough as far as anything practical goes. But busy enough otherwise."

"Otherwise . . . ?"

"Matt, you don't know what I'm up against here. I thought we were getting into the cattle business with Freidrich . . . I mean, I figured it would be *straight* cattle business without all these trimmings."

"Trimmings . . . ?"

"Well, if you can call them that. Actually, most of the things he keeps me busy with are pretty weird—not much connection with the stock business. I mean, things like hunting tarantulas, classifying cactus, editing his thesis for Columbia University, shipping food packages to stranded noblemen in Europe, liaison duty with the State Department and tracing shipments of tapestries from the castles of his grandfather's mistresses in Czechoslovakia. You can't tell me things like that come under the heading of cattle business."

Laughter echoed from the bathtub. "Bitten off more than you can chew, eh? Well, I thought all that letter writing wouldn't lead to any good."

"It isn't only the letter writing. I don't mind that. Matter of fact, he does most of the letter writing himself. Just listen . . ."

Matt turned off the tap for a moment, and we could hear Thurnwald's little typewriter clacking away in furious fits and starts.

"Sounds like he's really going at it with both hands and feet."

"It's like that all morning long. He works on his thesis and his mail. She reads and studies. After lunch he takes a nap, and she patrols to make sure he's not disturbed . . . his health, you know. It's really kind of pathetic. . . . Then in the afternoons we go hunting tarantulas in the desert. Now, I ask you, what's all that got to do with the cattle business?"

"Hell, boy, you never can tell a damn thing about what the cattle business will get you into. You ought to have found that out by now. I've been in all kinds of crazy situations in the last forty years. You just have to figure them out as they come along. That's what makes it fun."

"Well, maybe, out of your forty years' experience you can help me with today's homework. There's a new problem. Something really unique in our line."

"What's that?"

"Seems like we're playing nursemaid to a string of pearls . . . oh, nothing much. Just some hand-me-downs from Napoleon, but that boy didn't go in for costume jewelry. I'm sort of saddled with the responsibility . . . morally, at least. They're not insured, and Sophie wears them all the time, even to these border dives we've been visiting for the benefit of his thesis. Daytime, she wears them tarantula hunting. It's taken me a week to persuade her to put them in the bank vault. Today's the day. But she won't go into a bank. Just hates banks. Royalty stuff, you know. They're not supposed to have any truck with commerce personally, even when they're incognito."

"Now, to me, Ned, that don't make any kind of sense at all. From what I hear and read, royalty nowadays is usually damn glad to get their claws into any kind of business proposition."

"That's the pattern, I know. But here we've just got something off the pattern, that's all."

Matt considered the situation while buttoning himself into a fresh change of linen. Then he asked, "What's the problem about the pearls, anyway?"

"The problem is, she wants me to put them in the bank on my own responsibility, as if they were mine, without mentioning her name. I don't want the responsibility. Suppose something happened to me? And anyway, I'd look like an ass. You know, banks have to ask *some* questions. I'm down here on cattle business with you. They look us up. They know who we are. Can you blame them for asking how in hell I happen to have a string of Napoleonic pearls in my jeans? Sophie won't come into the bank to help explain anything, and she doesn't want their name on the records. She just washes her hands of the whole thing."

Matt saddle-soaped his boots while contemplating an answer, then ventured apologetically, "You know, Ned, the cattle business is getting to be a lot different now from what it was forty years ago. Why, in those days when I was a kid, a fellow often as not worried about how he could even *get* a good pair of jeans. Now, here we are worrying about stuffing Napoleonic pearls into them. You can't tell me that makes any sense."

"It may not make sense, but that's the way the dice are now. My question is what do we do about it?"

"You and I'll go into the bank together and take the safe-deposit box jointly. Then if anything happens to one of us, the other can get the pearls out."

"Suppose something happens to both of us?"

"We'll have a little talk with the bank officials about that. . . . Say, where are these pearls, anyway? I don't think I've ever seen pearls real close."

"She's bringing them in any moment." There was a knock on the door. "Maybe that's her, now."

"It is so nice to see you back again, Matt. We have been missing you. I'm so glad you have come in time for lunch with us. We should be leaving for town pretty soon now, if we're going to the bank first. I suppose Ned has told you about our mission there?" Sophie turned to me. "Here are the pearls. They will miss their daily sun, but perhaps you are right." She placed a bulbous mass on the table, wrapped up in a silk scarf.

It was a heavy little bundle. "How many pearls are there in this necklace, Sophie?"

"I think about a hundred."

"We ought to know exactly. Mind if we take a look?"

"No, no. Not at all. Perhaps it would be better to count them." We laid the necklace out on the table.

Matt took one look at the large oriental gems and turned to Sophie. "I've never seen real pearls before except in pictures. Mind if I pick them up?"

"Of course not."

He ran the long string through his fingers. "Kind of slippery and cold, aren't they? You know, I always thought pearls were much smaller than this."

"They come in different sizes," Sophie smiled.

"The oysters that made these must have been real brutes. Why, they're away bigger than the ones these fancy New York jewelers advertise in the magazines." He took them over to the window and looked more closely. "So that's what happens when a grain of sand tickles an oyster! Say, can you imagine living with things this size inside your shell? Those oysters must have spent all their time scratching." The pearls clicked softly as he placed them back on the scarf. "Funny sound they make, isn't it?" he observed, looking thoughtfully at the pile. "You say these things are alive?"

"Yes. They have to be worn or they get dull. And not everybody can wear them. I am fortunate for pearls. On some people with the wrong skin they turn yellow. Many people ask me to wear their pearls for them, and you can actually see the improvement."

"It is your noble soul from which they draw their luster, Sophie!" Friedrich suggested, coming up behind them.

"Friedrich! . . . He is always joking," she tittered.

"Nonsense, my dear. Everybody knows that. You have power over pearls just as I cast spells over tarantulas. Come, it is time to be starting off for town."

"We have to count the pearls, Friedrich."

Matt lifted his contemplative gaze from the jewels. "Of course, I've never counted pearls," he began, "but I've counted a lot of cattle, and I'd be willing to bet there's more than a hundred pearls in that necklace."

"Do you know, Friedrich?" his wife asked.

"I don't remember. It's one of those continuous strings without a clasp. I always lose my place counting."

"Why don't we count them?" I suggested.

Matt pinched the string between his thumb and forefinger and started counting silently. When he was about half way around, the telephone rang.

I picked it up. "For you, Matt. Some cattle broker in town."

"Here, hold my place." He passed the necklace over to me. "I make it seventy-six to there."

"I might as well go on counting while you're talking." I kept on pinching the pearls progressively and came full circle just as Matt hung up.

"Well, how many do you make it?" Matt asked.

"Did you count the two that you had your fingers on?"

"I think I counted one of them."

"Well, then it's either a hundred and sixty-five or a hundred and sixty-six."

Friedrich poked his wife gently with his malacca cane. "Sophie is not very bright at figures, you see. I am going to send her back to school. I heard her say, about a hundred. So, somebody could take off sixty-odd pearls, and she wouldn't know the difference. Now, if they are worth, say, two thousand dollars apiece, that would make quite a shortage."

Sophie looked up at him miserably and explained, "I thought it was one of the other strings."

A second count showed the total to be one hundred and sixty-six.

"Now that our school work is over, let us be off to this bank business and lunch," Friedrich announced. "I think Sophie would enjoy seeing the inside of a nice, American bank. It would be educational."

Once arrived at the bank, however, Sophie pleaded indisposition and preferred to stay in the car. Friedrich felt he couldn't leave her sitting there alone. So Matt and I, with the pearls stuffed into my blue jeans, went inside.

As we were making out the forms, a young woman secretary came up, smiling, with the message, "Mr. Grimes, our president, would like to see you in his office, if you can spare the time." We followed her in.

"I couldn't help overhearing your name a moment ago, Mr. Sheardon, out in the Safe-Deposit Department. We've been more or less keeping track of your cattle shipments here. You know, we do a lot of livestock financing. Glad to have you and your friend opening relations with us. I suppose that box will come in handy for all your cattle contracts."

Matt didn't answer but looked quizzically at me.

The bank president was a large, red-faced man lolling back in his swivel chair. "We've got a special situation here, Mr. Grimes, and we think you should know about it in case anything happens to both of us," I began. "What we're putting in this box doesn't belong to us." I worked the silk bundle from my jeans pocket and placed it on the president's desk. "Open it."

Mr. Grimes untied the handkerchief carefully and looked in amazement from one to the other of us. "Pearls?"

"You would do us a favor to count them."

Mr. Grimes spread the necklace out on his desk, marked a starting place with his paper knife and counted methodically around, then back again, while his secretary, bug-eyed, peered over his shoulder from a discreet distance. "A hundred and sixty-six," he announced, finally.

"I wish there were some way we could make a note of that, and a few other little facts we'd like to tell you about in confidence."

"Certainly, gentlemen, certainly! . . . Miss Phillips, would you get ready for some dictation, please?"

The dictation over, Mr. Grimes turned to us again. "And where, if I may ask, is Mrs. Thurnwald?"

"Right outside, in the car."

"Won't you invite her in?"

"We can invite her, Mr. Grimes, but she won't come," said Matt.

"Won't come? Why?"

"She hates banks."

"Hates banks?"

"You see . . ." I faltered, "It's sort of a mental thing. I think one caved in on her when she was a child, or something."

Mr. Grimes scratched his head. "I see. Of course. Well, then, I shall go out to her."

The Thurnwalds were reading assiduously when we came out of the bank. Sophie was especially warm in her conversation. "You have such a beautiful bank, Mr. Grimes," she concluded. "Perhaps some day I shall come in to see it. But today I have such a horrible cold . . ." she coughed convincingly, "that I would be afraid of infecting your employees." As we drove off, she smiled back sweetly at him and waved, palm up, in the manner of royalty.

22

Lencho the Hermit

Friedrich looked up from his breakfast coffee across the top of his Tucson paper. "Sophie!" he bellowed to his wife in the next room, "Come here at once!"

She appeared in the doorway clutching a wrapper about her, her hair still in disarray. "Yes, Friedrich! What is it? Are you all right?"

"There is here a most fantastic piece of news. It is something we must investigate. It is completely incredible. Here is an account of a man who just died in Tucson, who lived for nearly sixty years on a garbage pile and who ate absolutely nothing but garbage!"

"Friedrich, it cannot be true in this country where there is so much food. Surely, it is some joke."

"No, it is not a joke. Here . . ." he thrust the paper at her. "Read about Lencho the Hermit."

"It is horrible, *horrible!*" Sophie mumbled, taking the paper and sitting down by the window to peruse it. "The poor man must have been mad. He should have been put away. Imagine how he must have suffered!"

"Apparently, he didn't suffer at all, was quite healthy and perfectly sane. He did it by *choice!* Read on, you'll see."

Between exclamations of horror, Sophie read on, half mumbling aloud, with occasional short gasps. When she put the article down she seemed emotionally exhausted. "As a penance for sin!" she exclaimed. "So, that is it. But still, I do not believe this, even as a penance for sin."

213

"When one thinks of how nothing of any possible use is ever discarded in our countries, it is incredible to read that here in America a man can nourish himself for nearly sixty years just on what other people have thrown away!"

"Not only feed himself, Friedrich. It says here that this wretch also found all his clothes on the garbage pile and built a house there and lived in it! All from what was thrown away."

"Ach, what abundance! Of course, it was not much of a house, just built of packing cases. But apparently, to him, it was like our palace in Vienna. . . . Yes, we must get to the bottom of this. Imagine, what material for my thesis! What footnotes! We shall investigate immediately. Incidentally, isn't it today we go up to Tucson for my doctor's appointment?"

"Yes, Friedrich."

"Well, we shall leave early to allow extra time for the investigation. Ask Ned to telephone ahead to the City Garbage Battalion, or whatever it is called, for a guide to show us where this Lencho lived. Don't let them move anything. Bring the notebooks. Bring plenty of film for the camera. Hurry, hurry. We must get there before it's too late."

Friedrich did not don his ranch togs on the weekly trips to his doctor in Tucson, because the cowboy boots were too hard to pull off in the doctor's office when they wired him up for his electrical treatments. On these occasions he wore his smartly tailored suits, his Peal shoes and a homburg. He exchanged his black horn spectacles for his pince-nez with the black silk ribbon, splashed a dash of cologne on his fine silk handkerchief and took his malacca cane along.

"Couldn't we drive just a little faster?" he urged, as we rolled along through the desert. "There must be no question of our being late for the garbage appointment."

"Ah, yes . . . the garbage!" Sophie sighed expectantly. "What a pity it is that Matt cannot be with us on this expedition."

"He isn't of a very scientific turn of mind," said Friedrich. "He's better off inspecting those cattle at Piedras Negras."

"He's been having a lot of trouble lately," I explained. "The steer market's getting tougher every day. Then, writing a thesis isn't exactly up his alley."

"*Chacun à son goût*," Friedrich observed graciously. "After all, garbage has its unattractive side. But for us, the educational approach alleviates it. By the way, Ned, did you make satisfactory arrangements with the Garbage Battalion?"

"I'm to call them on arrival. The Sanitation Department will have an officer ready to meet us on the city dump. They seemed a little surprised, but they were very polite. I guess they don't have many visitors."

"While Friedrich was in the doctor's office, I called the city scavenger.

"Yes," said the scavenger. "We've got our man Gilhooley waiting for you with all the information. Sure, everybody in this department knew Lencho the Hermit. It's true, all right, no kidding. When do you want to take your friends out there, before lunch, or after? Of course, it ain't very appetizing just before you eat. I'd suggest after."

"Say, two o'clock then."

"Two o'clock, OK. Gilhooley'll meet you and your friends on the dump. Better allow plenty of time to get out there. It's quite a drive. And say, bring a Flit gun for your car. The flies are pretty bad."

"And now," Friedrich announced, emerging from the clinic, "Unlike Lencho the Hermit, we shall proceed to a delectable lunch at the Santa Rita Hotel, before embarking for our next . . . er . . . scholastic appointment!"

The hall porter at the Santa Rita couldn't have helped noticing the distinguished-looking couple coming toward his desk. He smiled obsequiously as Friedrich approached with military bearing. "Anything I can do for you, sir?"

With his cane, Friedrich indicated a map on the wall behind the porter's desk. "Perhaps, . . . my good man, is this a map of your city?"

"Yes, sir. Are you looking for some place in particular . . . ?"

"Very particular." As Friedrich wiped his pince-nez carefully with his large silk handkerchief, the porter got a fleeting glimpse of a tiny coronet and a delicious whiff of cologne.

"Could I help, sir? I have a full list of all the tourist attractions in town."

"This is not exactly a tourist attraction, and it is some miles out of town."

"Well, then, sir, perhaps it's not on that map. I have a larger map." He fumbled in the cabinet under his desk. "May I ask, sir, what . . . ?"

"We . . ." Friedrich indicated us all with his cane, ". . . have an appointment in half an hour at the city dump. Can you tell us how to get there?"

The porter looked from one of us to the other in astonishment. Sophie returned his gaze with a kindly smile.

"The city dump, sir? You mean . . . ?"

"I mean, where they throw the garbage, of course."

Since Gilhooley had been told that he was to receive distinguished foreigners, he was wearing what looked like a freshly laundered and sharply creased set of parade tans. He was waiting at the base of the city dump, which towered behind him. "It's quite a jaunt up this truck incline to the top of the dump, where Lencho lived," he explained. "I thought I'd better come along with you to show you the way."

"Oh, please do, Mr. Gilhooley." Sophie invitingly opened the rear door. "Come in and sit with me. We are all so interested to hear about Lencho the Hermit. Tell me, did you know him personally?"

"Oh, yes indeed, ma'am. We all knew him in the department. You see, he'd been living on this dump so long. Thirty years or more. Long before they made it fancy like it is now with all this modern machinery. Lencho used to tell us how it was when he first came. Pretty rugged, I guess, ma'am . . . If you know what I mean."

"You have certainly made it attractive now, Mr. Gilhooley," Sophie complimented him, as the car topped the incline, and we viewed a bulldozed miniature mountain of refuse, sweltering under the Arizona sun.

"Thank-you, ma'am. We do our best. We haven't got much to work with. But we try to keep it tidy. Burn what we can and use chemicals on the rest. Lencho always liked the system here. Said it was the best dump he ever lived on. And he should know dumps. He'd been living on them another thirty years before he even came here."

"Really, Mr. Gilhooley! How interesting! And could you tell us how he got started?"

"Yes, ma'am, in just a minute. But first, sir . . . before we pass it. If you don't mind stopping, I want to show you where he lived. Right here, sir, out on this little point. He always liked this view of the mountains. You see, over there to the northeast, that's Mount Lemmon. More than nine thousand feet high. Lencho said he never got tired of looking at it in the dawn."

"I can imagine that the sunrise would be beautiful from here," Friedrich conceded. "Tell me, was that his home?" The malacca cane pointed to a shack tacked together from packing cases and derelict leftovers of lumber.

"Yes, that was his . . . camp . . . as he called it. Not much, of course, and there's nothing in there to see now, because the department has taken out the few things he had, thinking some heirs might turn up. We got your message too late. But the city scavenger has Lencho's things, if you want to see them. We have orders to burn the shack."

"You were going to tell us how he got started living on dumps."

"Oh yes, Mr. . . . er . . . Well, anyway. You see, the story goes that when he was real young, in Mexico, his old man died, and he had an argument with his mother about using his old man's gun, and they were squabbling over it when the gun went off and killed her. So he came across the river as a wetback and wandered up and down this side of the border as a homeless kid until he was taken in by an old priest, who adopted him. When he couldn't stand thinking about shooting his mother any more, he confessed to the priest and asked what to do. Somehow, the old priest got it figured out that, for such an awful crime, the only way he could escape hell was by living the rest of his life on the most worthless things in the world: what other men threw away. Lencho figured that meant eating garbage. And after a few years—starting so young and all—his stomach got so that he couldn't eat regular food at all. It made him sick."

"Was he an old man, Mr. Gilhooley?" Sophie asked.

"He was seventy-seven when he died, ma'am. And it'd been about sixty years since he'd eaten anything but garbage. Of course, it wasn't all like what you see here, sir," Gilhooley addressed Friedrich, who had gotten out of the car and was poking around in the dump with his cane. "When the boys in the department caught on, we used to save him out the nicest bits when the trucks went around and put them on top of the load for Lencho."

"Have you made notes on all that?" Friedrich asked his wife, who was scribbling in her little book.

"Yes, Friedrich," she answered, still scribbling. "What finally killed him?" she asked, pencil poised.

"Some welfare people came up here and dragged him down to

the town and fed him fancy foods that they told him had been thrown out. Seems that made him sick . . . stomach got out of order, I guess . . . and he suspected they lied to him, and he ran away, back up here."

"That was just before he died, then?" Friedrich asked.

"Yes, and he'd never had a sick day in his life."

"It would be interesting to know what his last words were."

"Last thing I heard him say was that he hoped he wouldn't go to hell on account of he'd broken his promise in the end and spoiled his record, because he hadn't meant to."

"I wonder where he's buried?" Sophie remarked, putting her notebook away.

"Said he wanted his body to go to the medical school, where it would do some good, to make up for the bad thing he'd done."

When we got back to the Santa Rita, Sophie asked her husband, "Could I be excused for a while? I have some shopping to do."

"Run along, then," he dismissed her.

At a table in the bar, Friedrich continued, "It may be just as well that Sophie is not here at the moment. She hates to have me mention the matter of her extraterritorial rights, but I finally must. I am now at loggerheads with the State Department about our exit and reentry permits."

"They still refuse?"

"Under present circumstances, yes. My lawyers in Washington have done their utmost. As they point out, we are aliens and therefore we come under wartime restrictions as to crossing the border. We cannot cross over into Mexico under present circumstances. So I am going to have Sophie resurrect her extraterritorial rights. She will balk, I know, but she will do it for me. You may depend upon it. She has a kind heart, and she knows that I haven't too long to live, so she will do it."

We had just finished our second round when Sophie returned, carrying a small box of roses. On our way back to the Border Bungalows we stopped at a Catholic church, where she placed the roses on the altar of a shrine, knelt a moment in silent prayer and lighted a candle for the repose of Lencho's soul.

23

Another Undertaking for Don Francisco

It was not long before Friedrich returned to the subject of getting into Mexico, but we found it impossible to connect with the flighty Don Francisco de Portal-Mendoza for preliminary negotiations within what he considered a reasonable time. There were too many unexplained delays to suit Friedrich, and he summed up the situation.

"Writing and telephoning is no good in Mexico. We need action, and fast. Why wait for the State Department's blessing, which I know will come in the end? My plan would be to send you to Mexico City immediately to start negotiations in person. We shall see that it won't be a day too soon. Tell me, Ned, would you be willing to make this trip for us?"

"Certainly. But perhaps, with your diplomatic status, you wouldn't need me to clear the way for you."

Friedrich tapped the table in his baggage room–study and looked up at the ceiling thoughtfully. "Perhaps. But only *perhaps.* For us, in these days, it is always better to have friends strewn along the route ahead expecting us. Especially in Mexico. There's a special situation there, as you pointed out. In Mexico one never knows. But now, to get down to business, how soon could you start?"

"As soon as I can get in touch with Matt. If he doesn't need me . . . immediately."

Before long I was picking my way through the darting and noisy streets of downtown Mexico City to Don Francisco's new head-

219

quarters in a gleaming, modern office building. A bright-eyed little Mexican secretary led me to his walnut-paneled inner sanctum.

Like a spring released, Don Francisco popped out of his red leather swivel chair and clasped me in the two-position back-slapping technique of the Mexican *abrazo.* "I am so glad to see you, Don Edmundo! And so desolated to hear, just now, of all your efforts to reach me while I was away. But it was unavoidable. I was out of town."

"One of those inaccessible silver mines watched over by your mascot, there?" I indicated the little bronze elephant on his desk.

Don Francisco smiled roguishly. "He has been doing better for me lately. You see, the blindford and the rubber bands are removed. No, it was not in connection with silver mining that I was so far out of touch. . . . Rather, I should say, in the interests of diamond mining. That is, Emilia, my Brazilian diamond. You remember my telling you about her on your last visit?"

"She of the serenade with the lions? Indeed, I remember. I have wondered ever since how the expedition turned out."

"Excellently. Later I shall tell you in detail, my dear fellow. But for the moment, since I have delayed your business so long by my absence, let us get it started at once and discuss our lighter topics afterward." Don Francisco indicated a number of telegrams and messages on his desk. "I have only a hint from these as to the exact services needed by your friend, His Serene Highness, Prince Friedrich von Thurnwald."

"You have identified him, then?" I wondered at his having penetrated the incognito.

"My dear fellow, I have in here . . ." Don Francisco tapped his head ". . . reasonably complete statistics concerning every noble and royal house in Europe. It was part of my education. I know my Almanach de Gotha as thoroughly as, I imagine, you know your cattle brands. Naturally, I identified His Serene Highness and Her Royal Highness, his wife, at once. I know exactly who they are. I am . . ." he added gravely, ". . . deeply impressed and concerned. You know, some of my own forebears spring from sovereign families, though mostly the Spanish Bourbons." He dropped his meticulously barbered head in a gesture of homage.

"Yes, I know," I answered reverently and paused, suspecting that my friend was indulging in a moment of silent prayer for heads lopped off in the long ago.

Suddenly chipper again, he looked up and resumed, with an air of grave responsibility, "So now, we are charged with a royal mission. It is a singular honor, is it not? Imagine the distinction implied: of twenty million people in Mexico, it is I, Don Francisco de Portal-Mendoza, upon whose shoulders the royal favor falls like a glorious mantle from the past!" Already he was beating himself on the chest. "Ah, do not worry, my dear Ned, I shall acquit myself honorably in any matter which the family may dictate. What, incidentally, is Their Highnesses' pleasure? Rest assured, Mexico will be at their feet."

"It's not quite as complicated as that, Don Francisco. You see, Dr. and Mrs. Thurnwald have simple tastes. They are traveling incognito and, in fact, get very upset if anyone uses their titles. They insist upon being called simply, 'Dr. and Mrs.' So we'd better forget the Serene Highness and Royal Highness stuff. He is, actually, a cattleman, a partner of the Antler Ranch."

Don Francisco's face fell, but he took it bravely. "Who are we humble aristocracy to gainsay them? Ah, what a true sense of noblesse oblige! Well . . . ?" Resigned to the inevitable, he forced himself to smile. "Let us pursue the matter of their wishes then."

"They plan to visit your country here. Dr. Thurnwald has capital to invest, which he's salvaged from the wreckage of his estates in central Europe. He has invested in several countries. In ours it is cattle and New York real estate. In yours . . . well, he wants to look. He did mention mines."

Don Francisco perked up again at the mention of mines and fondled his little bronze elephant. "In this respect, the influence and services of all my mining organizations will be gratefully laid at the feet of His Serene Highness . . . I mean, Dr. Thurnwald."

"Yes, we must get used to calling him that."

"Except, perhaps, when he is not around," Don Francisco suggested hopefully. "Don't you suppose that then, just between ourselves, it might be permissible? Of course, when he is down here, I should not think of addressing him as anything but Dr. Thurnwald. As to his actually visiting Mexico from the United States, you know, there is a wartime problem for foreigners in both countries. In yours it is the reentry permit. And here in Mexico very special papers are required."

"Yes, we have been through long sessions with Dr. Thurnwald's Washington lawyers about that by mail and telephone for weeks.

I believe that they're claiming extraterritorial status to solve the problem on our side. But whether the Mexican Government will admit them past the usual limit, or give them exit permits . . . well, that's what I've come to see you about."

"It can be done. In Mexico anything can be done with the proper connections. The only thing is, it takes time, my dear Don Edmundo. However, I shall refer this matter to our mutual friend, Don Porfirio Ramirez. Perhaps he can save us some time."

"How is my old friend, Don Porfirio? I had a Christmas card from him. I should have returned one but didn't have the address."

"Don Porfirio is well. He has a new address now. His status is somewhat changed. He has asked several times about you. He lives now with fewer guards in a beautiful new villa in Chapultepec. His life is not so much in constant danger now, since several of his adversaries have . . . er . . . passed on. I shall arrange another meeting with him." Don Francisco picked up his telephone and after a brief conversation announced, "The secretary will let us know tomorrow. And now it is time for lunch."

"Today you will be my guest," I insisted, "though I'll miss the luxury of your club, which I enjoyed so on my last trip. Shall we lunch at, say, Prendes?"

Two days later at ten in the morning we drove up to Ramirez's new home.

"I must say that I feel a little odd about being invited to *breakfast* with Don Porfirio on a business matter."

"Actually, you are entitled to feel honored," Don Francisco explained, "because, you see, this makes it not a business but a personal matter. Don Porfirio is confirming to you the offer of his friendship, which he tendered on your previous visit. It is a very delicate distinction. . . . Well, here we are. Enrique will wait for us by the gate. Is this not a more elegant type of residence?"

Through the handsome wrought-iron gate the view was of a lush lawn with a modern villa against a mountain background.

"It certainly looks a little less like a fortress than the other place. I'll admit now that I was about half scared of that."

"You need have no fear anymore," he laughed, as a smiling *mozo* swung the gate open, and we started up the gentle slope toward the house. "The need for those security measures has passed, I assure you. You see, there's our host now, coming out on the balcony to meet us with only his faithful old *pistolero,* who now poses as a butler."

The great, dusky statesman beamed down at us from his balcony. "Welcome, Señores. I am honored that you have accepted to be the first breakfast guests in my new villa."

"It is such a beautiful location," I ventured.

"And, as you see, Don Edmundo, it is quite different from the other one. More easy of access, don't you think?" He seemed almost to have read my thoughts, as he smiled proudly.

I had practiced up on my Spanish since our first visit and now needed only occasional help from Portal-Mendoza.

The butler-pistolero showed us into the breakfast room deferentially, and Don Francisco seated me on our host's right at the great, round oak table. There was a huge masterpiece of a silver receptacle across the room, bearing the beautifully embossed seal of Mexico and seemingly out of place on the floor.

I couldn't help exclaiming, "What a handsome trophy! A racing cup?"

"Not exactly a cup. But for racing, yes, Señor." The great man smiled. "Only, this was a railroad race toward the end of my term in office. It is all that could be salvaged from my railway car when the Revolutionists dynamited it, as it raced for the border with a special engine. They thought I was aboard, but fortunately, I was not." He shrugged his shoulders and tore into the poached red snapper, as I realized that the object was a cuspidor, and then continued, "It is a handsome but grim reminder of what might have happened . . . ah, those were bad times! Things are much better now." He gazed out the window at his well-kept lawn. "But come, tell me about yourself. You will be here long?"

Portal-Mendoza politely interceded for the more complicated explanation of our present mission, sprinkling his conversation liberally with references from the Almanach de Gotha and concluding, "So you see, Excelencia, how we can help in bringing to Mexico the great honor of this royal visit."

"I see." The big, dark head nodded. "And I feel it safe to say that the Mexican government will look with favor upon such a visit already approved by your State Department. I shall arrange for the necessary papers to confer complete freedom of movement for your friends within Mexico, together with the proper border permits."

"I cannot thank you enough in behalf of my friends and myself, Excelencia. And if there are business dealings, could we assume that you might represent our interests?"

"*A sus ordenes!*" Ramirez answered politely. "And where shall I send the papers?"

"Why not send them to me for forwarding?" Francisco suggested. "I shall be in constant touch with Don Edmundo. And besides, it is traditional that my family act as aides to any branch of the Hapsburg dynasty, however distant."

"Ideal," I agreed, "if it won't cause any delay."

"On the contrary, I can have the papers specially flown to wherever you are."

24

Farewell to the Desert

MATT SHEARDON AND I RETURNED to the Border Bungalows from our respective missions on the same day. Friedrich and Sophie appeared genuinely relieved to see us, as if they had felt temporarily stranded in the desert and, perhaps, somewhat lonely while we were gone.

Friedrich broke out the bourbon, lifted his glass to us and said, "Let us drink to our reunion and proceed to the business of our various ventures." From his traveling file he withdrew the manila folder marked "Prospective Business."

Matt cocked the heels of his dusty boots on a chair and critically surveyed the now somewhat enlarged folder.

"Most of this correspondence you see is with my lawyers in Washington, who at least have been successful in getting our exit and reentry permits. So now we are all set for Mexico!" Friedrich announced, taking from his traveling file the block of legal-sized yellow sheets on which he had listed the ranches suggested as possible purchases by the Mexican Minister of Hacienda and, under his heading "Venture No. 2," printed MEXICO in underlined capitals. Then he wrote a short paragraph recording my trip to Mexico City, with more dates, and added underneath, "Results," and a colon. He divided up the rest of the page into numbered and lettered sections, finally announcing, "There! That will do for a start," and cocked his butterfly boots on the desk.

Matt cast a quizzical glance at the yellow sheet, tipped his little Borsalino slightly to the back of his head and remarked, "Hell,

I haven't done that much writing in all the deals I've ever made."

"Where shall we start?" I asked.

"First with your recent trip, recording its exact progress. Then we'll set down the blueprint for our own joint trip next week. Did you not say that is when the Mexican travel documents will arrive, *definitely?*

"I hate to use the word *definite* in any form regarding anything in Mexico, Friedrich."

"But it must be definite. It must be made definite. Get your friend Portal-Mendoza on the telephone. Find out if it is absolutely definite that he is sending the documents directly here by air courier next week. Impress upon him how my doctors are insisting that I return east for another examination, how I'm staving them off from week to week."

"I've been trying to get him on the telephone all day, Friedrich. As it stands now, his office has promised me a report this evening. It should be coming any time now."

"Very well. We'll leave that in abeyance for the moment and hope that the good news will come soon. Until then let us look ahead toward a glorious, extended and successful business trip in spite of what my doctors say about the altitude. . . . And, by the way, I have just read that the hearts of American race horses from sea level—Florida, for instance—improve and get stronger in the altitude of Mexico City. Why shouldn't mine?" He beamed at us hopefully.

"Friedrich! It is not the same thing. You are not a race horse," Sophie reminded him, waving a warning finger over her little glass of bourbon.

"We shall see, my dear. We shall see. I'm feeling better every day. Perhaps it is that you have no feeling for business opportunities. A woman never thinks clearly along business lines, like a man. A man thinks with his brain. A woman thinks with her uterus. It is an age-old truth." Friedrich then fastened his attention on the yellow sheet for a moment, grasped his pencil and looked up at me expectantly, poised to make further notes.

The subject seemed stymied, however, and I could only raise my glass to it, while Matt removed his little hat and retired to the sofa with a copy of the *Montana Stockman.* "I'm afraid you'll have to count me out on any extended trip to Mexico City," he announced pleasantly. "I've got to get back to the ranch soon to receive all these cattle we're shipping up."

Sophie excused herself and went into the laboratory–baggage room to plan packing her specimens of desert life, when the telephone rang. She picked it up. "For you, Ned," she announced. "Mexico City."

Amid crackling and momentary blank spaces, Don Francisco's secretary came on with a dim, hurried and complicated explanation as to why we had heard nothing from him, for which I could only thank her for calling and shake my head.

Despite my headshaking under Friedrich's critical gaze, he inquired eagerly, hoping against hope, "It is definite, then, about the documents, for next week?"

"His office can't reach him. He left two days ago for a place called Parícutin and hasn't returned yet."

Friedrich knitted his brows a moment. "Now what could that man be doing in Parícutin?"

"I believe he went there for lunch."

"Parícutin is that new volcano. I've just been reading about it in my research on Mexico. One does not go to a volcano for lunch."

The bald logic of the matter stunned me for a moment, as I remembered Francisco's having mentioned planning a romantic, surprise flight there with Emilia, his Brazilian Diamond, to illustrate the fires blazing in his heart for her. Perhaps, even at that moment, they might be clutching each other as the plane's engine conked out over the crater. But there was no use explaining the situation to Friedrich, bent as he was on the business angles. "He was going to do some exploring of real estate possibilities, I think, Friedrich."

"A volcano is not a real estate possibility. Not for me. I have enough hell as it is. Now, let us go on with our plans." He turned his attention to the sheet again . . . "Preparations for departure from Border Bungalows . . . Number one: Persuade Dr. Schmidt to extend our western visit by two weeks. Number two: Mexican travel documents to be received by . . . date still in abeyance. Number three: Retrieve pearls from bank. Number . . ."

Sophie called from the other room, "May I keep them out this time and wear them, Friedrich? Oh, I do hope they haven't started to die again! When can I get them back?"

"You may go for them tomorrow, if you wish, dear. We shall be leaving for Mexico City very soon, I hope."

For a moment Sophie was silent, standing in the doorway,

smiling sweetly at us. "I couldn't go to the bank tomorrow. It would be most inconvenient. But I should just adore to have my pearls back. Perhaps . . . perhaps Ned would be so kind . . ."

"Of course, Sophie, I'll get your pearls for you."

Sophie looked relieved at having escaped from the bank chore. "You are so nice," she smiled gratefully. "Because, you see, my *hentzi* . . . I still have not caught one, but I probably shall tomorrow with my new bait. Perhaps it will be my last chance, if we are leaving so soon."

"We might even be leaving before my next doctor's appointment in Tucson, I hope."

"Oh, no, Friedrich! Dr. Schmidt would not allow that. And I had been hoping that we could entertain the friends of Lencho in the Tucson garbage department."

Matt looked over the top of his *Montana Stockman* for an instant, frowned quizzically, then returned to his reading.

"You know, I still can't savvy this talk about the garbage deal," he said, as we were driving down to Nogales next morning, "even after what you told me last night. Are we in the garbage business too?"

"I've saved the newspaper article for you. They got a big kick out of the whole expedition. Friedrich says it's just the type of material he needs for his thesis."

"Didn't you tell me once you're *sure* there isn't a wire down somewhere? . . . Well, I suppose, as he said to you in French that time, each one to his own taste. If he likes it, he can have it. But I never heard of anyone studying garbage to get into college, or whatever he's trying to do."

"He just wants an American University degree to go with his others from London and Vienna. He sort of collects them, and in this particular thesis he's been looking for a subject that's kind of different."

"He's got it, all right. But what can he write about a bunch of garbage collectors?"

"Of course, only a small part of it's about that angle."

"I'd say even that's too much. I just can't savvy how folks like them, away up there on the ladder, can get such a kick out of setting up drinks for a bunch of garbage collectors. And did you hear what Sophie said to Friedrich: she feels *so close* to them?"

A royal princess, dripping with these pearls like we're going for now, and God knows what other loot they've got holed up back there in New York . . . I don't get it. Do you?"

"Friedrich has a French quotation that pretty well covers it. In English it means that sometimes the extremes meet."

"I guess they do at that. . . . Well, anyway, here we go. Time to switch over from garbage to pearls. . . . There's a good parking place right in front of the bank."

Returning to the Border Bungalows, we found Friedrich despondent over the time lost while we waited for the Mexican papers, which had given Dr. Schmidt the opportunity to write him a stern letter, reminding him that the span of his western vacation was already exceeded. He thumped out the days of waiting on his large wall calendar. "Ten days since we should have received our papers! Now, can you tell me, gentlemen, what sort of fiddle-faddle is this?"

"Down there they call it mañana." I repeated the old theme. "You just can't get away from it in Mexico."

"I thought your friend, Portal-Mendoza was so efficient. And that other one . . . what's-his-name . . . he of the dynamited spittoon . . . what could have happened to him? Assassinated, perhaps?"

"There's been a delay in issuing the papers because of wartime precautions and certain security measures they've got to arrange for you and Sophie, and there have been three feast days, when everything closes down. The papers will come soon, you'll see. Have patience."

"Patience . . . bah!" Friedrich growled. Let us get Portal-Mendoza's office on the wire again. Kick up a hell of a row . . . tell him . . ."

"It won't do any good, Friedrich. They still can't get in touch with him. Ever since his return from Parícutin, he's been out of the office in a highly nervous state. Overwork, I suppose."

"There's something fishy about this Parícutin trip! It doesn't sound businesslike to me. And to think that we've wasted a whole week sitting here, doing nothing, with the expiration date of our reentry permits getting closer all the time! And now Dr. Schmidt had ordered us to leave."

"Cheer up, Friedrich! It hasn't been wasted for me," Sophie

tried to console him, victoriously holding up a jar labeled *Eury-pelma hentzi*. Every day was worthwhile to me just to get this one specimen."

"I know, I know, my dear. But this is no time for spiders. I have given up these accommodations, and now we cannot get them back, so our whole plan is ruined. All because of this mysterious delay, when we should have had our traveling papers ten days ago. One cannot make plans like this from day to day, with all this wartime rationing. Now I have no more excuses for the doctor, and we must leave tomorrow."

"At least, you have finished your thesis, Friedrich. You should go back anyway to present it to the University."

"Ah, yes! That is so," he granted, cooling off a little and patting the bundle of script, which he then buried in one of his suitcases. "I guess we can still go to Mexico later, now that all the details are arranged for. After all, the cause is not a hopeless loss. But there is so little time." He pulled the strap taut on the suitcase, puffing as he sought to buckle it.

"Friedrich, you may *not* do that! . . . Your heart!" Sophie came over to relieve his efforts with a masterful jerk.

Next morning, as we wound up our business at the Bungalows' office, the manager handed Friedrich a large, red-white-and-green–bordered envelope. "For you, Doctor. Just arrived. Special Delivery. Would you mind signing here?"

As we pulled away for Tucson, the heart doctor and the train for New York, Friedrich tore it open feverishly. "A fine time to be getting our traveling permits for Mexico!" he fumed.

Sophie gazed at the jar in her hand. "I didn't have room for you in the case, little *hentzi*," she mused. "You shall sit in my lap."

They stood on the observation platform as the train pulled out, Friedrich waving his nutria Stetson, Sophie triumphantly clutching her preserved tarantula in one hand, while with the other she waved to us, palm up.

25

Fred Lauby Evaluates
Our Desert Activities

IT WAS THE WEEK after a rainy Easter when I got back to my cabin, where I found old Fred rocking contentedly in his "paradise chair." This was an old oaken swivel chair which tilted back and forward against a coil spring with adjustable tension. It was mounted on a crossbeam base to which he had fitted casters for easy mobility.

"I didn't expect to see you till the roads got better," he greeted me. "The mud's never been as bad as this week. Even the mail stage only got through once." To all Tongue River old-timers, the mail truck was doggedly referred to as the *stage*.

The place was littered with receptacles of all kinds filled with rainwater: buckets, jugs, dishpans, cooking utensils. Outside under the eaves were more receptacles being filled by trickles from the shed roof and a large barrel into which Fred would empty them periodically. He saw me taking in the situation.

"Ain't it just wonderful, boy," he beamed. "Never caught so much water since we built the outfit. I figure we've got damn near a hundred gallons."

"Well, I guess I'll take a bath then. How's the pumping system working?"

"Ain't working at all. Engine's busted down there." He nodded toward the ranch house. "I guess the reservoir's empty, except for a little rainwater. Damned if I know. Haven't had time to look. Not enough water for a bath, anyway."

I set up my typewriter and began to tackle the accumulation of mail. Fred indicated the pile of letters on the kitchen table and observed dryly, "Damnedest mess of stuff I ever saw. Looks like some of it's from that financial cowboy of yours. Say, how's he doing anyway?"

"Oh, he's doing all right. Had a big time down in the desert. They're back in New York now."

"How in hell can anybody have a big time in the desert? Ain't nothin' there but rattlesnakes."

"It's the climate. Doctor's orders. Then we drove around, up to Tucson and down to Nogales, and had some good meals across the border, before the wartime regulations closed it to foreigners. He saw Matt shipping some cattle out of Nogales and got a kick out of that. Then he keeps reading and studying and writing a thesis and working on his mail, which follows him around. He's busy all the time."

"What does his wife do in the desert?"

"She looks after him generally to see that he doesn't overexert. Then, they're both naturalists, and she helps him collect and mount specimens of plants and animals for their private museum in Europe."

"Rattlesnakes, too?"

"No, they didn't seem interested in rattlers. Too common. All museums have rattlers. Her particular hobby is tarantulas, but a special kind they don't have over there."

"Tarantulas? God, man, them damn things is sudden death! I hope none of 'em broke loose and got into your baggage. You'd better unpack it outside."

"Nonsense. She only got one, and that's in a jar. It was the wrong season for hunting tarantulas."

"Thank God for that. It sounds dumb as hell to me, hunting tarantulas in the wrong season."

"Well, they enjoy the outdoors. Sophie likes to sun herself and her pearls. When the tarantulas aren't biting, she spreads her pearls out on the sand, or hangs them up on cactus plants, and suns herself too, and reads, while the pearls get a kind of recharge from the sun. It sort of makes them look better."

"What . . . she took pearls down there and hung them up on cactus plants and thought they'd get recharged like automobile batteries? That just don't make no sense to me at all. Pussonally, I think they was wasting their time in the desert. And you, fighting that blizzard to get down there to help them and damn near freezing to death on the way. I can't savvy what all that's got to do with the cattle business. Seems like puttin' out a lot of good money for nothing. Say, who pays for all this tarantula hunting and book writing and all the rest? And how do you know you didn't get gypped? How about the bookkeeping?"

"Very simple. We got up a little pot and just kept sweetening it equally. I paid all our expenses out of it. When it was all over, we split the balance in the kitty three ways. No bookkeeping at all. The doctor paid me a hundred dollars a week for use of the car. Whatever it cost doesn't matter. It all comes out of the cattle anyway, and they're doing fine."

"I'm sure glad it turned out like this, after the bad start those steers got. You had good grass last summer. Then the winter was fairly easy up on the reservation, and Matt had plenty of hay. Now we're getting lots of rain again, so the grass is just about guaranteed for this year too. And the market's been rising all the time. Ideal, boy, just ideal."

"If this keeps up for another year, the doctor's likely to double his money. How can I get gypped? Hell, I've got a contract with him to look after his cattle investment for one quarter of his profit, instead of a salary. And nothing said about losses. If you don't put up anything, and don't take any losses, it's like having a twenty-five-thousand-dollar investment working for you for nothing, and earning about 30 percent. How can I get gypped? Isn't that worth spending a month or so out in the desert with pearls, tarantulas and college theses, and spending one night sleeping out on the way?"

Old Fred went back to his paradise chair and settled down with the *Pathfinder*, shaking his head and mumbling, "It's the goddamndest, craziest way to make money in the cattle business I ever heard of: running around in the desert with a couple of furriners, playing with tarantulas and pearls, and writing books and letters, without a cow or calf mixed up in it anywhere."

"It does seem kind of funny in a way, but there's one thing in favor of it: it's working. And anyway, they had fun, and it did Friedrich's health a lot of good. Now he's hoping his doctor might allow him to come out here this summer or fall. He's really looking forward to it and to investing more in the livestock business. He thinks it's a cinch."

"He should know how those steers of his started out," Fred sneered. "Did you ever tell him?"

"Hell no. What was the use? We just let him stay happy. The

poor fellow hasn't got much longer to live. He's happy in the business. Thinks the cattleman's yield is enormous, which it is, considering most other businesses back there and in Europe."

"Yes, but them fellers don't figure in the odds. It burns me up to hear some people talk this 'cattle baron' stuff, like it was the easiest life in the world. Well, they should know more about it. Most don't have no idea of the risks you fellers take. And the hell with them Indian leases and the rustling and the winters. They ought to ride with the wagon a while and polish saddle leather with their rumps for eighteen hours a day, like the old-timers used to do, or ride a caboose to Chicago with the beef. That'd learn them. The cowman deserves a big reward. He never knows what's coming next, and the very best of them has gone bust through no fault of their own."

Fred's obsession with economies had always suggested to me a certain worry that, some day, I might not be able to support both of us, so that he would find himself back on his own—old, jobless and poor. He was past the age of learning a new trade in the modern, motorized world, and his old trades of log building and horseshoeing were on the decline. Now, gazing around out the windows at his various receptacles gathering water from the dripping eaves, he seemed to be delving into the possibilities of a darker future.

"You know," he began, "I've often thought that, if you ever went bust out here, you might go back to that civilized stuff. I come from back there too, but I never could get anything very good from it. No lasting satisfaction, anyway. I tried going back there to the artificial life a couple of times, but it didn't work. It just won't for some, though others get by or think they do. Pussonally, I've always been a believer in the land. If you stick by the land, it'll stick by you. Of course, maybe it ain't so fancy a kind of life when things goes bad. But it's got a kind of respectable something to it that don't come from all them fancy trappings."

He was getting morose. There was one way to jolt him out of it. "How about going down to the ranch house to see if we can get the pump running?"

26

Mexico to Montana
in a Caboose

THE HUNT FOR REPLACEMENT steer calves never ended. After I had passed a few days of cabin life with old Fred, Matt sent his light plane to fetch me. It landed on the scraped-off sagebrush flat above the cabin, taxied down the hill and came to rest right at my yard gate. Matt was a man of few words, particularly written ones. No time to write anyway, and there was no telephone.

The pilot cut the switch and got out. It was Matt's son, Carl, who lived in Billings and sometimes had a ranch plane there. "Dad phoned last night and told me to come down here and pick you up. He wants you at the ranch right away."

Carl was a small, tanned, dark-haired man, not so outgoing as his father and not much given to conversation. There was a certain sadness about him, and for long periods he was not seen at the ranch at all, although he was building a house there for himself and his family. It could be some form of the ubiquitous in-law syndrome, I thought. But I never inquired about it.

"Right away?"

Carl nodded. "He's made a deal for some steer calves down on the border, and you're leaving in the morning. He says to pack light. You'll have to ride a caboose back. Sorry, but we're really shorthanded. Can't spare a paid hand for shipping. He thought you might help us out."

The words "pack light" brought back memories of that most uncomfortable of all modes of transportation, the caboose on a freight train. It meant, in fact, no baggage other than a small sack for one extra set of dry clothes, a toothbrush and razor: nothing more than could be carried on horseback and much less equipment than was allowable on a roundup wagon. So I gathered together the bare essentials in a little blue canvas bag and also packed a small case of extras for the trip down.

Carl was a whiz at handling a small plane and showed his typically western spirit of independence, inherited from his father, in cranking it singlehanded. Standing on the left side of the cockpit behind the propeller, where he could reach the throttle with his right hand and one propeller blade with his left, he snapped the blade down sharply. Still hot, the engine started right up, and he quickly throttled it back to where the plane remained stationary while he casually eased into the cockpit, without anyone to hold on the brakes. Soon we were airborne and heading southwest for the Crow Reservation. In half an hour we could see the Little Big Horn glimmering in the distance, and within the hour we had buzzed the ranch office and set down at the Antler "airport."

This was a much better-tended former sagebrush flat than mine. It was high over the ranch headquarters, with a three-plane metal hangar, into which we rolled our little Cub beside an almost identical one, the third space being for a "stagger-wing" Beechcraft used for long business trips and usually kept in Billings.

As we rolled the hangar doors shut, a pickup came honking up to us, driven by someone in the office we had buzzed according to the standard signal.

The supper bell was still an hour off, so Matt, Carl and I congregated in Matt's house by the gurgling irrigation flume, where Matt broke out some bourbon, and I got caught up on the tight labor situation at the ranch.

"All of our younger men have volunteered," Matt explained proudly if a little ruefully. "I'm too old, and you two are exempt as family men with young children, and I got a deferment for Jerry Flynn because we've got to have a wagon boss. Most of the cowpunchers we've got are retired old-timers who've agreed to saddle up again to help the war effort. We're going to have a mighty slim skeleton crew on roundup this year. We're even planning on using some of the ranch women who can ride. That'll be a tricky new angle."

We had early breakfast, after which Matt made a hurried telephone call, and we were on the gravel road to Wyola by six o'clock.

Jerry Flynn was in the back seat, also with his little caboose sack, and a small suitcase for the trip south. It was a drizzling April morning, cold enough to use the car heater. We were full of food, still a little sleepy, and conversation lagged. Matt was never one to give out much unnecessary information, Jerry was a traditional listener and I had learned to wait for things to happen before asking any questions. It was a rather typical, silent Antler operation. I wasn't even sure of exactly where we were going and was surprised when, reaching the main highway at Wyola, Matt turned north toward Billings instead of south toward Sheridan.

He volunteered the explanation, "We're going up the road a ways to see old Cousin Chet."

I had never even heard of old Cousin Chet and said so, wondering why, if we were in such a hurry to go south, we should suddenly turn north on an unscheduled visit to Cousin Chet. But one never really knew too much about Matt's plans ahead of time. It was the same on roundup. I remember instances when we would start off on morning circle at four o'clock, some fifteen strong, and half of us would not know where we were going. Matt would ride ahead with Jerry, neither apparently talking, and then perhaps an hour later up on some divide, Jerry would call us up alongside, two by two, and dispatch us with some such orders as, "Gather everything you can find along those two ridges and tip it off down such-and-such a creek, until you meet the wagon coming up." The main thing was to get going and not ask questions, whether you were employee, ranch guest or part owner.

"Old Chet's quite a character," Matt went on almost apologetically. "He's kind of a distant cousin, and somehow he got separated from the family and never got into the stock business. Salt of the earth, but he doesn't know much and he's never traveled anywhere farther than Billings or Sheridan. Always had to work hard, so he never had much time for schooling or reading on his own. Works for the highway department, section boss or something. His wife runs a little chicken farm up here. I just talked to him on the phone. Maybe he'll come along and help us with the shipping. He's got some time off."

Suddenly we turned off to the right, across a cattle guard and down a muddy lane to Chet's house. He was taking it easy, just finishing breakfast, a spare, bony graying man of about sixty, wearing a baggy suit.

We sat around and had several cups of coffee, during the consumption of which Matt outlined our proposed trip in a way that appealed to Chet's pent-up urge to travel. Matt cast a hint here and there, suggesting scenes that would "do you good, Chet," far beyond the banks of the Little Horn, even down to the banks of the Río Grande.

"That means big river, don't it?" Chet guessed. "I never seen a real big river, except the Yellowstone a few times. I sure like to see moving water. It kind of does something to you, even an irrigation ditch. What I'd really like to see, though, is an ocean. They say them big waves, high as a house, comes rollin' in on the beach, making such a racket it'd half scare you to death," he concluded, showing some trace of imagination although getting rather far away from the subject at hand.

His neat, plump little wife, apron over polka-dot, mail-order dress, was nursing the large pot of coffee, set back on the coal stove. She smiled at the very thought of an ocean and poured us all another cup.

But there was no changing the subject with Matt. "Chet," he said, with an engaging smile, leaning over the table and pausing slightly to let his cousin's imagination fire up a little, "do you *really* want to see an ocean?"

"Sure do, Matt . . . I sure do. But don't see how I'll ever git to one. Especially, on a trip like this."

"You never know," Matt said, truthfully enough. "I'll tell you what, Chet. If you'll come on this trip with us and help us ship these steer calves back up here, I'll guarantee to take you to see an ocean."

Even when one considered Matt's enviable record for keeping contracts, it did look as if he had bitten off more than he could chew this time. But his voice was as confident and firm as if he were betting on a poker hand.

"Aw, hell, Matt, there ain't no oceans south of here that I know of. You gotta go east or west."

"I'm telling you," Matt challenged. "Want to bet?"

"Nothin' much to bet with, Matt. You know that. I ain't got no big outfit like you, and I don't know much about them. Don't know nothing about shipping cattle either. Hardly ever been on a railroad, except the Burlington here far as Sheridan or Billings."

"That's easy. You got good health and common sense, and that's all it takes. My doctor won't let me ship on account of my diabetes. I got to eat regularly and take my shots on time."

"I like to eat regular too. Can't you eat regular when you're shippin'?"

"Not always. But look at it this way. Men from all over this country have been shipping with their cattle for half a century, and there's never been one died of hunger from it. You can come up to the ranch afterward, and we'll give you a big feed."

"I wanna get my garden going, and I always like to help the wife look after her chickens when I get some time off."

"I'm sending somebody over from the ranch to take care of all that."

"Go on, Chet," his wife urged from the background. "Go see the ocean."

"All right, boys, I'll help you out. When do we start?"

"We've already started. Grab your things and let's keep going."

Chet was a silent traveler and continued rather dazed, only slowly awakening to the fact that he was on his way to see the ocean, as we bore south to Denver, Amarillo and Fort Worth, where Matt had a meeting with some cattle brokers. There, looking at the wall map in a gasoline station, Chet openly despaired of seeing the ocean, until Matt announced that we had a little spare time, and that he wanted to see a friend in Corpus Christi, which was on the ocean and "only about two days farther down the road."

At the first glint of sun on sea, Matt declared triumphantly, "Look, Chet, there's the ocean."

"What ocean . . . where?"

"That shiny spot straight ahead."

"Don't look like much to me," Chet complained. "Where's the waves?"

"Too far away yet. But that's part of the Gulf of Mexico, which is part of the Atlantic Ocean."

As we drew closer, Chet was riding on the edge of the seat, all attention. "God, fellers, why didn't you tell me about this?"

"Tell you about what?"

"That it's so goddam *big!* You never told me how *big* it is."

"Oh, that's only a small part of one bay that we're seeing. It's much bigger than that."

"I reckon so. But I still don't see no waves."

"Well, I couldn't guarantee any waves. That depends on the wind. Maybe a storm'll blow up, or something, when we get there."

No storm did. The weather was hot, still and miserably muggy. Fog blew in, so we couldn't see whether there were any waves or not. But Matt had kept his promise. He had shown Chet the ocean, or part of it. Now it was Chet's turn to perform.

We returned north to Eagle Pass, Texas, on the border, where Matt contracted for some two thousand head of steers, which were being gathered and loaded in three groups at different points along the line. The first shipment of twenty-four carloads could be scheduled to pass through Del Rio the following evening, and the others of about fifteen carloads each were scheduled for a day or so later. It remained to be decided how these shipments had best be routed from there to Wyola, Montana.

There were three main routes. One was the shorter, mountainous route via Sante Fe and up Raton Pass in the Sangre de Cristo range. Although somewhat shorter in miles, it would be, perhaps, longer in hours because of slow going through the mountains, and there would also be long stretches of mountain freight rates of one and a half times normal rates.

The second would be an eastern route through Kansas, mostly all low country, which would save mountain freight rates, time and, consequently, feed bills. But much of Kansas was having very heavy rain just then, and both the Kansas and Arkansas rivers were threatened with flood conditions, which could complicate matters enormously and threaten the cattle.

Then there was an intermediate route, which shared some of the risks and advantages of the other two.

Matt decided to try them all, so as to average out the risks and expenses, and he put choice of routes up to us three. Chet was given first choice but passed the buck in bewilderment. Jerry Flynn scratched his head a while and said he'd rather take a chance on the flat route through Kansas. I voted for the mountain route, on the theory that a little extra money spent on freight and the safety of cattle that were increasingly harder to come by, would be a good investment.

This solved Chet's problem nicely, and he was dealt fifteen carloads to take up the intermediate route. Matt stressed that it would perhaps be the simplest; that there should be no complications, and that he would see Chet off properly, aboard the right caboose in the freight yards, and give him all necessary instructions and money.

So we broke up, I being the first to leave. We kept in touch with the Del Rio yardmaster by telephone as to the progress of this freight train. It had a late start from a place called Pavo, Texas, and seemed to be crawling. Eventually, the yardmaster reported that it had picked up a great many other cars besides our twenty-four, including some "hot stuff" (wartime railroad jargon for ammunition). The engineer didn't want to stop for one man to get on but said that, in view of the cattle, he would slow down enough for me to swing aboard the caboose if I were fairly spry and waiting at a certain grade crossing at 9:45 P.M., where he would lean out of the engine cab and holler at us.

We carefully checked on the grade crossing and arrived there early. After some time, we saw the headlight approaching and could hear the slow, determined chuffing. The whistle shrieked its long-drawn-out Morse code "Q" warning for the crossing. We waved flashlights wildly. The chuffing slowed down a little, as if the engineer were assuring us that he was not going to run away from us . . . that the deal was on. The great beam of light gleamed with incredible birghtness as it neared us.

"Don't stare at it," Matt warned. "You won't see too well to run."

As the great, double expansion engine thundered by, it seemed to be moving too fast for a man to jump aboard; but there was the engineer, waving to us understandingly and shouting, "OK. . . . Take it easy!" I looked toward the end of the train and for a while could not even see the caboose, while cars rattled and squeaked by interminably, including our twenty-four cars of steers, which were emitting an occasional bawl. I wondered which cars carried the "hot stuff," but there was no telling. Then in the dim distance I could see the faintly waving lantern of the freight conductor, and a red taillight on the caboose. The speed seemed much more reasonable now: about like a man jogging briskly. I looked ahead at where I would have to run: a rocky roadbed with ties to stumble over, and outside that, a narrow cinder strip. In the dark and with high heeled boots, that could be tricky. I played my flashlight beam along it and clutched my sack under my right arm.

"Don't wait too long and then try to catch up with it. Start plenty ahead of time and let it gradually catch up with you," Matt advised. "And don't try to jump aboard holding your sack. Throw it up on the platform first, so you have a free hand. Grab both the safety rails before you jump. Start running as the front end of the caboose comes by . . . Start now."

I found that, by then, I could easily keep up with the caboose, so I stuffed the small flashlight in my hip pocket—the conductor was lighting my path ahead with a more powerful one, anyway—and let the caboose slowly overtake me until its steps were alongside and I could toss my sack aboard. The conductor caught my sack, and I caught both the grab rails, with a wonderful feeling of safety, for it was then easy to jump onto the lower step and climb aboard.

The flashlights at the grade crossing were waving good-bye madly, and I waved back at them with mine. The conductor gave his prescribed two short jerks on the signal cord overhead. The engineer acknowledged with two short toots of his whistle. The soft puffs of the engine became louder and louder, ever closer together; there was a slight jerk as the couplings strained, and we began slowly picking up speed.

It was an old Texas Pacific caboose, smelling of the kerosene lamps firmly clamped into wall brackets, with odor variations of coal gas from a potbellied stove along one wall. Through the isinglass of the stove, a ruby glow from the coals was a welcome note in the otherwise ghastly interior. Atop the stove was a large, black coffeepot, which obviously could not be depended upon to stay there without help and so was slung from the roof by a length of toilet chain just long enough to keep it from crashing to the floor in a sudden jerk; and jerks are an established feature of caboose life.

The furnishings of a caboose are standard. Two boxlike seats flank the stove against one wall. The lids are hinged, and inside is the coal bin. Along the other wall are two more such seats, containing tools, signal flags, lanterns, kerosene cans, flares, torpedoes and other necessities. The torpedoes are little explosive devices which can be attached to the rails by bending flaps, to be exploded by a following train as a warning device. The wall space not occupied by these seats is taken up by the freight conductor's "office." This consists of a boxlike arrangement of cubbyholes affixed to the wall, with a cover hinged at the bottom to be let down to a horizontal position and thus serve as the conductor's desk. The cubbyholes are always stuffed with papers, presumably waybills for the freight aboard, for which the conductor is responsible. The chair, or stool, on which he sits for his office work is the only furniture aboard.

"Good hop," said the conductor, as I climbed aboard. "Come on in and have a cup of coffee." This was strictly southern hospitality, as there is usually an undeclared threat of war between freight conductors and ranchmen riding with their livestock. The railroad would much rather have livestock shippers sign a certain form of release (allowing the railroad to handle the stock as they see fit, with considerable elasticity of judgment) than be spied upon by a ranch representative who knows how often livestock should be unloaded, rested, fed and watered to keep within the laws of cruelty to animals, and who can threaten to invoke the law if his suggestions are not carried out, or actually invoke it to collect heavy damages in case of loss. Ranches are good freight customers, but their carloads of cattle and sheep have to be pampered, whereas carloads of coal or sugar beets don't, and won't talk back in case of trouble. So the ranch representative riding in the caboose is often a thorn in the freight conductor's side, on the verge of being a *persona non grata*.

Some freight conductors make clear their stance on this point right from the start. This one didn't. He was on the gentle side and had a polite, Texas drawl. "You with them twenty-four cars of steers, mister?" he asked.

"I am."

He poked around in his cubbyholes and pulled out some papers. "Antler Ranch. Billed through to Wyola, Montana. Gee, you've got a long way to go, mister. Have you shipped on this road before?"

"No, only on the Burlington to Omaha."

"Got your car numbers?"

I should have had them but didn't, and when I said so, he obligingly shuffled through his waybills, murmuring, "We'll soon fix that up." Then he handed me a list of the car numbers.

"How far up are they?"

"Quite a ways. But we'll be making a couple of long stops between here and El Paso, one to pick up water and another to let an express by. So you'll have plenty of time to see them. They looked pretty good when we loaded them on at Pavo. Been resting up for two days."

There is no such thing as a good sleep on a caboose. Sometimes there will be small, thin, hard and worn cushions on the benches. Your traveling sack is your pillow. For meals you are supposed to start with a full stomach, then depend on skimpy eateries near the railroad's freight yards and carry sandwiches. Only coffee and a few jugs of water are carried aboard. There is no latrine. For this, one substitutes the rear platform, taking advantage of a stop or executing a difficult gymnastic maneuver from the side steps.

One does, however, get a few hours' fitful rest despite the jarring ride, to which he becomes so accustomed that, when the train stops, he wakes up.

When I woke up, the conductor was calling to me from the opposite bench, where he was stretched out. "We'll be here about forty minutes, if you want to run up and see your stock."

The skies were clear, the stars bright and I had my flashlight to read the car numbers. I hardly needed it, as the bawling of steers identified their section from afar. But I checked them off anyway to make sure. Then I checked the cattle from the most forward car back by shining the flashlight through the lower slats along the floor to make sure that there were no animals down and likely to be trampled on. If there had been, the conductor would have had to order a stop to pick up railroad workers, who would enter the car through the roof manholes and get the animal up; or if it were hurt, unload it for later shipment. But everything seemed in order. The cattle had been properly loaded: just enough in a car so they could move around, but not so loosely that they could easily fall from a severe jolting.

The next day was an intolerable, dragging bore. I soon ran out of conversation with the conductor. The two brakemen were not very entertaining, except to each other when they played pinochle. All three men took turns on guard, sitting up in the lookout tower, whence there was nothing to see but vast, barren stretches of Texas and the long line of freight cars, rocking and clanking as they lumbered along, seemingly at snail's pace. The engine was barely visible, a tiny dot in the distance, issuing a jerky plume of smoke puffs.

Around noon we stopped again for water and picked up a second engine. That afforded me another look at the cattle and a quick meal at a sleazy small-town restaurant near the tracks, highly recommended by the conductor. When I saw the cattle by daylight, I lowered my estimate on the conductor's judgment of livestock. Some of the younger ones looked terrible, the rest only fair to middling. All looked thirsty, sunken in at the flanks. I decided to give them an extra long layover in El Paso.

My meal safely gulped down, I heard the engineer's long whistle blast, meaning that he would be ready to leave in about fifteen minutes. I ran back to the caboose, having heard that the crew of a freight train will sometimes conspire to leave a shipper stranded, if given half a chance. But I climbed aboard the caboose with several minutes to spare before the conductor looked at his great watch and pulled the signal cord. The engineer blew his "high-ball": those two short blasts that mean "I'm going to start up."

"Grab that safety ring," the conductor advised, nodding toward an iron ring in the wall. He and the two brakemen were all holding on to something. There was a loud rattling of loose couplings, as the inch or so of slack in each pair was taken up, rather more quickly than usual because of the two engines. At the last link of this chain reaction, the caboose leapt ahead with a crash, as if another train had run into us from behind. The jolt would have knocked a centipede off its feet.

"Throttle-happy sonofabitch," one of the brakemen growled.

I crossed my fingers for the cattle, wondering if any were down. They should have been riding next to the engine.

"Of course, them goddam engineers don't get none of this snap-the-whip up there," the other brakeman said. "They should worry."

"Must be a new man," the conductor suggested. "He don't realize he's got over a hundred cars behind him. Say there's only an inch of play in each coupling . . . well, that's a hundred inches. So the engine's moved more'n eight feet before we get started. It's a wonder we didn't pull a drawbar."

The afternoon and evening dragged on as slowly as the double-header power dragged us up the grade. I finished reading a paperback that I had brought along in my sack. I couldn't play pinochle. I ate two ham sandwiches and two bananas, bought at lunchtime. The conductor said I could sit up in the lookout for a change, but it wasn't any change. At that point, Texas looked the same from all the windows. You could just see more of it from the lookout, which didn't help. I looked around for something else to read, wondering whether any of this crew *did* read. Apparently not. In desperation, I looked in the coalbin. There were a few sticks of kindling wood . . . *and* a few random sheets from different old Texas newspapers, torn and coal-smirched. It was as if I had suddenly discovered the Congressional Library.

That night we pulled into the El Paso freight yards at about nine o'clock. While the yard crew was unloading my steers into large, well-lighted and equipped corrals, I watched them coming down the ramps and onto terra firma, with a trace of apprehension. The conductor was, I concluded, an optimist. They were not in top shape at all. I sought out the crew foreman and told him, "We'll lay over here tomorrow, and maybe Friday."

"How do you want to feed?" he asked.

"Bale and a half to the head."

"Bale and a *half?*" He wrote it down.

"And keep the water coming."

"No trouble there, We got automatic flow valves on all the troughs."

As the cars emptied out, I peered into each one. There were no dead or crippled steers. The water troughs, I could see, were all brimming. I went to the yardmaster's office to telephone.

I called up Juan Thacker, a genial livestock broker Matt and I knew, who lived there with his family in a very comfortable house.

"Matt Sheardon called up this morning from Del Rio. Said you'd be coming through with the steers and would give us a ring. We've got a room all ready for you. Be right down. Meet you there at the freight office."

Juan arrived in about fifteen minutes, a big man, with a big hat, big belt buckle he'd won somewhere and a big car. He was all smiles and courtesy—an oversize helping of Texas hospitality, worried that I might be hungry or need a drink, a pint of which he had brought with him for emergency.

The next day Juan talked with the railroad and made arrangements for our cars to be hooked into a freight that was due to pull out at about two o'clock the following morning on the Atchison, Topeka and Santa Fe line.

While the train was being made up, Juan had a talk with the yardmaster to make sure that our cars would ride next to the engine, and he saw me aboard the caboose. This was a shorter train with only one engine as we pulled out, so the start-up jolt, although still a "Hang on!" proposition, was considerably less. As we got into higher territory, however, we took on another engine to get us into Santa Fe the next morning at about six o'clock.

Santa Fe is at an altitude of over seven thousand feet and is the only state capital I know of to which you can travel on a freight but not on a passenger train. Passengers must drive some twenty miles to and from Lamy, New Mexico. But as we arrived there at about six in the morning, I decided that it would be a good place to lay over for the day to feed, water and rest up the stock, so I had our cars dropped off and said farewell to my "club car," its conductor and brakemen.

This was because, like El Paso, it was the end of a railroad division. In those days—although, perhaps, no longer— a caboose had to remain within a certain division. When it reached the end of that division, you had to get out and find the next caboose assigned to your train for the following division. That was one of the discomforts of shipping, and it could be a real chore in foul weather. It could mean sloshing about some strange freight yard in the cold, dark, early morning hours, looking over strings of cabooses by flashlight, hunting the one magic number that would mean your home for the next division. The key man was the yard-master, who had all the information, but he was sometimes as hard to find as the right caboose. Then there was gossip that irate railroad men sometimes used this situation as a means to "lose" livestock men conveniently.

At Santa Fe I unloaded, watered and fed the cattle another bale per head.

When we pulled out, my cars were riding behind two engines and comfortably protected from "hot stuff" (explosives) in the rear by several flatcars loaded with lumber.

The next day, as we neared Raton Pass and the grade became steeper, we stopped to pick up a third engine, a pusher. This was by far the most enormous piece of machinery I have ever seen outside the engine room of a great transatlantic liner. Unlike the highly polished and softly throbbing reciprocating engines of a steamer, however, this was a terrifying black and grimy monster, which came panting up behind us ominously, its bell tolling, its safety valve blasting steam, and coupled onto our fragile looking caboose with a gentle nudge as if afraid of smashing it. I learned later that it was one of the then new Mohawk, Class 0-5-A combination passenger-freight engines which, with tender, are 106 feet long and weigh 290 tons.

The full majesty of this overpowering machine was not immediately apparent. It started out as just a big noisy thing behind us, puffing out any hope of conversation or sleep. But as we got up into the canyon and the throttle was opened accordingly, the noise became earsplitting, and the view from the rear platform terrifying. The racket made one's innards vibrate, and one couldn't evade fears that the caboose, tiny by comparison, might not prove strong enough to withstand the terrific thrust, and might, at any moment, collapse like an accordion as this monster, spitting sparks up among the stars, snuffed out our lives, perhaps before anyone even knew about it. For several hours this continued, until we reached the more level plateau of Colorado.

My next layover was in Denver, and as we drew into the freight yards, I was surprised to see another string of cattle cars pulling up alongside us a couple of tracks away, also loaded with what looked very much like more Mexican steers. The two freights stopped at pens not very far apart and began unloading. When I had looked after my own cattle, I strolled over to peek at our competition and, perhaps, find out where they were going.

There was a hatless, disheveled-looking fellow wandering about in their pens, who seemed to have something to do with them in a vague way, so I headed for him. After a moment's staring at me, he shouted my name and came running over. "For God's sake, Ned, why didn't you fellers *tell* me about this?" It was Chet Sheardon, worn, torn and angry.

"Tell you about what?"

"About this goddam shipping business. You never told me what it was *like*. You and Matt talked like it was so easy. But I'll tell you, boy, I ain't never going to set foot in one of them damn cabooses again."

"What went wrong?"

"Everything was wrong. After the grub Matt gave me was gone, I nearly starved to death looking for a place to eat. The hide's all wore off my ass from sittin' on them board seats, and I haven't had any sleep for two days. Haven't seen a toilet since we left Del Rio. And say, have you ever tried hanging off them caboose steps? I lost my hat that way. Couldn't let go the rails to grab it."

"We'll go uptown and have a big feed," I tried to console him. "How did your stock make it?"

"Better'n I did. Take a look at them."

"How many times did you lay over to feed?"

"Once that I know of. But I guess they fed them another time or two when I wasn't around. I signed some kind of release paper they said would take care of that."

"What do you mean, when you weren't around?"

"Well, you see, we stopped at some little old junction out in the middle of Texas somewhere, and they told me I could find a restaurant there. But it was all nailed up—out of business. I looked around a long time, but couldn't find another, and when I got back to where I thought they said the train would be, it was gone. They run off and left me, plumb in the middle of nowhere . . . the bastards."

"How did you get back on again?"

"Well, there was this railroad feller working some switches, and he sure was decent. Said he was just about finished for the day and asked me to come home with him for supper. That was Friday and the last square meal I've had. He knew where the train was going, and he had a car and the weekend off. So I hired him to overtake the train and put me back on it. We drove all that night and until about eight o'clock next morning to some whistle-stop where he said he could flag it down. But the damn thing didn't stop, only slowed down, and I had to run like a coyote to catch up with it and jump on. Then I found it was a different caboose. They'd dropped the other one off, with my clothes sack in it, so all I've got left is what's on my back. And I had to pay the switchman all the money Matt gave me, so now I'm broke."

His tale of woe went on until we reached the freight office, where I telephoned for a taxi. We went uptown and outfitted him with a complete change of clothes, including a Stetson hat. Then we checked in at the old Shirley Hotel. I filled him up at the bar, and we went into the dining room. During supper he unburdened himself further about the trip, the ranching business and especially the shipping end of it. He stayed angry during the whole meal, but once upstairs in a comfortable bedroom and after a hot bath, he became relaxed and drowsy. I told him to sleep late next morning, not to worry about the cattle or how he'd get back home; that I would take care of everything.

When I got up, he was still asleep. I put on my last clean underwear, a fresh pair of jeans and a jacket. Then I left a note on the bureau, again saying not to worry that all expenses were on the ranch, to "eat hearty," that he would find fifty dollars in his new pants pocket, and that I'd telephone later. Then, with a good breakfast under my own belt, I took a taxi to the freight yards.

All was well with the steers, which were munching hay happily and lying around, obviously building up strength for the last lap from Denver to Wyola, about five hundred miles.

Not wishing to disturb what I hoped would be Chet's long slumber, I drove out to the local country club, where I had stopped on my chilly drive south thirteen weeks before, now verdant in the breath of early May. There I met a few casual acquaintances in the bar and telephoned to Chet.

He was just getting up and sounded still sleepy but more cheerful, since he had found my note and the fifty dollars.

"Look, I'm stuck out here for lunch, Chet. Are you all right."

He promised to eat well, and I promised to be back in an hour or so, adding, "By the way, I'm having your fifteen cars coupled onto mine. No use both of us riding a caboose up there, when I have to go anyway. So you can forget the cattle. You're riding home in a Pullman."

There were cheerful faces at the Wyola pens to meet me. Matt was there, and Jerry Flynn, with a few cowpunchers on horseback, and the bookkeeper, to make the tally on unloading. All the steers were accounted for alive, though there were a few from Chet's cars that had to be segregated into a hospital bunch for special treatment, but they all survived. Chet himself had also survived his Pullman trip, was met by Matt in Sheridan and taken up to the ranch for the promised feed. Jerry had arrived with his train the day before, having spent a whole day stalled in a Kansas flood so deep that water was coming into the cars. He lost a few head, and the balance took a greater shrink than Chet's and mine, but the overall percentage loss on the whole deal was low considering the circumstances. Matt's range, greening now after a wet spring, soon made up for that.

He had some good news of the Thurnwalds. Dr. Schmidt had pronounced a great improvement in Friedrich's health as a result of the western vacation and was now permitting him to visit the Antler Ranch. He and Sophie were expected in October.

27

The Thurnwalds Visit Montana

"FRIEDRICH! COME DOWN from that gate! Don't you know you're not supposed to sit on gates?" Sophie's sternly affectionate voice carried strong and clear in the cool, crisp October air, overriding the bawling of steers in loading pens, the shouting of cowhands and the clattering of freight cars.

"How is that, my dear? All cowboys sit on gates. I'm a financial cowboy. Therefore, I sit on gates. It's a simple syllogism."

"It is too much exertion for you. You know what Dr. Schmidt said. So come down immediately."

"There will be the same exertion if I come down immediately as if I come down an hour from now, and I want to see them load one more car."

Watching him draw the jeweled snuffbox from his blue jeans, she thought how cocky he was getting now that Dr. Schmidt had allowed him to have his snuff again. Poor Friedrich. Perhaps, after all, it was better not to oppose him and get him all worked up about the corral gate. He took such obvious pleasure in perching on it, but he did seem insecure, teetering now and again as the heavy animals surged against it, bracing himself by the high heels of his stockmen's boots hooked over the poles, his tall Stetson, a shade too large, rocking slightly on his head. He was happy, though, and hadn't Dr. Schmidt stressed that as very important? She could see the glint in his eye as he scribbled in his notebook and gloated over the stocky Antler two-year-olds scrambling up the ramps into the cars. So she just made a silent prayer about the gate and crossed herself.

Matt climbed up on the gate beside him. "This gives you a good idea of what your Open AO's will look like when we ship them out about this time next year, Friedrich. If you'd seen these cattle when we unloaded them from Mexico only two years ago, you'd never think they were the same steers, except for the Antler brand on them."

"They've gained that much, have they?"

"Come on over to the scales and I'll show you."

They both climbed down off the gate, and Sophie gave a little sigh of relief.

The ranch bookkeeper was hovering over the scales, recording weights and occasionally calling out for the scales to be balanced, whereupon the platform would be shoveled free of manure and dirt, and the beam readjusted so that it swung free, indicating zero. Then another draft of animals would be run onto the fenced platform.

"We've been weighing ten head to the draft," Matt explained, "to make the averaging easier."

"How are the weights running?"

"Pretty heavy, I'd say. Above expectations. Most of these steers are shipping out at well over a thousand pounds. They're averaging nearly eleven hundred. We weighed them in at under four hundred. And in this rising market that's plenty of profit."

"How much?" Friedrich's eyes sparkled at the prospects as he wiped the corral dust from his pince-nez glasses.

"It's hard to say exactly until the final weights are in. But, judging by these figures so far, I can give you an idea of what your AO's are doing."

"Will they do as well as these, do you think, Matt?"

"Perhaps better." Matt scribbled in his own little notebook for a moment and then announced confidently, "They're going to pay back your original hundred thousand, plus the 6 percent interest I've guaranteed you. They'll pay me for their running expenses, plus the same interest on that. They're going to pay their freight, taxes, all our traveling expenses and other overhead, and there'll be something like forty-two thousand dollars left over to split between us. Is that satisfactory?" he smiled questioningly.

"Satisfactory? . . . Mein Gott! . . . You Americans are stupendous!"

"It's not us particularly. It's just nature, work and grass. Of course, sometimes it don't turn out as well as this. A cattleman has lots of surprises. That's one thing we like about the business."

"Let us hope they continue to be surprises like this one. In the meantime . . . well, I guess we should be planning our next venture."

"Do you think we should make some plans for seeing the American bison?" Sophie asked, strolling over and meekly addressing Matt.

"Yes, I think you'd both enjoy a trip up to the buffalo range."

"Both? Ah, alas, poor Friedrich!" Sophie looked sadly at her husband. "It is not for you, dear Friedrich, but will you allow me to go?"

"The last of the vanishing American bison!" Friedrich sighed. "How I should love to see them! But I'm afraid Sophie's right. Eight thousand feet altitude is not for me. You must go, though, Sophie, and enjoy them."

"Never mind, dear Friedrich. Ned has arranged another trip for you, which will be equally interesting. He is going to take you over to his home on Tongue River. Is that not a strange name for a river? Perhaps you may be able to discover its derivation."

Friedrich glanced at his watch. "It is almost whiskey time," he announced. "Let us go to Matt's house for the observance, and there we can discuss our plans fully."

"Do you not think it would be polite to ask permission of the Indians before going to enjoy the sight of their fine bison on the domain which they also own?" Sophie asked. "We are only foreigners in a strange land, and we do not wish to trespass."

"I have the land leased," Matt reassured her.

"Leased, yes, I understand. But has it not been owned by them for centuries?"

"Well, if you want to look at it that way, yes, I suppose so."

"Who is their leader, their chief, as you say?"

"Oh, that's Bob Yellowtail; he's hereditary chief. His father was the last real chief. They don't have chiefs with feathered headdresses any more. Bob's a businessman, several college degrees, better educated than I am. Uncle Sam does pretty well by the Indians these days. They have their own universities, like Carlyle. Bob's something of an anthropologist."

"This Chief Bob is interested in anthropology?" Sophie gave one of her rare demonstrations of excitement, leaning forward in her chair, beaming over her bourbon with anticipation.

"Sure is, Sophie. Knows all about mankind and how we got to be this way, which is more than I do. He's also the Crow Agent, the only superintendent of an Indian reservation the government's ever appointed that's an Indian himself. All other agents are whites."

"He is very much the ruler, then, is he not? Appointed both by his own people and the U.S. Government," Friedrich suggested. "I think Sophie is right about getting his permission, if only as a mere formality."

"There's very little formality on the Crow Reservation, Friedrich. It's not necessary at all to ask him. Let's just drive up and look the herd over."

"Not absolutely necessary, perhaps, but still more polite. After all, he is, as Sophie says, a sort of ruler in the European sense. If we are to be his guests on the Reservation, we should acknowledge that fact by calling on him. Could you arrange a social visit, do you think? Where does this chief live?"

"Up at Crow Agency on the way to Billings. They don't go very strong on the social stuff up there, but I'll see if I can make an appointment with Bob."

Matt's low, modest voice came softly from the hallway telephone, "Hello. Crow Agency? Bob Yellowtail there? . . . Hello, Bob, this is Matt, at the Antler. We have a couple of guests here from Europe I'd like you to meet. Can I bring them around tomorrow? . . . Just fine. We'll be there. Thanks."

Matt strolled back into the living room, announcing, "Bob'll be in his office all morning tomorrow. We can go up right after breakfast."

The meeting lasted about half an hour in the bare, sparsely furnished agency office, decorated only by a few Custer Battlefield relics hanging on the walls. The agent was most cordial, and very much in charge of affairs, sitting at his desk, explaining the organization of the Reservation, discussing flora and fauna with Friedrich and the anthropology of the American aborigines with Sophie. It ended by his inviting her on a personally conducted trip to the buffalo range, which was set for the following day.

There was an indescribably strange, eerie aspect underlying this meeting, where one could sense a certain affinity between the Indian and the Europeans, as if each of the three knew that, despite their vastly different stations in life and the thousands of miles normally between them, they were somehow meeting on common ground in that they were all technically descended from hereditary rulers of ancient races. It was only the fortunes of war that had changed them from their hereditary power.

The next day we split up into two expeditions, one to the buffalo range and the other to Tongue River. Yellowtail arrived soon after breakfast. He and Matt then escorted Sophie to the high ranges with her notebook and camera, while I took charge of Friedrich, who was somewhat despondent because of not being able to go along with them. So I tried to think up a trip for him that would partially compensate, but along a route that would be generally downhill rather than up.

I decided on a surprise luncheon visit to old Fred at the cabin. Friedrich's diet, however, had to be considered because of Fred's somewhat sketchy and unpredictable inventory of groceries, which ran heavily to pork and beans, pig's knuckles, limburger cheese and sauerkraut, with heavy soda biscuits on the side, called "death wads" by old roundup cooks. Therefore, to guard against unforeseen culinary emergencies, we raided the Antler commissary for the ingredients of a completely independent food supply, including some fine cuts of lamb and beef which, if not needed, were to be left with Fred as a present from Matt.

In order to take in different types of scenery for Friedrich, I planned a looplike route. We drove north on the main highway from Wyola toward Billings but soon turned off on a little-used dirt road I knew of and worked east across the Crow Reservation to Indian Creek, which took us to the Rosebud River and the Birney road down Tongue River, a drive of about seventy-five miles. Friedrich's keen sense of history was aroused by the fact that much of this route was the country over which General Custer had marched to his fate. He was surprisingly well informed on Custer's battle and made notes on what I could tell him about the fatal march.

We came upon old Fred by surprise, sitting in his "paradise chair" at the kitchen table, enjoying the *Pathfinder,* with his telescope at the ready. He got up when he saw the car approaching and came lumbering out on the porch to greet us, with a sly smile and a trace of embarrassment. "I feel like I know you, Doctor," he said warmly. "Ned said he'd bring you over here from the Antler, but he didn't say when, and I'm not fixed up very well for entertaining guests, but I've got a load of food coming with the mail driver today, and I guess we can feed you."

"Don't worry about the food, my good man. We brought our own. We just wanted to pay you a little visit. We don't expect you to cook anything for us."

"Oh, Fred's a good cook," I explained. "Practically *cordon bleu.*"

"What in hell's that?" Fred asked.

"Blue ribbon stuff in France."

"We had a French cook on the roundup wagon years ago. Frenchie, we called him. He used to say, 'One hon-yon and one bucket-a-water mak-a de fine bouillon.' But he wasn't no blue ribbon cook." During this dissertation Fred was sizing up Friedrich from the too-polished toes of his still too-stiff cowboy boots with the yellow butterflies to the top of his too-big Stetson. "Yes, I've heard all about you, Doctor. You're the financial cowboy, aren't you?"

"It is really all I know about the business, so far, the financial side."

"Well, the rest of it'll come to you if you stick around here long enough. How long you going to be here?"

"Unfortunately, not long enough. My health, you see. I have to go back east to my doctor soon."

"Hell, man, you're in the healthiest place in the world right now. Lots of people from the east come out here to get well, but I never heard of anyone going the other way. Ned says you're getting better all the time. You don't look sick to me. You got a nice ruddy face."

Friedrich was also sizing up his new acquaintance, probably surprised that he didn't match up with the movie versions of strong, silent western men. "So you're Ned's chef. I used to have a good chef, too, at home in Vienna, but that goddam *schweinhund* of a Hitler took him away from me and put him in the army. I hope he puts vitriol in all their sauerkraut. . . . As a chef, what is your specialty, Mr. . . . er . . . Fred?"

"I don't have any particular specialty, Doctor, but when I cooked on the roundup, I used to have a reputation for throwing together a pretty good batch of sonofabitch."

"What's that? A regional specialty of some kind? What do you put in it?"

"No, it's just a mess of stuff all thrown together. It's not so much what you put in it as how you throw it together. There's sort of a knack to it. Hard to explain, but I had the knack. Lost it now, though, it's so many years since I've made sonofabitch. I could make you something else, though, soon as the mail driver gets here with the grub. In the meantime, how about a little drink?" He produced a bottle of Old Yellowstone from the kitchen cabinet.

"I am allowed two ounces of whiskey a day, and it will be a great pleasure to have one of them with you, Mr. Fred."

"Sorry I don't have any ice, Doctor. Have to lug it up the hill from the ranch icehouse down there. All I can offer you is bourbon and ditch."

"Ditch? What is that?"

"Ditch water. Of course, it isn't really that, we just call it that. Don't worry, your doctor would okay this water."

"Excellent! Ditch water for me, please. I shall remember that when I get home . . . if I ever do." He lifted his glass in a toast, "Against Hitler!"

"Against Hitler!" Fred and I joined in.

"I understand your home is in Vienna, Doctor. That sure must be different from here."

"Yes, it is vastly different. We do not have this beautiful log work over there. I like this better. I find it more quaint. And your view of the countryside is magnificent."

"What's your house made of?"

"It's made of stone."

"Well, stone houses are nice too, but they're hell to build. You must have had a lot of fellers helping you build it."

"Oh, I didn't build it myself. It was built long before my time. Yes, it required a number of workmen."

"I hope they got it facing the right way, so you have a good view."

"Well, of course, it's in the city, so we don't have any view like this; but it does overlook some beautiful gardens on one side and a pretty plaza on the other, with nice, wide streets, one of which goes right past the Opera House, a magnificent building. In general it overlooks what we call the Inner City."

"Cities is nice to live in for some folks," Fred conceded. "But as for me, I like looking out over the meadows and the river and them old hills across the river, with all the streaky colors in them. . . . Well, I guess the mailman's late. Getting hungry? I'll just throw something together." He shook down the stove grates, laid some wood on the hot coals, opened the chimney draft and soon had a crackling fire.

"I've got an idea!" Friedrich announced, looking from one to the other of us. "I'll cook for you two. Let me see if I can remember something of what my chef taught me in Vienna."

"No, Doctor, you mustn't exert yourself. I know where everything is. It's much easier for me," Fred objected.

"But I insist that I am still capable of producing an edible meal, and we have all the food with us. We do not have to wait for this mailman."

"Drag it out, then, and I'll cook it."

When I got back from the car with the box of food, they were still arguing. Then Friedrich had a brilliant suggestion. "We will have a contest," he suggested. Fred will cook one course and I shall cook another. Ned will be the judge as to which is the better."

There was to be no peeking. The doors between the kitchen and bed-sitting-room were to be closed while each contestant prepared his offering. After another round of bourbon, Fred disappeared into the kitchen for a half hour, secretly prepared his course and put it in the warming oven. Then Friedrich took a pinch of snuff, as if to stimulate his culinary reminiscences, sneezed mightily and disappeared with a flourish behind the double doors. When he opened them, it was to present a tempting dish of shish kebab, with apologies for not having skewers.

Fred's entry turned out to be a much more humble dish of spaghetti, but it was made according to his own very special recipe, which he would never divulge to me. Each contestant gallantly praised the other's production. Both were really delicious, and I finally pronounced the contest a tie.

After lunch Friedrich took some medicine and explained that he must lie down for half an hour on doctor's orders.

"I take a siesta too every afternoon. You know, Doctor, some of my ancestors was Spanish, and it just seems to come sort of natural to me," Fred explained, stretching out on the other corner bed diagonally opposite.

I left them in peace, mumbling to each other like old pals, and closed the double doors while I did the dishes. Occasionally, I could catch something of what they were saying. Fred was explaining basic cattle ranching theory: ". . . because, you see, Doctor, every time a cow has a calf . . ."

Then I took my stack of accumulated mail out on the porch to work on it in those peaceful surroundings. Even then, I could get snatches of their siesta conversation, such as Friedrich seeking the derivation of "Tongue" for the river's name and Fred's explanation, "Because so many Indians around here used it, like the Crows, Cheyennes, Sioux and others just traveling through the country, all speaking different languages. They called it the River of Many Tongues, then it got shortened." That little bit of information would surely get to Columbia University some day.

When siesta was over, we didn't have much time left to get back to the ranch, so we said hurried good-byes, and the two chefs congratulated each other again on their skills. While Friedrich was fumbling in a bag he'd brought along, Fred got me aside and giggled, "Say, he ain't a bad old guy for a prince, or whatever it is. I sure hope he comes out on top with them steers. Don't let him get in too deep with Matt. You know, Matt's a gambler. He's been broke once, and he might go broke again. He's got no calf crop coming along as a cushion."

From the bag in the car, Friedrich produced a pinchbottle of Scotch and gave it to Fred, ". . . because I feel you really won the cooking contest with that spaghetti, and you ought to have this as a memento."

We took the longer, but safer, route back, along the old red shale Birney road to the highway north of Sheridan, then up to Wyola, arriving at the Antler just before whiskey time. Friedrich dutifully confessed that he had already consumed his ration for that day and so was ineligible for the "observance."

Toward the end of October the Thurnwalds returned to their winter headquarters in New York. On the long drive from the Antler Ranch to Billings they were bubbling over with happy reminiscences and the obviously beneficial effects on Friedrich's health of their two western trips. Their gratitude was touching.

"I'll always remember this trip . . . always," Friedrich said with feeling.

"And you'll always be remembered here, Friedrich . . . both of you. You are, after all, now part of Crow Indian Reservation history."

"If I am ever remembered for anything here, I hope it will be for the fact that I never submitted an inch to Hitler. I never gave up any of my lands to him. They are my ancient birthright and came to me by inheritance, purchase or treaty. Not one acre by conquest, such as he is now carrying on all over Europe. I have not signed over a single title. They are all in my vaults in neutral countries, except a few that I could not save from the palace in time. For this he hunts me like a fox and would execute me if he could."

In Billings, Friedrich and Sophie boarded the Great Northern's luxurious all-Pullman "Empire Builder" and glided down the shining rails on their way to New York.

28

Taps for Fred Lauby

THE FOLLOWING YEAR, when the war ended, the Thurnwalds returned to Europe to see what could be salvaged of their former domains. Friedrich sold out all his American interests except the cattle, concerning which our correspondence now blossomed again. Zurich was his new headquarters. In New York the faithful paperwork slave, Mr. Erlander, faded out of the picture.

Friedrich's first string of steers arrived at the ranch in May, 1943, so they had now been double-wintered. They had put on a good gain and were almost all ready to ship that fall of 1945. Matt made an early test shipment of a few head on September 3, and the results were so gratifying that I immediately cabled Friedrich in Zurich, thinking that it would do his heart good in the midst of what must have been a sad return to his estates. I asked him what to do with the cash and future checks which would be coming in. He answered to bank it in New York after deducting my share, saying that he planned to go into another steer deal with Matt. It would thus be immediately available under my power of attorney.

After the wagon's annual lay-up for repairs in August, it went out on the range again as usual on September 1 to start gathering the steers for shipping and for general "working" of the herd. That could mean cutting out other people's cattle which had strayed in with ours, working out our own brands and segregating them according to the various owners' wishes (Matt allowed several of his employees to run their own brands with him) and

Antler steers on the range. *Courtesy Roahen Photos, Billings, Montana*

sometimes even working with cows and calves that Matt was looking after for others. The cows, when driven long distances, would lose track of their calves, necessitating the tedious process of close herding them, sometimes for hours on end, until they "mothered up" and all the bawling had ceased. The more experienced a cowman is, the more he can speed the mothering-up process.

That year I joined the roundup October 17. On the twenty-third it snowed so hard that we couldn't see any cattle. Visibility was zero for two days, so seven of us had to sit in the mess tent, where there was nothing to do but play poker and tell stories. We used kitchen matches for chips, but they were really just counters, representing no value, and all had to be returned to the cook after the game. Jerry Flynn was a strict wagon boss. He allowed no gambling, liquor or ladies on the wagon, except guests or relatives of the Sheardon family, introduced by Matt or somehow connected with the outfit, and then only for day visits. During the war a few exceptions were made out of sheer necessity. He considered women, like cameras, out of place on a serious, commercial roundup.

Another taboo he had was criticizing the outfit's horses. If you didn't have your own string (seven horses) you rode what he dealt out for you in his own best judgment. In my own case (being a non-professional rider) I could usually count on getting a horse that was "plumb gentle" or nearly so. Being bucked off was not considered funny, and he wouldn't risk putting me on any horse he didn't think I could handle. He was always, however, trying to graduate me to better horses, and the challenge was fun. But the professionals had no such treatment. Some were rodeo riders or "bronc twisters" by trade and vied with each other in riding the meaner horses. Sometimes, especially on cold mornings, as we saddled up to start off on morning circle, there would be quite a display of showmanship, with good-natured kidding of each other. But no rider, whether he got hurt or not, ever criticized the outfit's horses. I only saw one instance where a rider (who was a new man), after being badly thrown several times, cussed out an Antler horse. He was instantly dismissed and told that he could walk to the nearest highway, carrying his saddle, to thumb a ride.

The boys on the wagon were all very loyal to the outfit, no matter who was or wasn't within earshot. To them it was the only outfit. Differences of opinion did sometimes arise, but they would always spit them out at each other, usually with some humorous twist to take the edge off. There was no harboring of grudges, and a sort of unspoken rule against fighting seemed to be in the air.

These boys gave a good example of their loyalty when a labor organizer got into camp under some false pretext and tried to talk them into joining a union, with the expectation of more money, less work and easier living. He met with seven cold shoulders all at once and was given just enough grub to speed him out of camp and on his way back to Billings.

I stayed with the wagon until we had shipped most of Friedrich's steers. On November 2 we shipped 1,079 head of mixed brands from Spear Siding, including some AO's, representing most of the remainder of Friedrich's herd, after the light end had been cut off to hold over for shipment next year. They brought $120,659. By then it was time for me to head for my winter quarters in New York.

Friedrich kept reinvesting the proceeds of his cattle sales in more steers, but did not return to this country. His operations now became more or less routine under his contracts with Matt and me. Matt had complete charge of the ranching operation and I of the financial end. I also served as their channel of communication. But his correspondence fell off, so that after a year or two I would hear from him only occasionally. The bank in Zurich seemed to take over more and more. After a while the bankers appointed a Swiss law firm in New York to represent them, and I would correspond mostly with this firm, which was annoying, because a Swiss lawyer in New York cannot be expected to know much about cattle, except possibly the dear Brown Swiss cows which are so picturesque coming down from Alpine summer pastures, with garlands of flowers decorating their horns, to amble through the little towns and turn in at their owners' gates without any cowpunchers at all. These lawyers simply didn't know what was going on out in Montana, and there was much explaining to do.

In the winter of 1946–47, while I was in Acapulco, Mexico, word came of old Fred Lauby's death—no one ever knew exactly on what day.

I had never known very much about Fred's background, except that he was born somewhere in New Jersey and that he was descended on his mother's side from the historic Van Ness family of Kinderhook, New York. I had once made an investigation of old files in a New Jersey newspaper office and corroborated various bits of information he had given me about relatives. I wondered if he had any heirs or any estate. I had always considered him poor, which he was. But he had sold his quarter-section homestead a few years past and also his small herd of horses. For twenty-three years he lived with me, rent free, board free and tax free. Although he would never accept a salary from me, I paid him standard wages for any work he did around the place, as I had paid him for his building work. Possibly, he had savings from his younger days.

I knew that, a few years earlier, he had two thousand dollars in cash, because he asked me to buy him two U.S. Savings Bonds. These he deposited with a Sheridan bank after much deliberation, a special trip to town (for which he put on his necktie at the city limits) and, accompanied by the bank president, an inspection of the bank's vaults where they would be kept, plus my repeated assurances that the bank president was on the square, even though they had no private safe-deposit box available. He was afraid that his bonds might somehow get mixed up with the bank's bonds and be lost in the shuffle. So we made three copies of his numbers. One he put in a wax-sealed bottle in my vault under the cabin, another he put in a mason jar stashed away in the outhouse (as the place least likely to burn) and the third he kept mysteriously to himself.

I knew that he had a sister, long dead, who left children, one of whom he particularly disliked and often cussed out, saying that he would never leave him anything. I tried to have him draw up a will, but he procrastinated too long. There were some mineral rights which he had reserved from the sale of his homestead. He had also reserved the right to move his cabin, but that had long since fallen to ruin. There were some personal effects in an old trunk in my coal shed, which were practically valueless except as family mementos. There was one grim memento: a black steel can, looking very much like a can of blasting powder and rattling the same way when shaken. He told me not to worry about an explosion in case of fire; that it contained the ashes of his brother-in-law, who died in 1915. The family had just never gotten around to a funeral.

Fred Lauby as barber

Fred did leave a small estate, settled by a Birney cowboy lawyer. In the end, the hated relative did get some money. He also got the mineral rights, which although considered worthless then, are now in the strip-mining age quite valuable. I often wonder whether he held on to them long enough. I once tried unsuccessfully to buy them.

In due time, the facts of old Fred's demise revealed themselves. It had been a bitter winter, and Fred, according to custom, had "holed up." Often in winter no one saw him for long periods. But my neighbors down at the ranch house always kept a kindly eye peeled for him. They invited him down for Christmas dinner, and he was his usual old self. Following Christmas there was a blizzard, so they knew he was holed up tightly and didn't think much of not seeing him around the cabin.

An old Cheyenne squaw, caught in the blizzard on her way to Sheridan, decided to camp near the ranch house until it blew itself out. During the first few days of January, she came to the house with dark forebodings: "Something wrong with old man up on hill. Three days, no smoke from chimney, three nights no light in window."

My good friend Al Harris plodded up the hill. With no answer to his knock, no tracks about, and only the dead silence of falling snow in answer to his shouts, he tried unsuccessfully to force the doors. Then he went around to one of the small, square bedroom windows and looked in. He saw old Fred, sitting on the edge of the bed in a position suggesting that he was about to lace a shoe, but frozen solid. The hot-water tank attached to the stove had frozen and burst, and water flowing from the hilltop reservoir had gushed up against the doors, freezing them shut. There was an egg on the stove, frozen solid. Old Fred must have been contemplating breakfast, found a frozen egg and placed it there to thaw while he put on his shoes.

He died instantly, as he had always wanted to, and where he had wanted to, overlooking those "old streaky hills," and was buried in the little local cemetery only four miles away, surrounded by many of his old cronies.

The burial itself had been something of a tour de force. The road was impassable in both directions: to Sheridan and to the county seat at Forsyth, Montana, from where the coroner said he would send a hearse right behind the first snowplow, adding that

Fred would be perfectly all right as long as nobody went up there and built a fire. The road to Sheridan was opened first for the U.S. mail to get through, and since the distance was only fifty-three miles, Fred went to a Sheridan mortuary. Since he was a huge man and frozen in a rather spread out position, the undertaker faced a problem in getting him through the two-and-a-half-foot doorway. This was solved when he spied an axe on the woodpile and sent his assistant for it, despite the protests of some kindhearted person who pleaded against their "whittling" on the corpse. The axe, however, was used only to tap him gently into a more amenable position.

The next problem was digging a grave, since the ground was frozen solid a third of the way down. Stalwart friends dynamited the first two feet, then dug to four feet, but the earth they threw up froze solid almost as fast as they dug, so that it would be impossible to replace by the time of the funeral. They, therefore, left the last two feet for further consideration.

On the day of the funeral there was another blizzard, with sub-zero temperatures and a high wind. The hearse got stuck at the cemetery entrance; so, at least, the hardy mourners got some slightly warming exercise while laboring to free it. Two old-timers fortified with bourbon arrived on horseback. The simple ceremony was quickly performed, and the mourners were asked to stand back for the final shot of dynamite. At this point, one of the old-timers raised a technical question as to the rated strength of the dynamite and how many sticks should be used. He was tactfully quieted and the shot boomed. The loosened earth was quickly picked, shoveled and heaved out in great chunks, and the coffin was lowered.

"It was the most unusual burial service I've ever conducted," said the officiating minister in the spring on his daily rounds at the Sheridan Hospital, where I was recuperating from a streptococcus throat infection on my way up from Mexico. "Despite the weather," he said, "I had determined to remove my fur coat, bare my head in respect, and consecrate the grave in my surplice. For the few moments required, I've never been so cold in my life, and the surplice was flapping out straight behind me. I scratched around for some earth to sprinkle over the coffin, but it was all frozen tight, and I had to substitute a handful of snow, packing it a little, so it would go down."

No time was allowed for the newly dynamited clods to become frozen to the others. They were unceremoniously tossed back in a hurry, landing on the coffin with ominous thuds, as if threatening to break through. But what little coverage they afforded was better than none and represented all that would be available until the first spring thaw.

When the gravediggers had done their utmost, they proceeded to the Birney bar for copious toasts to Fred. One of them later told me that they had ordered a case of beer and charged it to me, but I cannot remember ever having received the bill.

The kindly cemetery committee had filled in the rest of the earth before I arrived to check on the grave, which was by then a respectable mound with a great, irregular piece of native slab rock standing up on end at the head. Today, thirty years later, three large growths of sagebrush cover old Fred. One must stoop down and part them to see the little marker with his dates, "1875–1947." The cemetery is still exactly as it was, surrounded by its woven-wire fence and corral-type gate fastened by a chain and harness snap, still serenaded by coyotes on a cold evening.

29

Ranching by Mail

A VERY PLEASANT SIDE of the ranching business went out of my life with the Thurnwalds. As war had crossed our paths, so peace had separated them. I hoped that they would be happy again in returning to their native lands, but did not hear much about their readjustments except that some of their family estates, being in the postwar "American Zone," were returned to them.

Friedrich and Sophie continued to live in Zurich, but they sometimes wrote from a villa on the Italian Riviera. He seemed to have lost some of his effervescence, and I feared that his health might be going downhill. A snapshot showed him sitting with a nurse on the sun porch of a sanitarium. His cattle business was reduced to a routine operation, with correspondence carried on through his Swiss lawyers in New York, but it continued to prosper through another two ventures. Then there were no further instructions to reinvest.

I corresponded with these lawyers as little as possible, since their rather bossy attitude did not sit well with me. They could not possibly understand the Antler operation and, it seemed, were always fishing for information about our directors' meetings or anything that would help them run up a large bill for time spent on useless correspondence. They would have been shocked to know of the actual informality of these meetings, there being so few partners involved in the running of Friedrich's steers; actually, just Matt, two members of his family and myself. We were likely to have a directors' meeting anywhere, at any time, because we always agreed on everything beforehand. Sometimes they were held in a rush, and unnecessary proceedings were cut very short or skipped altogether.

On one occasion, we had a meeting in the roundup mess tent out on the range. This was a fast one, and we galloped off, having forgotten to declare a dividend. Then someone remembered the omission, and the rectification was just as fast. We simply drew up our horses together, announced an extension of the meeting, and declared the dividend. This definitely was not the Swiss way.

By now, life had taken on a sort of four-cornered pattern, as I divided my time between Mexico City, New York, Birney, and the Antler Ranch, where I would go out with the wagon spring and fall. It was a good life, healthful, active and productive and interesting in that it provided opportunities to meet all kinds of people and to practice languages. Thus it went on for another three years, with the Thurnwalds faintly fading into the background, although I always kept in touch with them.

Friedrich's letters, however, became spasmodic and then ceased altogether. I feared the worst, but it was several weeks before my fears proved to have been justified, because the Swiss lawyers, for some obscure reason of their own, never notified me of his death. Friedrich had been dead nearly two weeks before our lawyers in Billings knew about it. This was a considerable shock to me, and it was difficult to learn any details.

I remembered that Friedrich had once mentioned belonging to some monastic order to which he was particularly devoted. One of its customs required that the members all be buried together, dressed in their monastic robes and hoods. Later, I found out that he had thus been laid away somewhere in Styria. It was hard for me to imagine his jolly face (especially, sniffing snuff at whiskey time) now still and solemn in its hood.

With Friedrich gone and my power of attorney consequently voided, the Swiss lawyers had even less regard for me and now bypassed me completely. The matter of payments to Friedrich's estate for the final shipment of Open AO steers was progressing nicely when the ranch bookkeeper received a letter from these lawyers, representing themselves as attorneys for the Zurich bank handling the estate and instructing the bookkeeper to make checks for the proceeds payable to them personally, disregarding his former method. Matt was not even consulted.

The bookkeeper called our lawyer in Billings to inquire and was asked to wait while our lawyer looked up the power of attorney issued to the Swiss lawyers by the Zurich bank. It turned out that full "powers of endorsement" were not included in that power, and the bookkeeper was told to postpone action until the matter could be clarified, to protect the Antler interests.

A series of snippy letters, telegrams and cables then flew around the circuit between Zurich, New York and the ranch, no one wishing to take responsibility for the delay, which irked the bank. In the meantime, I had something over $16,000 coming to me as my share of the last shipment of steers and received my money without fuss, which may have rubbed our foreign friends the wrong way. At the same time, they had turned down perfectly good money from the ranch, because the check was drawn in the regular form and not to them personally. This matter was finally resolved by the issuance of a proper power of attorney.

I then received a letter from the lawyers, enclosing copies of their statement to the bank for legal services in putting the deal through, with a request for my signature to approve. This I refused to give, on the grounds that, with my former power of attorney dead, I was now an outsider to matters concerning the Thurnwald estate, the bank handling it and themselves as representatives of that bank. Second, I was not putting my signature on any paper approving their actions and laying blame for the delay on our side, when it actually resulted from their presenting our lawyer with a sour power. I further objected to endorsing the $1,500 legal fee for their services, which I did not engage, was not consulted about and did not need in order to handle the cattle business as I had always handled it for Prince Thurnwald, without any complaints. That was what I was paid for, and I did not need any help, especially with the Sheardon interests. In short, I did not like to see his widow charged twice for the conduct of affairs entrusted to me.

I further objected to their trying to wiggle out of reimbursing us for $165.79 in taxes which we had mistakenly paid for them, citing several instances where Matt had given the AO account the break on steers that were doubtful in the tally or could not immediately be located: a generous gesture of many times the tax item value, and one which was not strictly necessary.

Then, leaving my correspondence on this matter in the hands

of my old friend and Sheridan attorney, Barry Marshall, I took off by automobile for New York, via Texas, and that was the end of the matter.

When the Thurnwald business was settled in early 1951, I began to take stock of my position in the ranch and the prospects I might expect in continuing it indefinitely. Matt was then sixty-five years old and in failing health from diabetes neglected in his youth. Insulin and the hypodermic needle were his constant companions, and he took other medications. His flying trips to the Mayo Clinic were becoming more and more frequent. He was subject to comas if his diet was violated, as it sometimes had been when we traveled off the beaten track. In fact, I had had a harrowing experience with him when we were roaming the Mexican State of Chihuahua in search of the La Plata ranch headquarters, and his doctor had thereafter forbidden him to drive long distances alone. He had told me that his medications and treatments would probably see him into his eighties, *if* he did not develop any other illness, but that his medications would clash, probably fatally, with those required for some of the more common ailments.

It was a big *if* for me, since he was absolute boss of the Antler and I doubted whether anyone else could run it. I realized that there was a great deal of complication in the ranch setup about which I knew nothing, and I gathered from his casual remarks that he would welcome a chance to simplify the operation. Half a million acres was a lot of ranch for a sick man to have on his hands at that age. He had vaguely mentioned dropping all the Indian leases and reducing his domain to fifty thousand acres of deeded land. The Indians were becoming more difficult to deal with. Labor was getting scarce and expensive. The drying up of the Mexican market as a source of supply and the steadily rising price of beef, tempting banks to loan huge sums on that commodity, were making too much of a gamble out of the livestock industry.

There were also internal rumblings within the Sheardon family. Black moods concerning the business obsessed Carl, who finally had a mental breakdown. Martha, Matt's daughter, had always been a pale, delicate young woman, something of a religious fanatic. She and her husband, Willie, lived a sort of semisecluded life and rarely appeared in the mess house for meals. Willie could not see eye to eye with Matt on anything.

I had long known, in a vague sort of way, that enmities existed in the family, but I had not tried to pry into them, considering them none of my business. I strove to be civil and polite to all members of the family, as they were to me, and neither side dwelt particularly upon their differences. Now, however, it occurred to me that these differences and enmities would come into full flower upon Matt's death and might split the ranch wide open, leaving me in an uncomfortable, and perhaps even financially dangerous position.

I had had two good runs in the cattle business: in the 1920s and again in the 1940s. I was getting into my fifties, and, if this cycle of rising beef prices should break — which it would have to do eventually — I might lose all my advantage and then be too old to make a comeback. Also, my wife did not care for ranch life. I had entered into it in my younger days and had become used to it, but I knew that I could not keep it up forever. So, in 1951, when a good chance for me to sell out came along, I took it.

30

The Handwriting on the Wall

UNSADDLING AT THE BURLINGTON shipping point of Benteen, when the last of Friedrich's steers rolled out, gave me a creepy feeling of the sort that sometimes comes over one when he knows that a major change is taking place in his life. I knew that I should never again saddle up to ride for the interests of a great, going cattle outfit wherein I had a slice, be it ever so small. I knew that Matt's roundup wagons were the last purely horseflesh operation in the state, and probably in the country. When they went, that indescribable spirit of the range—made up of what its men call "good-heartedness," of close relationships between man and beast, and of discipline—would go too; and already there were rumors of mechanization. There is just something intangible, but very real, that goes with the old range life, which does not go with carburetors and spark plugs, blessings though the latter may be.

I decided then and there, however, to keep in touch with Matt and the outfit as long as he should live and not to let memories die unnecessarily, but to preserve them as mental fodder. Part of this mental fodder came about as the result of a business trip Matt made to Boston in connection with a contract for the sale of his wool crop. On his way he stopped off in New York to visit me.

Matt didn't know much about New York and was anxious to see the financial district, so I took him along on a chore to my bank and then to the Visitor's Gallery of the Stock Exchange. He was surprised to see members on the trading floor below cavorting about in paper hats and carrying wooden swords, but it was one of those slack trading days when they decide to have a little nonsense, sometimes to welcome a new member. Walking back up Broad Street toward Wall, he spied the old J. P. Morgan building. We crossed over for a closer look, and he was most impressed by a glimpse of the magnificent ceiling that can be seen from the street.

I'll bet there's a lot of good information under a ceiling like that," he said.

"What kind of information do you want?"

"Wool. Those Billings wool buyers were twisting my arm before I left, trying to contract this year's wool crop, but I wouldn't contract for thirty-six cents, and they wouldn't pay thirty-seven. Maybe we could go in here and get the outlook for the wool market from one of these Morgan men."

"We can't just walk in cold without some kind of appointment, and it's too late today."

"I'm going up to Boston tonight to see some wool people there, and I'd like to have two sources of information to compare, before tackling those Billings buyers again."

"I'll try to get a morning appointment for the day after tomorrow."

One of the Morgan Guaranty's commodities department managers, specializing in wool, kindly dated us up, and we arrived well ahead of time. This officer's young woman secretary, who appeared to be new at her job and somewhat impressed by it, undertook to inform us of the importance of her boss and the value of his time. "All his appointments are strictly limited to fifteen minutes," she emphasized, "except by special arrangement. You must remember not to stay longer." I promised her to keep track of the time.

When we got into the sanctum, its occupant couldn't have been more friendly and interested, questioning Matt closely about his entire livestock operation, banking connections and general mode of life. He had spent some time researching livestock commodities out west and regretted never having seen a big ranching operation at first hand; so Matt invited him to the Antler, and he accepted, acting as if he were ready to pack his bag right then. He ended up asking Matt for more information than Matt was asking of him.

As the deadline approached, I began throwing hints about leaving, but our newfound friend would not hear of it. His telephone rang, and he told the secretary quietly that he was still busy and couldn't see anyone. After half an hour I got up and started apologizing about taking up so much of his time and was told not to worry, which I didn't, since it seemed that the wool prospects looked pretty bright.

After nearly an hour Matt arose, against further protestations, picked up his little Borsalino hat and said meekly, "I'm sorry sir, but I've run out of time, The plane's waiting for me, and my pilot wants his orders. We have to get to the Mayo Clinic in Rochester this afternoon and out to the ranch tomorrow."

The Morgan man followed us into the outer office, smiling and promising to come out for a visit, while several customers cooled their heels in the waiting room, and the fresh secretary gave us a dirty look.

On his return, the Billings wool buyers pestered him again. Matt later told me the outcome. "They'd changed their minds about thirty-six cents a pound and said they were willing to meet me at thirty-seven. So I told them how you and I had been on an extensive trip, analyzing world market conditions in Boston and New York. I said we'd just come back from an interview with the head commodities partner of the Morgan bank on Wall Street, and that now I didn't want to sell my wool at all. They offered me thirty-eight cents, and I took it—for three hundred thousand pounds."

Incidentally, that deal topped the market.

On his home scene, the livestock industry had been undergoing a recession. Cattle prices had fallen sharply, and his son's dark moods had developed further.

On business trips to Chicago, Carl had formed strange acquaintances, some of whom showed up at the ranch, where they were distinctly out of place, especially one unmarried couple who staged a minor stabbing. Another strange guest arrived in a large, black car with a large black driver, whose name was given only as Gold Dollar. This guest, upon hearing that Matt had a bothersome neighbor, offered to have Gold Dollar "wipe him out," if Matt wished. Less alarming was the oddball who, at first meeting and without even having been introduced, offered to give me what appeared to be a very thin, platinum Patek-Philippe pocket watch in, perhaps, the $2,000 price range. When I refused it on the grounds of some misunderstanding, he said, "Don't worry, I have a whole suitcase full of them. They're marvelous imitations that cost me only a dollar, but they're good for a year." The watch was very accurate, but it stopped forever after exactly one year.

The operational side of the ranch continued much as usual, with Matt wheeling and dealing in all kinds of propositions to utilize his range, culminating in 1957, when he staged what is generally considered the last big traditional beef roundup of modern times; the last that even remotely approached those fabled roundups in the days of the great cattle barons.

He was then in partnership with a Nebraska cattle syndicate which suddenly had to be dissolved in order to settle the estates of some members who had perished simultaneously in an automobile accident. There were two contracts to be met. One was with Armour & Company, assessed as the largest order ever bought by that packing firm from one source at one time. It called for the delivery in Billings of 7,500 two-year-old steers at the rate of 740 head per day, all in one brand, the syndicate's T Slash.

The other contract was under the personal brand of a syndicate member, 2 Bar, and called for three thousand head. Matt, according to his custom (as with my own little deals) had provided all the range, handled the operational end and was then running the roundup that was to gather and ship this beef.

The price was $19.75 per hundredweight, or about $1,500,000 for the package. The down payment was a study in contrast between the openhanded trustworthiness of old-time cattlemen and our present era of business chicanery and distrust. It was one silver dollar. The C., B. & Q. railroad guaranteed a special train of thirty-three cars (750 head total capacity) every day until the job should be done.

At early dawn on September 4 the mess and bed wagons were moving. Bill Greenough, the wagon boss at that time and his eighteen Antler cowpunchers fanned out over the sagebrush; the day wranglers took charge of their 165 horses; Matt's pilot revved up the scouting plane and searched the range to report the distribution of cattle (the only really modern touch, but it saved manpower and horseflesh).

Three shipping points were to be used: Benteen and Aberdeen for the 2 Bar steers that ranged on the east side of the Big Horn River, and Rowley for the T Slash contract, which steers were

on the west side of the river. All went well with the 2 Bar herd.
The T Slash herd, however, was a bitter struggle, since some
Reservation leases had recently changed hands, and the new
leasees threw up a fence that barred the old, accustomed Antler
shipping trail to Rowley.

There was only one alternative: a thirty-five-mile trucking haul
to the Burlington at Billings. This would cost time, money and
manpower, besides posing the problem of building special makeshift corrals for loading trucks on the range. In addition, the plan
depended upon continued good, dry weather over the equinox
period when rain was likely, because, although fifteen miles of
the route was directly accessible to all-weather highways, the
other twenty miles stretched over open range which would hopelessly bog down the heavy trailer trucks.

Nothing daunted, the cattlemen took on their gamble. They
leased every monster diesel semitrailer truck they could get their
hands on, and some of them may have prayed for the first time in
their lives as they build corrals from army surplus portable air-
strip material at the Cashen Ranch, an Antler stronghold on the
Reservation, their loading point.

The weather held until September 30. Then, as the last truckload pulled away for hard ground, the black clouds rolled up.
The best-timed "moisture" that any cattleman ever enjoyed burst
upon them just as soon as this last load was safely on the highway.

The roundup ended October 18. Both contracts had been fulfilled, with a few head to spare. Actual delivery was 7,543 head,
with a weight of 6,830,636 pounds in the T Slash brand and
3,142 head of 2 Bars, weighing 2,776,951 pounds, for a grand
total of 10,685 head, or 9,607,587 pounds of beef on the hoof.

Matt gave further evidence of curtailing his domain by selling
a "pasture" of 147,000 acres on the west side of the river for
$1,500,000. It consisted of mixed leases and deeded land. But
then he suddenly turned around and took on another 100,000
acres of leases elsewhere. It looked as if he might be trimming
down the outfit in preparation for death. Not long afterward, I
heard that he had developed heart trouble.

I saw less of Martha and her husband in those days, but made
no attempt to shun them. I could not totally forget our erstwhile
pleasant relations and, although it was impossible to doubt anything Matt told me, still I had not heard much of their side. They

were sober, excellent parents and might feel that they v.ere in some way working for their children's future. They already had the sadness of their daughter's becoming an epileptic. Their position, on the whole, was far from enviable; and I had observed that they were deeply in love. It was also possible that Matt, being a diabetic in the days when not so much was known of this disease, should never have had any children. Who could tell how these streams of misfortune might be mingling together to cause the sad family relationships I was just then beginning to realize? I kept silent and hoped against hope that some ray of sunlight might break through the clouds.

Matt died in August, 1961, of heart failure complicated by diabetes. The plane I took out of Denver to attend his funeral developed engine trouble and had to turn back. There was no other plane that could put me in Billings in time.

Fifteen months later, in November, on my way to Sheridan I stopped for gasoline at the Decker, Montana, post office and noticed the Big Horn County Sheriff's car parked there. As I walked in, the postmaster was talking to the Sheriff, "You don't need any more directions," he said, "there's your man now."

"The Antler Ranch office sent me to find you," the Sherriff said. "They couldn't locate you by phone. Sorry, but I have to give you bad news. Mrs. Sheardon was found dead in bed yesterday morning. I think it was a heart attack. The funeral is in Billings tomorrow."

"Tell them I'll be there."

"Yes, I will, Ned." he said kindly, though I didn't know him. "I'll radio Hardin right now, and they'll phone." Hardin is the county seat.

One night less than two weeks later, there was a severe explosion and fire in a combination tool and storage shed housing drums of diesel fuel, attached to which was a bedroom and bath occupied by Harry, the long-time Japanese ranch handyman, who was trapped and died of smoke inhalation. I never heard the cause of this tragedy.

It seemed that the premonition of disaster to follow Matt's death, which I had experienced at the time I decided to sell out, was developing into reality.

From that point on, the Antler Ranch—if it still exists as such— has faded from my life. The paths of its people have diverged from mine as unpredictably as they had merged in the first place. The ranch itself has been sold twice since then and is now owned by Texas oil and cattle interests. I no longer take the Wyola turnoff, but can never drive by it without mixed memories of the way of life that used to be there, something that was very real to me, but that can never be really expressed on the superficial, two-dimensional level of words on paper. It is of a separate order of experience, existing, perhaps, only in the subconscious, not in our usual, conscious experience of the workaday world, even though everybody and everything concerned was definitely of the workaday world.

Until the 1970s, Wyoming and Montana had escaped the general desecration of wilderness fairly well, particularly in their respective northeast and southeast corners between the Powder and the Big Horn rivers. Today, however, the country is split wide open between the coal-mining interests and the environmentalists. With already enough coal above ground to last us several centuries, the threat of strip mining, which would indeed eventually wipe out the last of our wilderness and rangeland, is a horror. However it may be dressed up in sheep's clothing by paltry exhibits of vegetation, forced under artificial circumstances and labeled "reclamation," the fact remains that rangeland, once destroyed, can never be replaced. Range grass is one blessing that the Creator placed only in certain parts of our country, where certain semiarid conditions exist. It will not thrive elsewhere, and it cannot be moved. Centuries of grazing by both wild and domestic animals (including much overgrazing) have failed to destroy it. Man can destroy it, but the penalty is that he cannot replace it, despite all his scientific knowledge. It was meant to thrive and has always thriven without his help.

No range, no beef. No beef, no shoes, saddles or other leather, just plastics supreme. In fact, without growing plants and animals that feed on them, food could come only from the ocean. Even that is now being polluted in the supposedly sacred name of energy, which we throw away or use for unnecessary purposes, as witnessed by the per capita energy consumption figures of other countries. Some foreigners live happily on less than half our bloated per capita energy consumption.

As for our waste of food, it has long been proverbial. Friedrich and Sophie von Thurnwald were not so ridiculous as they may have seemed during their inspection of the Tucson city dump and in the interest they showed in Lencho the Hermit. Witness the *Energy Office Newsletter* for March 28, 1975:

> A group of anthropology students have recently concluded a two-year survey of the "garbage habits" of the population of Tucson, Arizona. By sorting and cataloguing the garbage of 380 selected households, the group learned that the people of Tucson throw away over 9,500 TONS of perfectly edible food per year (estimated cost was around $10 million at retail prices). Estimates are that some 17% of this nation's solid waste comes from America's dining table.

Witness further, as noted in *Parade Magazine, Rocky Mountain News,* May 18, 1980, that a study of society through its garbage called garbology has been added to the college curriculum by Dr. William Rathje (Ph.D., Harvard). Now an anthropologist at the University of Arizona, Rathje has performed most of his garbage analysis in Tucson.

With the elimination of this waste in food and energy, our irreplaceable rangeland would not have to be so drastically invaded by the strip miners, some of whom seem bent on refusing to learn that farm or ranchland once worn out and disturbed by machines *is* irreplaceable. The late, famed author, Louis Bromfield's classic failure with his Malabar Farm, near Lucas, Ohio, into which he poured big money from novels and motion pictures, reaping nothing but bitter disappointment instead of bringing the land back onto a reasonable production basis, is a recommended exhibit for overenthusiastic strip miners. Incidentally, it is open to the public.

Despite the dark shadow cast ahead by the progress of strip mining, one must face the fact that today we live in the age of metals. There is no question of turning back to the "days of wooden ships and iron men." The age of wood destroyed the forests, but modern methods of reforestation by the great lumber companies are correcting that. The age of metals, however, requires the destruction of minerals, and there is no replacing them at the source. Our only salvation is to reduce the destruction of minerals, as well as that of the life-giving grass, to the barest minimum; to eliminate the shocking waste of food in city dumps and metal in automobile junk piles; to curb the greedy consumption of power for profit motives and the irresponsible advertising and promotion that whips it up, also for profit motives. The environmentalists are not trying to deny that the increasing population of a growing country must require a corresponding consumption of minerals for power and metals. They are only asking why, after two hundred years of flagrant waste, the people should suddenly be told that in the next decade they must provide several hundred times as much basic fossil fuel—coal, to be exact—as was ever produced before, and this at the price of eventually destroying their food.

Who is to blame for all the range- and forestland being held in escrow, so to speak, for the great mining operators? Not the little rancher on the Big Horn River, the Rosebud or the Tongue, who sells or leases his few hundred or few thousand acres under unbearable economic pressure, because the needs of his ever-increasing descendants can no longer be met by the area of his land, which is static. The number of cattle his land can support does not increase, while his family increases by geometric proportion and in the face of hopelessly demanding labor conditions.

Practically full blame must be borne by the tens of millions of acres of public domain quietly tied up for mining interests by huge government leases, made years in advance: land to lie fallow possibly for centuries to assure fantastic future profits, in the face of constitutional regulations that mineral leases must be worked within a very few years or be forfeited.

Closely following upon the heels of the strip mine itself there is not only the desecration of the land from a food-producing standpoint, but also the desecration of a way of life.

Panning our hypothetical camera along the afore-mentioned corners of Wyoming and Montana, we can zoom in on two examples of character desecration all too familiar to those who know the country and, incidentally, well documented by the *Wall Street Journal* in December, 1975, as follows:

> Psychologists have taken soundings among residents of the new energy boom towns in the West, and have found a sort of "future shock."
>
> A study made for the state of Montana says residents of the town of Colstrip have feelings of "powerlessness, futility and despair which come from sweeping social changes over which those con-

cerned have little or no control and which they consider to be essentially oppressive."

One Colstrip trailer resident is quoted in the study as saying, "The whole town is on wheels. I expect to wake up some day and see half of it gone."

Other Western boom towns share this state of mind. A Wyoming psychologist has coined the term "Gillette syndrome" to refer to the drinking, depression and crime caused by sudden change at Gillette, Wyo., where strip mining of coal is fast expanding.

In addition to this, as of 1975 and regardless of the dates on their titles, approximately 2,150 owners of somewhere between 20 and 25 million acres of western lands have been served with summonses by U.S. marshals, requesting them to show cause why they should not relinquish all their water rights, on which their very existence depends, both above and below ground, to certain Indian tribes controlled by the government. This is in spite of the fact that some such water rights have been in effect for over a century, are based on patents to original public domain dating back to the Louisiana Purchase and signed by every president since Thomas Jefferson. They had never been questioned until the matter of strip mining came up, bringing along with it the fantastic water requirements of coal gasification plants. These and their companion electro-generating plants are already on the drawing boards and are slated to crisscross the western rangelands with their plumes of poisonous emissions and network of transmission lines carrying the unavoidable danger of multimillion-volt charges. All this may be called "progress"; but, if unchecked, it can only mean progress toward an ultimate economy wherein we will have no food, but plenty of electric toothbrushes.

Already, food for animals is shrinking alarmingly. No longer can cattle be run on lush Crow Indian rangeland leased for fifteen cents an acre, so that six dollars a year will see a steer through and turn a profit besides, as Matt Sheardon and I used to figure. Farmers are paid subsidies to reduce crops, and they shy away from animal husbandry because the price of feed is so high.

In the wilder, less exploited areas of the animal kingdom the same indications abound. A paltry 12,440 acres of range were grudgingly doled out to wild horses in the Pryor Mountains of Montana by the government in 1975. It was limited to 140 head, excluding foals, with roping permits on sale and mountain lion predation encouraged. Our American bison, or "buffalo," have not done even that well. In fact, they have fallen from their once vaunted status of animal nobility to the depths of ignominy. By the Taylor Grazing Act, all rangeland, once their birthright, has been denied them in favor of domestic livestock. They may still be found on some old coins, but they no longer have any "Home on the Range."

And as for good old leather, where does one find it nowadays? Old stock saddles, well polished by blue jeans, glow wistfully in secondhand stores and ask us the same question.

UNIVERSITY OF OKLAHOMA PRESS
NORMAN